# 100 Wonders of the World

# 100 Wonders of the World

*The Finest Treasures of Civilization and Nature on Five Continents*

CHARTWELL
BOOKS, INC.

This edition published in 2004 by
CHARTWELL BOOKS
A division of BOOK SALES, INC.
114 Northfield Avenue
Edison, New Jersey 08837

© Naumann & Göbel Verlagsgesellschaft GmbH,
  in der VEMAG Verlags und Medien Aktiengesellschaft,
  Köln

© 1999 Rebo International b.v., The Netherlands

Original title: 100 Weltwunder
English text by Stephen Challacombe based on
a translation by Dr. John N. Kraay
Cover design Minkowsky Graphics, Enkhuizen, The Netherlands

Publisher and responsible for the concept: Dr. Manfred Leier
Redaction advice: Anne Benthues
Text: Winfried Maass, Nicolaus Neumann, Hans Obertländer,
Jörn Voss, Anne Benthues
Design: Wolf Dammann, Teresa Nunes/Redaction 4 GmbH
Photographs: Hamburger Verlagskontor GmbH
Documentation: Peter Münch
Production: Naumann & Göbel Verlagsgesellschaft GmbH, Köln

ISBN 0-7858-1889-8

# Preface

*The ancients knew seven wonders of the world, among which were the Pharos of Alexandria, the Colossus of Rhodes, and the pyramids of the Nile. The pyramids still exist: their dimensions are such that they withstood the ravages of time. Neither nature nor human hands have been able to destroy them.*

*Why did the Greeks speak of the "wonders of the world?" They admired the great cultural monuments of their age because of the importance in their culture of marrying artistic vision with the architectural skill necessary to create such enormous structures.*

*The "Wonders of the World" were wrought with human hands. This book adopts this same criterion for selecting its wonders of today's world. The technological advance of humankind though has brought with it a threat to the natural magnificence of this world. Hence we also feature the national parks and nature reserves established on every continent to protect the natural wonders of nature which are at least as important as those monuments to our modern technology.*

*Both natural and cultural monuments are listed by UNESCO as monuments that humankind must strive earnestly to protect, but this book ranges wider than the UNESCO list because there are many examples of architecture and landscape that do not have a world cultural heritage designation. Such inclusions by us that UNESCO omits are the Eiffel Tower in Paris, the Manhattan skyline, prehistoric cave paintings of Lascaux, and the limestone cliffs of Rügen.*

*There are a great many wonders in our world and therefore the choice is of necessity subjective. Travel with us through these pages to visit one hundred of the most magnificent wonders on earth.*

*The publisher*

# Contents

## ASIA

## AUSTRALIA

## AFRICA

# The forgotten Machu Picchu

*The ancient Inca settlement in the Peruvian Andes was discovered in 1911*

PERU

**Machu Picchu**

SOUTH AMERICA

Pacific
Ocean

Atlantic
Ocean

**ROUTE**

Flight from Lima to Cuzco,
train to Machu Picchu

**BEST TIMES**

June–October

**ALSO WORTH SEEING**

Ruins from the
Sacsayhuaman Inca
settlement near Cuzco

On the eastern side of the Andes in Peru, where the mountain river Urubamba flows to the Amazon basin, the American explorer Hiram Bingham made the most important discovery of his career on July 24, 1911. He was searching for relics of the Inca culture which was destroyed by the Spanish *conquistadores* in the sixteenth century. After climbing a steep mountain wall at one of the many bends in the river, the young history professor from Yale finally reach a mountain path at about 7,500 feet that was surrounded by large rocks and not visible from the valley. The entrance had been blocked by an earthquake many years earlier. The many walls draped with foliage and high tiered terraces sug-gested a large city had once stood there.

### In the center of the temple complex

Bingham named his discovery Machu Picchu which means "Old Top" in the Quechua native American language. Research later showed that this indeed was a former Inca settlement which had been inten-tionally built in an inaccessible place in an effort to hide from the plundering conquistadors who had already conquered the Inca capital of Cuzco, only 75 Miles away to the northwest. In the years following Bingham's discovery, archaeologists uncovered the overgrown temple and palace whose walls were magnificently constructed from granite blocks.

At what was obviously the center of the settlement stands the temple complex and here at the highest point there is a terrace carved from the granite with spiral steps hewn from granite leading to it. The archaeologists identified a monolith as an *Intihuatana* or sacred stone of the Incas, that "captures the sun." Similar structures of rock were used by the Incas as a sun dial, which was central to their cult of the sun.

Not far from the Intihuatana, archaeologists found three well-preserved walls of a sun temple with an altar formed from three slabs of rock. Another important structure within the palace is the *Torreón*, a half

round tower with sacrificial altar, beneath which is a pit that Bingham dubbed the "King's Mausoleum." Close by they found 142 skeletons, mainly of women who were probably *Ajillas* as the maidens were known who were selected for the sun cult. There are other parts of the settlement that are more simply constructed and were probably inhabited by soldiers and workers. A large open area, now known as *Plaza Principal*, was probably a meeting place for festivals such as the winter solstice.

The hundreds of tiered terraces that lead upwards to the city itself were cultivated for crops such as potatoes, corn, and other vegetables in small fields enclosed by rocky walls. It is thought the soil for these was brought up over sixteen hundred feet from the Urubamba valley. Calculations show that the fields could produce sufficient food for ten thousand people.

*The Incas built the settlement of Machu Picchu on a mountain path and so well hidden by rocks that the conquistadors did not find it. Stairways and tombs were hewn from rock, like the "King's Mausoleum" bottom left. Other buildings are constructed of stone dressed to fit precisely without use of mortar (bottom right).*

# The mysterious giant pictures of Nazca

*Why were they etched in the desert 1,500 years ago?*

Strange grooves in the desert created by unknown hands are one of the biggest archaeological mysteries in South America. They were formed about fifteen hundred years ago over an area of about 200 square miles between the present-day towns of Nazca and Ica in southern Peru. Some grooves run straight across the flat plains of the Peruvian pampas, while others form huge designs on the high planes and steep surrounding hills. These can only be recognized as giant drawings from the air.

## Drawings of huge creatures

These geometric forms were first discovered in 1939 by the American cultural historian Paul Kosok during an exploratory flight.

The observations that Kosok made inspired the German mathematician Maria Reiche to devote her life to studying these patterns in the desert. She discovered that once these grooves in the yellow sand of about eight inches deep and at least three feet wide were cleared of their covering of red earth they became much more apparent. By this means scientists exposed a drawing of a condor that is more than 390 feet wide. The drawing had to be photographed from the air to reveal its subject. Later other creatures were uncovered such as a spider with legs of over 130 feet and other giant depictions of humans, fish, cacti, and flowers.

Most of these drawings are etched as a single line, which sometimes runs for hundreds of yards or even miles across the desert. The survival of these ancient etchings is due to the good fortune of the local climate and geography. Very little rain falls in the Pampa de las Figuras between Nazca and Ica and the area is shielded against sandstorms by the line of mountains running along the

coast to the west and by spurs of the Andes to the east.

What is so striking about these etchings—apart from their size—is both the accuracy of the drawings and the artistic flair with which they have been performed. Similar designs, attaining the same aesthetic standard, are also found in the ceramics of the Nazca culture that flourished in southern Peru between the fourth and fifth centuries. This makes it certain that Nazca artists also created the desert etchings.

## Astronomical drawings

Quite how the early Peruvians—from before the time of the Incas—were able to make these drawings which they could not oversee at a single glance remains a mystery.

It is certain that they used ropes to help them draw straight lines and circles but no-one has provided a complete explanation of the meaning or purpose of these drawings. Most scientists agree that they are astronomical drawings and Maria Reiche believes they are accounts of cosmic observations. One of the grooves she discovered leads straight to spot at which the sun sets in the southern hemisphere during the June solstice. Other lines that are not precisely parallel relate to the different points at which the sun sets during the solstice for the years 300 through to 650 of our calendar. Even with these theories the mystery remains as to the cultural significance of these drawings. This gives plenty of scope for the imagination such as the Swiss writer Erich von Däniken, who believes these drawings are signals to and landing strips for aliens.

*Most of the drawings made in the Nazca desert 1,500 years ago by unknown artists can only be seen from the air. The etching on the right is of a bird.*

# Riches amidst poverty

*Havana is still the jewel of the Caribbean despite its decline*

NORTH AMERICA

**Havana**

CUBA

CENTRAL AMERICA

*Pacific Ocean*

SOUTH AMERICA

**ROUTE**

Tourists traveling individually must book minimum of three nights

**BEST TIMES**

November–April

**ACCOMMODATIONS**

Hotel Nacional de Cuba (legendary for its rich and famous)

**ALSO WORTH SEEING**

Museo Casa Ernest Hemingway (writer's home, now a museum)

No one agrees on the origin of the name Havana or La Habana for the Cuban metropolis but all Habaneras agree that they know not of a more beautiful city. Even though the beauty has faded and crumbling since it was the richest colonial city in the Caribbean, Havana is still very impressive.

## Old Havana is protected by St. Christopher

The virtues of Cuba's beauty were first extolled when Christopher Columbus discovered the island on October 28, 1492. He noted in the ship's log: "This island is the most beautiful ever seen by human eye." Spanish colonists established their first settlement in 1515, which they traditionally called Villa de San Cristobal de la Habana but four years later they moved because of the climate to a first-class natural harbor to the north that is today's Havana. Historians suspect the name "La Habana" refers to the Ciboney tribal chief Habaguanex who ruled over the western part of Cuba at that time. Another legend refers to a beautiful Arawak woman who cried out "Habana!" with arms outstretched while the Spanish ship was anchoring.

In the sixteenth century another pretty native woman became the wife of the Spanish governor, who failed to return from a voyage up the Mississippi. The legend has it that the woman peered out to sea for her returning husband for so many years that she eventually became blind. She is immortalized in bronze as "Girradilla", decorating the bell-tower of El Castillo de la Real Fuerza.

The old fortress of La Fuerza was of little strategic significance—it was the headquarters of the Spanish governors—but came into its own in the twentieth century as a tourist attraction on the edge of the old city, where the greatest collection of Spanish colonial buildings in the Caribbean are to be found. The lively Old Havana, La Habana Vieja, with its artistically decorated facades, archways, old wells, and hidden courtyards, was declared a

world heritage site by UNESCO in 1982. Extensive renovation saved it from the threat of decay and buildings that had already deteriorated were restored to their original condition.

Palaces, traders' houses, and churches evidence the wealth of Havana through the seventeenth and eighteenth centuries when Spanish ships laden with gold and silver used Havana as a refuge on their voyages home. Cuba also flourished from the sale of its sugar cane, rum, and cigars.

The attractive old town is a blend of Spanish architecture with the bright colors and forms of the Caribbean. The cathedral of San Christóbal, with its pillared frontage has clear signs of late baroque Italianate influences. The glazing bars are reminiscent of the wrought-

iron talents of Andalusian blacksmiths and there is a trading house as grand as a mosque. Given the parlous state of Havana's other old quarters, the restoration of the historic city center seems wholly inadequate. Havana is in desperate need of economic growth to enable the tremendous damage that

dictators of the right and the left have inflicted on such beautiful avenues as the Carenas Boulevard. In cheerful bars such as Bodeguita del Medio, many people will raise their Daiquiris to toast the hope that this may soon happen.

*Old Havana has the largest collection of Spanish colonial architecture in the Caribbean. They are a magnificent assortment of fine churches, noble palaces, and traders' houses. The historical quarter—known as Habana Vieja—with its narrow alleys and cozy cafés, has been significantly restored in the past few years.*

# The prehistoric world of the Galapagos

*How prehistoric animals survived in isolation*

Three to six million years ago volcanoes erupted more than 400 miles off the coast of Ecuador causing lava to spew from open craters in the bed of the Pacific Ocean to form the Galapagos archipelago. The archipelago consists of some sixty or so islands of varying size. The Galapagos Islands are still mainly dominated by volcanoes with desert-like coast lines and impenetrable rain forests in the interior. The plant and animal life that developed here under ecological conditions that were different from the continental land mass of South America is markedly distinguished from species that developed elsewhere under similar conditions.

## A paradise for tortoises

The first reports about these islands—which became known as Las Encantadas (the enchanted)—reached the Occident in 1535 from the bishop of Panama, Tomas de Berlanga. This cleric made notes of his observations during a voyage of discovery along the unexplored coast in which he records dragon-headed sea lizards, enormous tortoises, and many exotic birds. These creatures had no feature of humankind, inhabiting a paradise that was to change only when seamen started to come ashore regularly to replenish their stocks of fresh meat from the giant elephant tortoises weighing up to 550 pounds. The islands were given the Spanish name for tortoise, which is *galapago*.

The British naturalist Charles Darwin first encountered the islands in 1835. The larva and ash fields formed an uninviting brown desert but on closer inspection he became fascinated at the way different species of animals had adapted to their environment across time. One such example was an unusual finch that sought its food of insect larvae among rotten wood by cleverly using a cactus spine in its beak as a spear. Darwin assumed that the ancestors of these birds had become isolated on these islands a very long time ago and had learned through evolution to use the spines as tools in order to survive. Other birds, also known as Darwin finches, have developed different types of beak that are specialized for obtaining food under differing circumstances, such as collecting seeds, sucking nectar from cactus flowers, or catching insects. Such observations about *natural selection* formed the basis for Darwin's earth-shaking book, *On the Origin of Species*.

Today it is still possible to see creatures on the Galapagos that have evolved quite differently from others. There are graceful "sea lizards" that resemble dinosaurs but are really land animals that have learned to derive nourishment from algae and seaweed. These creatures probably stem from iguanas from the mainland that landed here, perhaps on driftwood, many thousands of years ago.

A smaller colony of five-foot-long tortoises has also survived on these islands. There are cormorants that can no longer fly because they fear no predators, dwarf Galapagos penguins, strange sea lions, seals, and more than one hundred species of birds that are peculiar to these islands. This includes twenty-eight different types of Darwin finches only found on these islands. Of the plants, forty-seven percent are found nowhere else, and the same is true of thirty-seven percent of the fish species in the waters around the Galapagos.

In 1959 the government of Ecuador declared the Galapagos Islands—officially known in Spanish as Archipielago de Colon—as a national park to protect the islands' unique flora and fauna.

*The naturalist Charles Darwin discovered an almost prehistoric animal kingdom on the volcanic Galapagos Islands. There are lizards akin to dinosaurs.*

# At the wells of Itza

*Traces of the Mayas and Tolteks on the Yucatan peninsula*

**ROUTE**

Almost 75 miles (120 km)
east of Merida and Cancun

**BEST TIMES**

October–January

**ACCOMMODATIONS**

Hotel Mayaland, Villas
Arqueológicas

**ALSO WORTH SEEING**

Mayan cities on Yucatan
peninsula: Coba, Tulum, and
Uyma

I t was night, with only the light of the moon penetrating the darkness of the jungle as the amateur American archaeologist Edward Herbert Thompson climbed the one hundred foot pyramid of Chichén Itzá for the first time in the late nineteenth century. Then, the Mayan city to the north of the Yucatan peninsula was a crumbling mass beneath a covering of green foliage. Shadows of enormous great buildings of stone—temples, palaces, colonnaded galleries, and superbly crafted walls—could be seen above the treetops which the researcher inspected more closely the following morning. Discovering the people behind the construction of the city was to become Thompson's life's work.

The name of this city of Chichén Itzá predates Columbian times, harking back to the Mayan civilization and language in which it means "at the well of Itza." The Itzas are thought to have been people of noble birth who established a new religious metropolis here within the first centuries of the first millennium AD. Following them the Mayans flourished here until the fourteenth century when the city was conquered by the Tolteks who added their architectural style to that of the Mayans. Hence Thompson was looking down on the remnants of two South American civilizations from the top of the pyramid in the moonlight.

Later archaeological digs by the American uncovered a processional avenue twenty feet wide and almost one thousand feet long, paved with red bricks. This leads from the edge of the ruins to a natural limestone basin about two hundred feet across and more than 130 feet deep that is half full of water. Thompson was certain this had been a sacrificial well about which he had read in the notes of a sixteenth-century Spanish missionary who reported that virgins were thrown into the well of Chichén Itzá at times of great

drought to appease the rain god. Thompson's investigation was meticulous. Jewelry which appeared to have broken when the sacrifices were made was recovered from the well. Jade was also found, together with clay pots, and gum copal, from which the Mayans made incense.

### In the observatory

Together with two professional divers, the maritime archaeologist also recovered human remains which were probably from sacrifices. These were not solely of young women but also included skeletons of boys and men. The circumstances surrounding their deaths is difficult to ascertain. Were they thrown into the well by priests or did they jump willingly in the hope their sacrifice would make the rain god Chac more benevolent towards their people?

Perhaps it is this kind of unanswered question which draws masses of tourists to see Chichén Itzá today with the impressive structures uncovered and carefully restored in the past decade. There is much to see here beneath the burning sun of the Yucatan peninsula. Like Thompson you can climb to the top of the stepped pyramid that was built by the Mayans and which is surmounted by a temple of the Tolteks. There are also frightening monuments with feathered serpent deities that have enormous jaws and tails that point towards heaven. There are many tombs, the remains of a hall of a thousand columns, and more than seven areas for playing ball games. Here teams once competed by trying to throw a rubber ball through a ring of stone. One of the principal attractions is an elevated dome that is built on two

stone terraces. This acted as an observatory for the Mayans. A spiral stairway leads to three openings in the tower of the observatory. These apertures align precisely with points at which the sun and moon set and have enabled archaeologists to reconstruct a system with which the Mayans drew up their calendar.

The most dreadful building at Chichén Itzá is the Tzompantli—skull platform—of about two hundred feet by forty feet. This rectangular building has the appearance of a large sarcophagus and the reddish brown walls are decorated with a relief of four rows of a skull design. Archaeologists believe this represents the severed heads of enemy captives that were kept in the inner part of the Tzompantli.

*The tablet at the center of Chac Mool— one of the Mayan deities— shown top left, was probably used to receive hearts as offerings. Tourists climb the stepped pyramid, top right, surmounted by a Toltek temple. Below is one of the courts at which inhabitants played an ancient ball game.*

# Where people became gods

*The ancient town of Teotihuacán remains a Mexican mystery*

NORTH AMERICA

**Teotihuacán**

MEXICO

*Pacific Ocean*

SOUTH AMERICA

**ROUTE**

Sited 31 miles north of Mexico City; bus from metro station Indios Verdes

**BEST TIMES**

October–January

**GOOD FOOD**

Restaurant in culture center

**ALSO WORTH SEEING**

Acolmen convent, pyramid at Place Tenayuca

Three questions for a quiz game. Who commissioned the building two thousand years ago of the first important metropolis of the Americas? What is that city called? What do you call the people who lived there? The answer to all three questions is that nobody knows. The city in question is an impressive array of pyramids that was probably already abandoned and derelict before the Aztecs started a new settlement around the start of the fourteenth century just thirty-one miles to the south that became Mexico City.

## Sun pyramid as tomb

The Aztecs kept the neighboring ghost town as a mythical burial ground and gave it the name by which it is still known today: Teotihuacán. This means "Where the people became gods." The latest archaeological discoveries suggest that the history of Teotihuacán dates back to before the beginning of our first millennium. Around 100 BC the unknown builders started construction of a city laid out like a chess board at an altitude of over 7,500 feet. There was a temple complex, a processional avenue flanked with palaces, and wide residential areas. The city grew so big that it eventually spread over more than seven square miles.

The residents of Teotihuacán completed their most important building in the first century BC. For this they moved and carried in millions of tons of soil to form a large volcano-like cone that is the Pyramid of the Sun. The pyramid's base is similar in size to the Cheops pyramid at 728 feet by 738 feet but it is only half the height at 206 feet.

The Pyramid of the Sun is crowned by a temple that has survived centuries of erosion and earthquakes. This was probably used within the Meso-American civilization for a cult of the sun. This assumption is based on the alignment of the structure with the point on the horizon where the sun sets at the summer solstice. The name of the Pyramid of the Sun therefore appears to be entirely appropriate. A similar but smaller building with sides about 138 feet shorter is known as the Pyramid of the Moon. This building, which has no temple, has withstood the elements for that past two thousand years.

In the first century AD the people of Teotihuacán also built the Quetzalcoatl temple in the form of a pyramid. Giant stone heads of the feathered serpent deity Quetzalcoatl

and the rain god Tlaloc projected from the top of the temple. The archaeology suggests that large parts of the city consisted of living quarters where workers and craftsmen lived. From one of these *barrios* it appears tools and weapons were made of obsidian—a glass-like volcanic crystal that is extremely hard. Objects of earthenware and gold exhibit craftsmanship of the highest order. The city flourished and became both a religious and trading center in the first and second centuries, at which time the population of Teotihuacán had reached around 150,000. The walls of their religious buildings and palaces were magnificently decorated with frescos and images of their deities. Superb stone-carved masks were decorated with turquoise, obsidian, red mussel shells, and mother-of-pearl.

In the course of the next two centuries Teotihuacán fell into ever-increasing decline. Perhaps this was due to the felling of the surrounding forests which created a steppe-like landscape and conditions which coincided with long periods of droughts, causing famine. One can imagine that the starving population rebelled against the priests and rulers and many left the city in search of better living conditions. By 750 the first metropolis of the western hemisphere was completely deserted and the buildings gradually became buried beneath sand and wind-blown soil. The man-made mountains of the pyramids soon took on the appearance of real mountains.

It took the tourism of the twentieth century to bring the hustle and bustle of life back to Teotihuacán.

*View from the Pyramid of the Moon shows the sacred heart of Teotihuacán, surrounded by further pyramids. The Avenue of the Dead leads past a number of smaller tombs to the Quetzalcoatl. The 206 ft high Pyramid of the Sun can be seen at the top left of the main photo. It was built in the first century BC.*

# The place where the clouds are born

*The Iguaçu Falls are the world's mightiest*

If you drifted silently in a boat along the upper reaches of the Iguaçu River—through the Brazilian jungle—you would at first hear nothing but the screeches of monkeys and the shrieks, whistles, and strident song of exotic birds. Eventually though above this you would hear the distant sound of thunder, coming ever nearer until it is deafening. It is time to turn back before the sound gets any closer.

## Through the Devil's Gorge

The hellish thundering is created by the Iguaçu Falls at the border of Brazil, Paraguay, and Argentina where the river plunges 230 to 260 feet across a crescent of basalt escarpment two miles wide. The clouds of vapor that rise from the spume cause lush vegetation on islands in the river as water races through the Devil's Gorge before the Iguaçu gasps its last breath as it merges with the Paraná River. This is not just another waterfall but a legion of cataracts, with twenty-one major falls and some 250 lesser ones. Huge veils of mist rise up, often with the myriad colors of the rainbow. The native Guarini people who inhabit the area call this "the place where the clouds are born." They bury their dead here.

The Brazilians celebrate the *Saltos do Iguaçu* as they call the falls, as one of the world's greatest wonders, in which Niagara Falls could easily be lost. The Iguaçu Falls are three times wider than Niagara and the 111 million gallons of water which passes over the falls every minute is more than two and a half times the flow at Niagara. The Spanish name for the falls is *Cataratas del Iguazú*. The Iguaçu River (also Iguazú and Iguassú) flows inland from the Serro do Mar away from Brazil's Atlantic coast. Much of the 820-mile course of the river is navigable until it reaches its confluence with the Paraná, which is 2,300 miles long.

The remote location of the falls in the flora-and-fauna-rich rain forest has retained its natural splendor. Small areas on both the Brazilian and Argentine side of the falls have been designated as nature reserves.

From the tourist hotels sited at the borders of the three countries it is possible to watch the unusual behavior of swallows that build their nests in rocks behind the Iguaçu's curtain of water. This protects them from predators. During the day one can observe large flocks of swallows wheeling above the torrents as they catch insects to feed their young before returning to their brood with their catches.

## Rare butterflies

The many different butterflies provide further colorful visual splendor in this tropical paradise. They can be seen everywhere: bright blue, yellow, white with red spots, and many other magnificent colors. At least the butterflies are less at risk here of being captured by native butterfly hunters who earn a living from selling these beautiful butterflies which are close to extinction elsewhere. Giant species with wingspans of almost eight inches are so sought after in the area around the falls that they are threatened with extinction.

**ROUTE**

Flights from Buenos Aires, São Paulo, and Rio de Janeiro

**BEST TIMES**

November–March

**ACCOMMODATIONS**

Hotel das Cataratas (next to falls) and Hotel Rodovia das Cataratas (17 miles)

**ALSO WORTH SEEING**

Itaipu, the world's largest hydro-power station (book through hotels and travel agents)

*There are 21 major and 250 lesser falls at the borders with Brazil, Argentina, and Paraguay spread across a crescent of 2 miles and plunging 260 ft into the Devil's Gorge*

# A lot of ice in Patagonia

*Wild natural beauty at the southern tip of the inhabited world*

**SOUTH AMERICA**

ARGENTINA
*Pacific Ocean*

**Patagonia**
*Atlantic Ocean*

## ROUTE

To San Carlos Bariloche by air from Buenos Aires to El Calafate, entrance to nature reserve Los Glaciares and Torres del Paine from Buenos Aires via Rio Gallegos

## BEST TIMES

October–March

## ACCOMMODATIONS

Hotel Llao-Llao (one of Argentina's best) on lake Nahuel Huapi near San Carlos Bariloche, where there is also more budget accommodation

A large block of ice that has broken away floats in the wild sea like some giant claw of a predator. Anyone who comes too close will be irretrievably lost for this is close to the notorious Cape Horn, where the great storms of the Southern Ocean collide with those of the Pacific and Atlantic. The wilderness of Patagonia was first reconnoitered by air in the 1920s by the German adventurer Gunther Pluschow in his "Silver Condor" aircraft.

This wild tip of Argentina and Chile got its name from the Portuguese seafarer Ferdinand Magellan who dubbed it Patagonia because of the *patagones* or big feet from the tracks they discovered everywhere. These tracks were made by the primitive footwear of the native Tehuelche people which they made from *guanacos*' skins (a type of llama).

### The Cordillera a boundary

Neither Magellan or the British naturalist Charles Darwin (in 1834) found the summit of the Cordillera particularly attractive. Darwin recorded that "an infertility curse lies over this land." The German aviator-explorer Pluschow on the other hand found the richly tinted landscape very exciting. His descriptions started to fuel the eventual growth in interest in tourism to this far-flung corner of our planet with its fiords, glaciers, primeval forests, semi-deserts, seal islands, and largest sheep pastures in the world.

Patagonia extends over 1,242 miles from the Colorado wells to Cape Horn. The eastern part is Chilean while the less mountainous and more extensive western part is Argentine. The ice encrusted mountains running from north to south form the boundary between the two countries. In Argentina parts of Patagonia consist of steppe-like

plains across which strong icy winds blow, but despite this harsh climate the land is fertile and supports around twenty million sheep. Admittedly more than twelve acres of land are needed per sheep, but land is plentiful in this part of the world. The woolly flocks share the land with the native guanacos and nandoes (the Patagonian ostrich).

On the mountainous Chilean west coast rainfall is much more abundant and everything is covered in greenery. The northwestern part of these mountains resemble the European Alps, leading to the name of "the South American Switzerland." Milking cows graze Alpine meadows and there are also "Alpine" views and farms that resemble

buildings in the Black Forest and Swiss chalets. In common with the Alps there is also the panorama of snow-capped mountains.

Further south the mountains that form the border are covered with the largest ice sheet of the world except for that at the two poles. Continuous heavy snowfall has formed twice the depth of ice here that is found in Iceland. This is why such enormous glaciers have formed here, threading their way to the lower land. On the Chilean side the glaciers feed regular crops of new icebergs into the sea while on the Argentine side enormous glaciers of blue ice thunder downwards, leading to severe flooding. The largest of the Patagonian glaciers, the Perito

Moreno, surges continuously forward with a two-and-one-half-mile-wide and 230-foot-high wall of ice into the two elongated crescents that are the lake known as Lago Argentino.

The Moreno Glacier has left a memorial to Gunther Pluschow untouched. He died nearby when his Heinkel seaplane crashed in the Lago Argentino on January 28, 1931. His last flight had been over the ice sheets, swamps, mountainous seas, and glaciers of Patagonia.

*Three views of Patagonia: the summit of Cerro Fitzroy (11,072 ft.) above is considered one of the five most difficult peaks to scale by mountaineers. The Moreno glacier (left) pushes a 2½-mile-wide and 230-foot-high wall of ice into the Lago Argentino. A vast steppe-like landscape characterizes the southeast of Patagonia.*

# Highway to adventure

*The Pan-American Highway runs from Alaska to the southern mountains ranges of Argentina*

## ROUTE

By well-equipped and well-maintained vehicle from the highways of the U.S. and Canada. Take important spare parts, replacing them en route could prove very expensive. By boat or air around the missing portion through the Darien Gap

## BEST TIMES

Ideally a year-long journey but aim to travel from the north during spring and be in the south by December

The Pan-American Highway appears in travel guides as an "ideal" road to adventure. The famous (and infamous) highway is not a single road but interconnecting series of roads from the Alaskan Highway in the far north of the U.S. through the Inter-American Highway of Mexico and Central America into South America on the final leg of the Pan-American route. Depending on the starting point and route chosen, the trip can be from over 15,000 to around 28,000 miles.

The original intention of North and South American countries in the nineteenth century was to construct a Pan-American railroad. At a joint conference at Santiago, Chile in 1923 preference was given for a Pan-American freeway, known in Spanish as *Carretera Interamericana*. The U.S. contributed its western coastal freeway to the project, but it was difficult to complete an unbroken link through the difficult terrain of Central and South America, with much of the proposed route running through swamp and tropical rain forest. Part of the proposed highway between eastern Panama and Colombia has still not been constructed and may never be because of both political and environmental issues.

## Also passable in winter

The main extension of the Pan-American Highway was made by the U.S. with the building of the Alaska Highway. This was constructed in 1942 in a matter of months to make it easier to defend the northernmost state of the Union in the event of a Japanese invasion. Since then civilians have also benefited from this highway that is also passable in winter, linking Alaska across Canada with the North

*The northern part of the Pan-American highway is the Alaska Highway that was constructed during World War II to help defend the most northerly state of the U.S.*

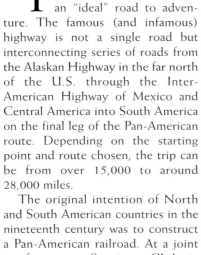

American coastal road Highway 101 that forms part of the Pan-American route. In his book *Panamericana*, Roland E. Jung describes a journey by car in forty-two days from Alaska across the Equator to Tierra del Fuego.

The Swiss motoring writer Peter Ruch took five months on a motorbike along the highway on a similar journey traveling about 15,500 miles. The high-points for Ruch were the enormous Matanuska Glacier in Alaska, the wild landscape of the Fraser Valley in Canada, attractive Mexican towns such as Guadalajara and Putzcuaro, the Mayan ruins of Copan in Honduras, the old colonial town of Cartagena in Colombia, and the snow-covered peaks of volcanoes to the east of the highway in Chile.

## The journey's toll

Most travelers along the Pan-American Highway find that they pay a high price in order to see its beauty. The searing heat or biting cold, mechanical problems, blocked side roads, unbelievably high tolls apart from bribes to corrupt police and other officials, together with some hatred and envy of foreigners all make the journey a major challenge.

But the lure of adventure continually draws people to it. Clemens Carles, who was born in Germany, did the journey in the opposite direction on a cycle. He started his epic mountain bike adventure at Ushaia—the southernmost town in South America— and pedaled north towards the polar circle and the Arctic Ocean. He more or less followed the line of the Pan-American Highway—apart from

an excursion to the east to view the Iguaçu Falls on the borders of Brazil, Paraguay, and Argentina.

His journey took him through eighteen different countries and was filled with all manner of trouble, political unrest, robberies, torrential rain, and copious amounts of bureaucratic wrangling. Close to exhaustion on a worse than usual road in Columbia the German cyclist wrestled his way through the jungle of the Darien Gap to Panama. It took Clemens three years to complete his journey which he has since recalled in books and articles.

When he finished the journey the odometer on his mountain bike read 44,620 kilometers (27,725 miles).

*In the north of Chile the Pan-American Highway follows route CH 11 that links Chile across the Andes with Bolivia. Between Big Sur and Morro Bay in California the route follows Highway A1 for splendid panoramas of the Pacific coastline. The total length of the Pan-American is up to about 24,800 miles, depending on the route chosen.*

# Hawaii, land of fire from the belly of the earth

*The mountains of Hawaii are higher even than Everest*

HAWAIIAN ISLANDS

**Mauna Kea**

*Pacific Ocean*

**ROUTE**

Flight from Oahu via Honolulu or direct from West Coast of America (San Francisco, Los Angeles, or Vancouver), to Hilo

**BEST TIME**

All year round (peak season is Christmas)

**ACCOMMODATIONS**

Kilauea Chalet, Carson's Volcano Cottage, Volcano House (all sited in the Hawaii Volcanoes National Park)

**ALSO WORTH SEEING**

The Jaggar Museum

From the air the almost 1,500 mile long chain of the Hawaiian islands resembles a long wound that is crusted around the edges and still bloody at its heart, set against the endless blue of the Pacific Ocean. Only when you descend do you realize that the dominant color is green, interrupted by the black of lava, fiery volcanic craters and lava flows, and by snow-covered mountain tops.

## Platform for observatories

The landscape of the eight larger and twenty-six smaller islands of the archipelago—which also includes towering cliffs delineated by the spume of breaking seas and great stretches of picturesque sand banks—was formed thirty million years ago when molten rock from the center of the earth made its way to the surface, building until the lava and smoking fumaroles broke the surface of the ocean. The islands of Hawaii are the peaks of volcanoes that extend deep underwater. The people who live on the main island of Hawaii, from which the chain gets its name, boast that the giant volcano Mauna Kea is in reality the world's tallest mountain, measuring about 32,000 feet from its base to the summit, with

the majority of the mountain—about 18,000 feet—being hidden underwater. The mountain rates a mere 13,796 feet above sea level. The forces that formed such a massive basalt edifice are incomprehensible. The last eruption of Mauna Kea was fifteen million years ago and the volcano is classified by vulcanologists today as inactive. On the snow-covered mountain top of the dormant volcano the U.S. has established the Mauna Kea Observatory, with contributions from a number of other countries, and there are other observatories here too because this is the best place on earth to look at space because of the almost complete absence of any water particles (97% free).

Many of the other smaller volcanoes of the forty or so on the islands are still active. Kilauea alone on the main island has erupted more than fifty times in recent decades. Its crater is 3,646 feet up the side of Mauna Kea and is more than three miles wide. The seared rock face plunges about five hundred feet almost perpendicularly to the lava crust that forms a thin skin of rock over the infernal glow. Walking on the craters is one of the island's main attractions. Although thick "mist" can in an instant obscure visibility or tourists can suddenly find themselves peering into the fiery mouth of a crater, such activities are deemed relatively safe as the volcano usually gives warning of impending eruptions.

## Polynesians passed this way

The volcanic activity is closely monitored from a special observatory at the rim of Kilauea. This center registers seismic activity below ground over a large area from which predictions are made. Even a volcano that cannot be seen above the surface of the sea is constantly monitored. Loihi at the southern extremity of the group of islands lies approximately 3,100 feet below the surface of the ocean, but this does not prevent it being a future threat.

The first inhabitants of these islands were the Polynesians who sailed to Hawaii in about 700 AD, finding the volcanic soil and lush tropical forests to be a good place to settle. These days the fiery archipelago, with its four thousand mountain tops mainly covered with snow, attracts vulcanologists, astronomers, and legions of tourists.

*Three views of Hawaii: molten lava, fertile volcanic soil, and (right) a helicopter flight over the smoking crater of Pu-Cu*

# Manhattan, the city of all cities

*Manhattan's skyscrapers acclaim the New Yorker's zest for life*

NORTH AMERICA

USA

**New York**

*Pacific Ocean*

**ROUTE**

Bus from JFK Airport to Grand Central Terminal

**BEST TIMES**

April–June and September–October

**OPENING TIMES**

View locations: Empire State building – daily 9.30 a.m.– 11.30 p.m.

**ALSO WORTH SEEING**

Statue of Liberty, Long Island, Hudson River Valley

Manhattan was once just a small settlement. However, right from the outset, the town on Manhattan Island between the Hudson and East Rivers was a melting pot of people of many racial backgrounds. In 1524 Giovanni da Verrazano, a Florentine in the service of the French king Francis I, landed in what is now New York Bay. The Englishman Henry Hudson, who worked for the East India Company also landed there in 1609, but the first colony was founded in 1624 when Dutch settlers established New Amsterdam on Manhattan Island. By 1643 the colony numbered about five hundred persons, who spoke eighteen different languages. The settlement was taken over by the English in 1664, who renamed the town for the English king's brother, the Duke of York. In 1788 New York became the capital of the eponymous state, which was the eleventh of the initial thir-

teen states of the United States. Two years later the city was easily the largest in North America with 31,131 inhabitants. The city spread from the island of Manhattan to the mainland so that a bridge was urgently needed. In 1883, the newly built Brooklyn Bridge was at that time the longest suspension bridge in the world. The bridge linked the island of Manhattan with Brooklyn and Queens to form Greater New York City.

*The golden apex of the Fuller Building, erected in 1929.*

These days Manhattan is a city of two faces: one is hectic and glittering with busy streets, bars, cinemas, theaters, museums, galleries, cheap stores, and classy boutiques, the other is a commercial center trying to turn that extra buck, usually way way up above the street level. Since the end of the nineteenth century Manhattan has increasingly been shaped by office blocks, rising ever higher into the sky to maximize returns on the enormous cost of land there. This has made Manhattan the world capital of skyscrapers.

## The peaks were decorated

Ever-higher buildings were made possible with the advent of the steel-frame of girders that enabled increasing numbers of storeys to be piled one on top of another. The style with which some architects executed such miracles is part of what makes Manhattan so exciting. The Flatiron Build-

ing of 1902 is a particularly fine example of the sculptural form that can be created with a building. In the 1930s architects returned from Europe with decorative motifs which they used to embellish their skyscrapers. Such an example is the General Electric Building of Cross & Cross. The apex of this office complex was decorated by them with a fine Gothic tracery of red bricks, enriched with glazed earthenware. The most famous building of them all—though no longer the tallest—the Empire State, is embellished with an Art Deco facade that reveals architecture as an aesthetic art form.

When skyscrapers started to be built in other cities, Manhattan developed the "international style" as this European-influenced but essentially American architecture was described. An architect who is now regarded as the "grand old man" of skyscrapers built his first at this time. He is Philip Johnson who gained his first international recognition in 1958 for the Seagram Building that he designed with his colleague Mies van der Rohe. Twenty

*Until their tragic destruction in September 2001, the twin towers of the World Trade Center dominated the skyline of Lower Manhattan.*
*The Chrysler Building (above) is exuberantly decorated in Art Deco style.*

years later in 1978, the architectural team of Hugh Stubbins & Associates set new standards with the forty-six-storey Citicorp Center that has become a striking feature of the Manhattan skyline with its four gigantic towers high above Lexington Avenue with the arresting peak at an angle of forty-five degrees. The following year Johnson

returned to start construction of the first post-modernist skyscraper for AT&T. The office block, in the form of a Chippendale chest, was completed in 1983. Johnson dared to experiment with different forms and set new standards that freed architecture from a rigid set of aesthetic "rules."

# The "thundering water"

*Niagara's cliffs are a spectacular backdrop to adventure*

NORTH AMERICA

NIAGARA FALLS

USA

*Atlantic Ocean*

*Pacific Ocean*

### ROUTE
Internal flight to Buffalo, New York. Daily shuttle flights from Toronto. By road from Toronto or New York

### BEST TIMES
June–August

### ACCOMODATION
Hotels and motels in all price categories. Book well in advance

### ALSO WORTH SEEING
Trips on the "Maid of the Mist", hovercraft trips on the Niagara River, and helicopter flights over the falls

Every minute around forty-five million gallons of water cascade over the 164 feet high horseshoe escarpment of the Niagara Falls from Lake Erie to Lake Ontario. The two lakes are linked by the Niagara River. A heavy mist is always present above the abyss and conceals the tourist boat "Maid of the Mist" from which thousands of people clad in multi-hued rainwear each year get a grandstand view of the magnificent natural spectacle.

Native Americans called the world's most famous waterfall "the water that thunders." The falls are situated on the border between the United States and Canada and are actually two cataracts: the Horseshoe Falls in Canada and the American Falls in the U.S. Between them they are a Mecca for tourists, seekers of Dutch metal, and a magnet for those planning suicide. Charles Dickens was so impressed by the awesome power the falls reveal of nature and wrote: "It was as if I had left the earth and cast a glance in heaven." His fellow countryman Oscar Wilde on the other hand—commenting on the flourishing marital tourism—observed: "The Niagara Falls are the biggest disappointment of American married life."

### Ice from Lake Erie
Few people can tear themselves away from the spectacle. The sound of the water tumbling can be heard from some way off and closer you can actually feel the ground vibrate. The Niagara Falls are most impressive at the start of spring when the Niagara River transports great floes of ice from Lake Erie that tumble over the falls with a great crashing sound to form a great barrier of ice.

The main tourist season starts in May with 35,000 people per day at the peak and around thirteen million in total visiting the cataracts each year. Not everyone comes to look, some come to be seen because the falls are such a spectacular stage backdrop for those who wish to perform. Many have attempted to ride the falls in a boat while others have tried barrels such as the mad Englishman Charles Stephens. This father of eleven allowed himself to be thrown over the Falls tied to an oak barrel. Niagara only relinquished his arm, still tied to the lid of the barrel.

### Border skirmishes on the banks
The main drama here in earlier times was between soldiers. When America joined in war with its British colonial masters in 1812, the Americans quickly seized the town on the Niagara peninsula and the banks of the falls that were in the British province of Canada. It took two years before the governor of Upper Canada, Isaac Brock was able to force the Americans to retreat. There are a number of historical monuments on the western bank of the Niagara River that remind us of this conflict, which gave the Canadians their first sense of a separate identity from America.

There are twin cities of Niagara Falls on both sides of the border but nobody really cares today whether the thundering water falls on American or Canadian soil although people still hunt for relics of the British colonial past.

After a visit to the Falls a drive around the wine region and the beautiful landscape of the peninsula, or through the attractive town center of Niagara on the lake are a must. This was once the capital of Upper Canada and the town is still very traditional and decidedly British in style.

*The road from which tourists can watch the spectacle of Niagara Falls is on the water-front. The panorama (left) shows the grandeur of the landscape.*

# The American Dead Sea

*The size of the Great Salt Lake depends on the rain*

NORTH AMERICA

**Salt Lake City**

USA

*Pacific Ocean*

**ROUTE**

Flight to Salt Lake City from throughout U.S. San Francisco to Salt Lake City is about 750 miles

**BEST TIMES**

April–June, September–November

**OPENING TIMES**

Visitor Center at Great Salt Lake City State Park on Antelope Island open 9 a.m.–5 p.m.

**ALSO WORTH SEEING**

Salt Lake City: Temple Square (entry for Mormons only), Pioneer Trail State Park

The lake, sixty-two miles long and around thirty miles wide, covers a large area of the northern part of the state of Utah but it is a fraction of the size it once was. This inland sea was almost 20,000 square miles and once stretched far into Nevada and Idaho. There is a very real risk that America's dead sea—the Great Salt Lake—may shrink still further because the inflow from the Bear River, Weber River, and Jordan River that rise in the Wasatch mountains and the Rockies is no longer sufficient to replenish the water in the lake.

Once the lake was almost one thousand feet deep but today it is barely sixteen feet in depth. Changes in inflow and evaporation have caused the level to drop at a rate of about two feet each year. Any sudden change in the level of water entering the lake immediately effects the size of the lake because the banks of the lake are so shallow. The lake is regarded as a sensitive climatic indicator because a loss of just two feet in depth results in a loss of almost one hundred square miles of surface area. This is why the lake expanded to more than 2,300 square miles in the wet 1980s but was a mere 965 square miles in the much drier years of the 1960s.

The Mormons, who colonized this area and made Salt Lake City the capital of both their land and the state of Utah, have never concerned themselves much about the volume of their "holy" lake. It was here that their prophet Brigham Young heard God's call on July 24, 1847 in which he was told how life was to be led in this "holy" community. Today's Mormons still adhere to strict codes established by their founder and their temple complex is still the center of the city, with its population of 160,000.

## Railroad crosses the lake on a dike

The lake posed a major problem for those building the railroads across America and for a long time it stood in the way of the great east–west route New York–Chicago–Omaha–Cheyenne–Ogden–San Francisco. The Union Pacific line through Utah between Ogden and Lucin could not be linked directly until the Lucin Cut-

off was built between 1902 and 1904 to carry the railroad over the lake on a dike. This runs for more than twelve miles across the lake.

Despite the high salinity of the water in the lake—which can be as high as twenty-seven percent—there is life in the lake; not in the water, but on islands in the lake where bison and pelicans have found refuge from people. Since the 1950s, large quantities of cooking salt have been recovered from the lake—over 165,000 tons each year. At Grantsville on the southern shore a flourishing industry has sprung up producing chemical salts from the bed of the lake.

The lake has found a wide range of other uses from early on. The salt flats were soon used by the U.S. Army as a testing ground for new vehicles and this lured privateers here too which soon resulted in the creation of the "Bonneville Speedway". This seemingly endless flat track has been the scene of many world speed records. The track is

marked with a black line in the salt but if no records are planned, or if heavy rain has washed out the markings then anyone can use the speedway. In a country that is so strict on speeding on the highway the salt flats are a great draw for those seeking the thrill of speed.

*The Great Salt Lake was once much bigger—stretching way into Idaho and Nevada. The reduced flow of water into the lake these days is not enough to compensate for evaporation. The salt industry (below) benefits though and the car industry tests new automobiles here. The salt flats are often used for attempts at the world speed record.*

# The cliff dwellings of Mesa Verde

*Ancient cave settlements found in Colorado cliffs*

NORTH AMERICA

USA

**Mesa Verde**

*Pacific
Ocean*

### ROUTE

Nearest airport: Cortez-
Montezuma. Reach the
National Park via U.S. Route
160 Durango–Cortez

### BEST TIMES

May–October (the visitor
center is close in winter)

### ACCOMMODATIONS

Far View Motor Lodge
(summer only)

### ALSO WORTH SEEING

Monument Valley, Arches
National Park (Utah)

O ne clear December morning in 1888, two cattlemen rode across the wild landscape of the Mesa Verde in southwest Colorado searching for stray cattle. Richard Wetherhill and Charlie Mason were crossing the "green table" as the Spanish name describes this plateau that rises two thousand feet from the surrounding flat landscape. The Mesa Verde is some twenty miles by fifteen miles across and at an altitude of around 7,500 feet. In the millions of years since the Mesa was formed deep fissures have opened up in the sandstone and niches, caves, and natural overhangs have formed in the rock walls. The two cattlemen ascended the steep canyon and found themselves looking straight into an enormous oval cave that was lit by the morning sun. They had discovered an abandoned settlement that appeared to float half way up the cliff face. This was to become known as Cliff Palace.

According to legends of the Navajo native Americans, this inaccessible area was once inhabited by people who were highly developed. The Navajo settled this area in the sixteenth century and found the settlements intact but without any trace of their original inhabitants. The Navajo called these people "Anasazi", meaning "those who were here before us." Archaeologists and anthropologists have adopted this name when referring to a tribe of Pueblo native Americans.

## Entry only by ladders

The cliff dwellings had remained empty for more than six hundred years and Wetherhill found two more large settlements that same year. After this though the Mesa Verde was stormed by gold prospectors and increasing numbers of these villages were discovered and plundered. There were no riches to be found— except in the archaeological sense— just skeletons wrapped in rugs, and articles that would have been of everyday use. In 1906 the U.S. government declared the Mesa Verde a National Park to put an end to the vandalism.

In the years since the chance discovery, archaeologists have traced the Anasazi and their history back to early times. In the sixth century, the Anasazi formed village communities and constructed dwellings close together of several floors. These homes were carved from the sandstone, built into the steep sides of canyons, constructed in caves, or in inaccessible valleys with flowing water. Entry to these settlements was only possible by means of ladders through the roof. At sign of danger the ladder was pulled inside the dwelling. These are ancient burglar-proof penthouses. Alongside each house there are usually several large circular buildings, partially sunk into the ground. It is thought these were used for religious ceremonies.

The area was probably much more densely populated in ancient times. Recent estimates from research suggest on the order of fifty thousand Anasazi-Pueblo native Americans once lived on the area of New Mexico and Arizona. Not all the ruined settlements have yet been identified, and fewer fully explored. Very little is known about the former inhabitants. They grew corn, beans, and pumpkins, kept turkeys, and used dogs for herding and for food. They wove fine fabrics from cotton, and their ceramics are decorated with black and white designs. They also made double baskets which they decorated lavishly. Water for about sixteen villages in the area was provided by constructing canals and reservoirs. It appears that they led a peaceful existence for archaeologists have found no traces of warfare, oppression, slavery, or other violence.

The Anasazi departed their settlements at the end of the thirteenth century. The reason for this was a mystery for a long time but experts believe they now know the reason. Tree rings from the period show that there was a severe drought from 1274 to 1299. The Anasazi presumably moved south and became the forefathers of the Hopi, who still live in the region today.

*Cliff Palace is hidden behind an oval opening in the rock (opposite page and left). This early settlement of the Anasazi native Americans is considered to be the most important evidence of a pre-Columbian culture. The circular kivas were used for religious ceremonies. More such settlements probably await discovery and others have yet to be archaeologically surveyed. Drawings were found in some of the caves but these are of a later date. The archer sits on a horse, which were introduced to the New World by the Spanish.*

# Grand Canyon National Park

## The Colorado River creates a glimpse of our earth's history

CANADA

**Grand Canyon**

USA

MEXICO

*Pacific Ocean*

### ROUTE

Flights from Los Angeles and Las Vegas to Grand Canyon. By road: 81 miles north from Flagstaff, Arizona on Arizona 64

### BEST TIMES

South rim closed October–May. Extremely hot at the height of summer

### ACCOMMODATIONS

Grand Canyon National Park Lodges

### ALSO WORTH SEEING

Canyonlands National Park, Utah

*The steep walls of the Grand Canyon glisten colorfully as if lit by the sun. The strata revealed by the Colorado River's erosion expose the history of the earth*

The Grand Canyon is 217 miles of territory from another world. In 1898, the Scottish writer John Muir wrote of the Grand Canyon: "Its architecture is so unworldly, it is as if one has landed on an extinct place on another planet. A play of nature, wonderful, bizarre, huge. Unbelievable colours, dramatic contrasts, the intense aromas of nature, the deadly silence."

The Colorado River has carved its way through rock for more than ten million years, revealing the history of our earth as recorded in the strata in the canyon's walls. The wonderful natural spectacle was created by the river but its beauty has been preserved by the low rainfall of Arizona. If there was more the superb colors of the canyon walls would have been washed away.

### The gorge is more than a mile deep

The magnificence of the Grand Canyon does not impress from a distance. It is just a chain of rocks, like so many others between Utah and Arizona, until one nears the rim of the canyon and looks into its depth. The best vantage point is Desert View. Only then do you see layer upon layer of glowing shades of red that form a stark contrast with the ponderosa pine forest. This inverted mountain is growing downwards through the flow of the shimmering ribbon of silver at its base: the Colorado River.

The river's current has dissected a cross-section through the earth's crust, as if with a scalpel, allowing us a glimpse into millions of years of the

*Panoramic view of the Grand Canyon. The Colorado flows at about 12 m.p.h., tumbling through*

earth's history. The geology spans many eras but the canyon is also impressive for its sheer size. It is more than one mile deep and the Colorado River which formed it transports around 44,000 tons of soil through the canyon each day much of which is deposited lower down. This has caused the Clen Canyon to form through deposits of around 800,000 tons of sediment. The canyon bottom can reach temperatures as high as 113°F (45°C) in summer—as high as the deserts of Mexico—while it is a more comfortable 75°F (24°C) outside the canyon.

The first Europeans to see the canyon were a group of Spanish led by Francisco Vasquez de Coronado in 1540 exploring the territory of the

*160 rapids in its course.*

Hopi native Americans. The canyon was an unbridgeable obstacle for them. The most spectacular section of the canyon became a National Park in 1919, covering an area of over 1,900 square miles.

Around 30,000 people visit the view points each day during the main season (about four million each year). These are scattered around the gorge and there are also places where it is possible to descend into the canyon. One of the most popular places for holiday snapshots is Hopi Point, a protruding rock platform from which you can see from west to east.

Today some five hundred Havasupai native Americans live in the bottom of the gorge. This tribe came here in the twelfth century as a refuge and one of the attractions of a visit to their reservation is the chance to see the three emerald green waterfalls from which the tribe derive their name—"people of the green water." The Havasupai have been able to ward off all attempts at infringement into their gorge during the course of their history. There were plans to lay a railroad across their land in 1889, intentions for a Christian chapel in one of the canyon walls with a lift, and proposals in 1961 for developers to build an eighteen-storey hotel into the south wall. The people of the green water are resigned to such attempts, but then they have been patiently dwelling in the Grand Canyon for eight hundred years.

*View points like these attract 30,000 visitors each day in season.*

# The Golden Gate Bridge

*A technical miracle spanning San Francisco Bay*

NORTH AMERICA

USA

San Francisco

*Pacific Ocean*

**ROUTE**

Buses for Golden Gate, change Market Street/corner 7th Street for Golden Gate Bridge

**BEST TIMES**

September–October

**ACCOMMODATIONS**

Sherman House, 2160 Green St. (Victorian villa with view of Alcatraz and the bridge)

**ALSO WORTH SEEING**

Golden Gate Park, Alcatraz, Fisherman's Wharf, View from Telegraph Hill

Bridge builder Joseph Baermann took on a battle against the elements with the construction of a suspension bridge across San Francisco Bay. He had to cope with the tides of the Pacific Ocean, the furious storms that can batter America's west coast, and the risk of earthquakes and he triumphed over all of them. The final rivet of the project Americans consider as the "seventh wonder of the world wrought by human hands" was driven on May 27, 1937: San Francisco's Golden Gate Bridge was finally completed.

The Golden Gate is the strait at the entrance to San Francisco Bay that separates the bay from the Pacific Ocean. The promoters of the bridge decided to raise steel towers of 745 feet on either side of the strait on which to attach thick steel cables to support a suspension bridge. The bridge is 9,186 feet long with a central span of 4,200 feet. The bridge deck needed to be 220 feet above the surface of the bay to enable ships to pass through.

### Risk of collapse during construction

Construction of the bridge started in 1933 and ran into immediate difficulties. The first attempts to form a foundation for the southern pylon on a platform three hundred feet below water failed because of the strong tidal flow. During one of San Francisco Bay's notorious fogs a ship rammed a work platform and sank. Soon after this three huge blocks of concrete needed for the foundations and some construction equipment fell into the sea. Storms in the fall swept away more equipment, and workers suffered from sea-sickness.

One especially hazardous operation was the stringing of the thirty-six inch thick cables that are made up of 27,000 separate strands of wire. There was a continuous risk of collapse because of gusts of wind or carelessness so a safety net was rigged part-way through the operation. This act saved the lives of nineteen men who fell. These nineteen workers who survived the fall formed the "Halfway to Hell Club." The bridge builders Ed Murphy and Ed Stanley wanted the final rivet to be driven on May 27, 1937 to be one of gold but the golden rivet was too soft and it

broke, disappearing into the depths. Therefore the final rivet to be hammered home was of steel, like the countless others in this million ton structure. The opening of the bridge was celebrated for many days and tens of thousands of pedestrians crossed the new construction.

The Golden Gate Bridge quickly recovered its investment. In the early years an average of four million motorists crossed the bridge each year. Half a century later in 1987 ten times as many were using the bridge. This does not include the many pedestrians and joggers who cross

toll free while enjoying one of the world's most amazing vistas.

The Golden Gate Bridge has withstood the risks that Baermann had to overcome, such as bad weather, and the passage of time, and remains in reasonable condition despite all the pessimistic predictions. Severe storms can cause the road deck to sway considerably. During World War II the R.M.S. Queen Elizabeth passed through the strait laden with troops with barely forty inches to spare between her funnels and the bridge deck.

The world's most famous suspension bridge also attracts those

with suicide on their mind. More than a thousand people have jumped from the bridge. When fogs rolls in from the Pacific only the towering pylons can sometimes be seen rising out of the mist. Another ethereal character to the strait is lent by the water organ of the Golden Gate Yacht Club which automatically pipes to announce the turn of the tide.

*The Golden Gate Bridge—built between 1933 and 1937—saves motorists driving between San Francisco and Marin County from a long detour. The bridge is 9,186 feet long with a central span of 4,200 feet. The height of the deck above the sea varies from 216–236 feet, depending on the tide.*

# The mammoth trees of America

*Sequoias grow 440 feet high and live for thousands of years*

NORTH AMERICA

USA
**Sequoia
National Park**

*Pacific
Ocean*

**ROUTE**

From Los Angeles via
Interstate 5 to Bakersfield,
Highway 99 and 63 to
Visalia, Highway 198 through
the Sequoia National Park.
Total journey 218 miles

**BEST TIMES**

June–September (closed in
winter)

**ACCOMMODATIONS**

Giant Forest Lodge, Grant
Grove Lodge, motels at Three
Rivers

**ALSO WORTH SEEING**

Kings Canyon National Park
(northern neighbor to
Sequoia N.P.), Yosemite
National Park (125 miles to
the north)

Fur trappers were the first people who claimed to have seen giant redwoods with trunks as thick as an elephant. They swore they had seen such trees with their own eyes and this was the God's honest truth. These trees were on the western escarpment of the Sierra Nevada. They should have kept quiet about them for soon lumberjacks were felling great swathes of these trees.

The giant Californian redwood or "big tree" is known to scientists as *Sequoiadendron giganteum* and is related to the swamp cypress. They can reach heights of 440 feet. Some of the enormous trees that were felled were three to four thousand years old. Their lumber ended up as dance floors or bowling alleys. Two of the largest specimens were auctioned to be exhibited as wonders of the world.

The survival of the remaining "big trees" in Southern California is due to the activity of a few men who established the Sequoia national Park in 1890 against the wishes of the lumber industry. The Giant Forest area became the showpiece of the National park to the north of Los Angeles. It was here that the native American Monachi brought the cattle breeder Hale Tharp in 1858. He moved into the burnt out trunk of a sequoia, bought a piece of ground, and then refused to sell despite offers of huge sums until the government took over the land to form a national park.

There is a thrilling walking trail through the middle of this forest of mammoths, the Congress Trail. Taken at an easy pace it takes about two hours to complete. You will see that the trees are just as those fur trappers described them: as tall as church spires, and as thick as an elephant. The name sequoia is derived from Cherokee Chief Sequoyah who drafted the native American alphabet from which the botanists took the name. An individual tree is also named for him and others are named for prominent politicians and generals of United States history.

## Drive straight through the tree

One particularly large example is known as General Sherman of the Union army during the civil war of 1861–1865 who decisively won the final victory for the Union against the Confederates with his troops. The celebrated sequoia known as "The Largest Living Thing" is 2,500–3,000 years old with a diameter of its trunk at the base of more than 102 feet. The trunk reaches upwards to almost 275 feet and the diameter of the upper trunk is more then thirty-six feet. It has been calculated that the tree contains 52,477 cubic feet of lumber, weighing about 1,384 tons.

Trees of a similar size can be found in the two neighboring national parks. In Kings Canyon National Park the tree known as General Grant—Union commanding general and one-time president—is just over 267 feet tall with a trunk that is just over 107 feet in diameter. In Yosemite National Park you can admire the Grizzly Giant that is about 2,700 years old and about 210 feet tall. Close by this specimen is a tree with a tunnel bored through its trunk large enough to allow buses to pass through after the tree fell in 1968.

*The tallest trees in the Sequoia National Park are between 2,500 and 3,000 years old and more than 260 feet high. If allowed to continue to grow they will live for several thousand years more. These mammoth trees do not die of old age but when the roots can no longer support the 100-plus tons of their trunks, or when destroyed by fire.*

# Castle fit for a newspaper king

*Hearst Castle is opulently decorated in the European manner*

NORTH AMERICA

USA

● **Hearst Castle**

*Pacific Ocean*

**ROUTE**

Highway No. 1 to San Simeon, approx. 237 miles north of Los Angeles. By bus from parking lot to the castle.

**BEST TIMES**

September–October

**OPENING TIMES**

Daily 8 a.m.–3.30 p.m.

**ALSO WORTH SEEING**

Big Sur, Monterey Bay, aquarium at Monterey

Hearst Castle is the kind of fairy tale castle from which a princess is rescued, like the fantasy of Schloss Neuschwanstein in Germany. Although William Randolph Hearst may not have been of royal blood he was far wealthier than the Bavarian King Ludwig II who also indulged his fantasies. The guests at Hearst Castle were certainly of at least equal standing with Ludwig's at Castle Neuschwanstein. The illustrious guests included Winston Churchill, Charles Lindbergh, Charlie Chaplin, and George Bernard Shaw to name but a few of the people that the "King of the West Coast" invited to his court. These days Hearst Castle—officially Hearst San Simeon State Historical Monument—is a tourist attraction, outdone only by Disneyland.

## Blue hours with Gershwin

The castle—which Hearst modestly called "the ranch"—lies forty-five miles north of San Luis Obispo, halfway between San Francisco and Los Angeles, on a hill overlooking the Pacific. This summer home is set in almost 250,000 acres of land inherited from his mother. In reality the "castle" is a complex of buildings. Four guest houses are grouped around the *Casa Grande* or main house, which has more than one hundred rooms. What makes Hearst Castle so significant is that it is the greatest collection of European architectural detail and artifacts anywhere. Hearst had entire walls, roofs, and floors stripped from European churches and cloistered buildings to add to his dream of an idealized Europe in California. Gothic chimneys and Moorish tiles, medieval art, and antique vases decorate the 115 rooms and halls of the house, built in Moorish style. Hearst's inner sanctum—the playroom—is complete with carved oak choir stool in which Hearst sat while he had George Gershwin play piano for him during his "blue hours." A safari park

surrounds the immediate grounds of the house that today is only home to manageable herbivores. The lions and cheetahs that roamed the park in Hearst's time were transferred to zoos following Hearst's death.

Hearst started to build his "palace" in 1919, when he was at the peak of his power. Orson Welles modeled himself on Hearst as the hard-nosed newspaper magnate in *Citizen Kane.* Hearst at one time controlled twenty-three percent of America's daily newspapers of which as much as sixty percent were in California.

The building of the California summer home became the life's work for architect Julia Morgen and was not finished in Hearst's lifetime. Hearst died in 1951 at the age of eighty-eight. Every time Hearst returned from a trip to Europe with a new "trophy," parts of the "castle"

which had long been completed had to be rebuilt. There are parts of the castle today that are still at the design stage. The building is a cultural puzzle, a glittering monstrosity of juxtaposed objects and parts of buildings gleaned from Europe.

## Valuable objects in every room

The facade of the Casa Grande, modeled on the twin tower Mudejar design of a Spanish cathedral, rises up in front of a swimming pool filled with water from a spring, which is surrounded by Grecian columns and statues. In the grandly decorated dining room the tables are laid with porcelain from France and China. Colorful banners from the classical Siennese horse race or *palio* and Flemish tapestries adorn the walls. One needs two hours to view all the "trinkets." There are genuine valuables too, such as a Spanish refectory chair, the bed of French

statesman Cardinal Richelieu, twenty-two carat gold mosaic in the baths, antique Persian tiles in the billiard room, heavy baroque chandeliers, doors from a Florentine palace, and figures of Venus in the guests' toilets. In order to hear what his guests were saying about him out of his sight "W.R." as he liked to be called installed microphones in all the guest quarters. Hearst was convinced that his collection was of "high cultural value" and believed no progress was possible "without European culture."

*The design for Hearst's swimming pool is based on the square and colonnade in front of St. Peter's in Rome. The facade of his Casa Grande is decorated with a reproduction of a church door and the many rooms are also copied from originals in castles and monasteries.*

# Chambord: a dream turned to stone

*This château on the Loire became the model for grand absolutist architecture*

EUROPE

**Chambord**

Atlantic
Ocean    **FRANCE**

*Mediterranean*

## ROUTE

From Paris on the A10 via Orléans to Mer, then cross the Loire and take D112 to Chambord (distance 94 miles). Closest rail stations at Mer and Blois

## OPENING TIMES

Daily from 9.30 a.m.–4.45 p.m. or 6.45 p.m. depending on time of year

## ALSO WORTH SEEING

Châteaux on the Loire, including Blois and Orléans

When a power conscious ruler, inveterate womanizer, and unstoppable visionary builds himself a hunting lodge then it must be something very special. Francis I (1494–1547) created a dream in stone when he built Chambord. It is a splendid work of fantasy, like a tale from the *Thousand and One Nights*. When the Holy Roman Emperor Charles V visited this most pompous of all royal hunting lodges in 1539, with its 440 rooms, eighty-three stairways, and overall dimensions of 512 feet by 384 feet, it moved him to state: "Chambord is the paragon of the works of art humans can create."

Francis I, king of France, was constantly at war with the Habsburgs for control of Europe and developed his desire for a Renaissance châteaux while campaigning in Italy. It was important for him that he and his hunting friends should be as well cared for as they were at . court. The southwest of the Sologne was considered the best location for such a château because the king could indulge his passion for hunting there. The area then was filled with wild boar and deer and remains one of the best places for hunting in France to this day. Since the site chosen for the palace was marshland, building it was more of a nightmare

than a dream, and when a plan to divert the Loire proved unsuccessful an entirely new river bed was dug at Cosson. It was essential to the king that the beauty of the château be reflected in water.

The plans for the château were drawn by Italian architects with the medieval style of French castle as their starting point. A monumental tower was sited in a large square structure to mimic the *donjon* or lookout tower of earlier settlements. This central feature remains the heart of the château today. A roof terrace is reached by means of a stairway, but not just any stairway. Part of the wonder of Chambord is this truly

royal entrance through the *escalier meridional*. It is believed that the plans for this were drawn by Leonardo da Vinci. It is certainly true that Francis persuaded the original "Renaissance man" to come to the Loire and a love for architecture is one of the many things for which the master was renowned. Double helix stairways spiral in opposing directions, with deep windows that enable you to see both ascending and descending visitors without them meeting one another. This part of the château is also said to represent the globe, while rooms on one floor are grouped in a Grecian circle.

### Revolutionary plunder

The roof terrace was designed for festivities. The château served as the pedestal to the roof terrace rising above it like a giant centerpiece, with 365 chimneys, hundreds of spires, capitals, lanterns, and bell towers.

People partied on the roof, played games there, walked around beneath parasols, got drunk, or looked out for returning hunting parties to see if they had been successful.

Francis I did not live to see his château completed. His successors reluctantly continued with the building of it, but it was Louis XIV who added some sparkle to Chambord when he rediscovered the place during the construction of his palace at Versailles. The French revolutionaries of 1789 were opposed to the grandeur of Chambord and they plundered the château of its furniture, wall hangings, and paintings. Under state ownership and stewardship efforts have been made to restore Chambord's decaying glory, partly funded by tourism. A visit to Chambord is an absolute must for anyone visiting the Loire.

*The Loire was diverted so that Chambord's beauty could be reflected in it when the château was built between 1519 and 1537. Francis I was inspired by the palaces of the Italian Renaissance. The enormmous building has 440 rooms, 83 stairways, and is the largest of the châteaux of the Loire. The imposing towers and turrets emphasize the building's grandeur and enclose a roof terrace where elaborate court parties were held.*

# The Eiffel Tower: the best-known face of Paris

*The most important structure of the 19th century looks out across Paris*

There was a struggle at first. As soon as it became known there were plans to build a 984 foot tower in the center of Paris for the World's Fair of 1889 architects, artists, and politicians got the "Petition of 300" together. This warned of disfigurement to the capital and described the plans to build what they described as a "pitch-black chimney" as a "fraud like ugliness." The tower was built in spite of these protests and subsequently contributed much to the fame of both France and Paris.

The initial plans were made by Maurice Koch, a technical assistant employed by Alexandre Gustave Eiffel's (1832–1923) engineering and construction company. Eiffel, a descendent of German immigrants from the Eiffel region, was awarded the lucrative contract for the World's Fair when his company won the architectural competition held by the department of commerce.

## Champs de Mars building site

The city of Paris provided an old training ground on the banks of the Seine, known as the Champs de Mars, as site for the new structure and the foundations were established in 1887. Eiffel had four huge concrete anchors, each fifty feet by twenty-six feet, set in the natural gravel bed of the waterside site to carry the burden of the four "elephant legs" and the entire weight of the tower of some 10,700 tons. Erection of the steel work started on July 1, 1887 to a carefully prepared plan. Workers had to join together twelve thousand separate pieces that were then partially assembled at an ironworks in Clichy.

It was an amazing puzzle which Parisians watched rise before their gaze. Eiffel's planning was so sound that he used a surplus crane to

construct the lifts which take people to the viewing platforms at heights of 187, 377, and 899 feet above the ground.

As the tower grew higher it cast its shadow across Paris like a sun dial but the vociferous group of protesters got smaller and smaller. The vast majority of Parisians were now acclaiming and admiring the apparent elegance of the edifice with its web-like structure which enables this colossus to give an impression of delicate tracery in spite of its significant mass.

When the tower was completed on time on March 31, 1889, and Eiffel had the French tricolor run up at a height of 985 feet 10 inches, newspapers celebrated the tower as a "triumph of the modern industrial culture" and as a grand secular counterpart to the Sacre-Coeur—that other elevated monument that can be seen from much of Paris.

From the highest observation point it was possible not just to see all of Paris but on a clear day to see far into the countryside surrounding the city.

## Monument of the Revolution

For the opening of the World's Fair in 1889 the steel structure that quickly became known as the Eiffel Tower was illuminated with ten thousand gas lamps which competed with the fireworks display for the Fair.

Gustave Eiffel declared that for him the tower was a monument to the French Revolution of 1789 which created the conditions for "the century of industry and technique," which was so emphatically celebrated at the World's Fair.

In addition to great renown, the *Tour Eiffel* brought great financial rewards to its creator. The company owning the tower earned more than the construction costs in the first

year alone. The Eiffel Tower quickly became the "trade mark" of Paris and has helped to make Paris one of the most popular city destinations for tourists. In 1929 a radio mast was added to the top of the tower, followed in 1935 by a television transmitter, increasing the height of the tower to 1,052 feet. There is a laboratory, meteorological station, equipment for air traffic, and a small apartment on the top platform. Eiffel once used the apartment.

*The original height of the Eiffel Tower was 984 ft but it is now 1,052 ft with its television antenna. The original weight of 10,700 tons was reduced by 1,477 tons after renovation. Some five million people visit the tower each year, which is the city's biggest attraction and its world "trade mark."*

# Palace of the Sun King

*Versailles' pomp was created to reflect the power and glory of Louis XIV*

Louis XIII had a hunting lodge built in the wilderness-like landscape of Versailles. This was a simple brick-built building of three wings that was surrounded by water. His son Louis XIV had many fond boyhood memories of this château and so he chose it as a refuge where he could conduct his affair with Mademoiselle de la Valiere. The outside of the château was adorned for him with all manner of finery and he had the interior modernized and added a separate new wing.

When Louis XIV decided to make the château his palace and to move the court there from Paris in 1668, he needed much more space in which to hold court and give recep-

tions and grand state occasions. Therefore, Louis Le Vau was commissioned to give the new palace a scale more becoming such a royal purpose. Further embellishments in the form of the grand exterior windows were executed by the architect Jules Mansart ten years later in order to further enhance the brilliance of *Le Roi Soleil*—the Sun King—as Louis XIV was now known.

## A triumph of obsession

The palace had to be grand by design with "scale, design, and beauty which would remain throughout the centuries as a testimony to the self-esteem of the most powerful king in Europe," and in this it certainly succeeded. It was a tremendous testimo-

ny to the power of Louis XIV. His court at Versailles in 1682 numbered twenty thousand, at least five thousand of which lived in the palace itself, which has 1,300 rooms heated by fires from 1,252 chimneys. The stables alone can house 2,500 horses and two hundred coaches. The Sun King's power was not solely reflected by the palace but by his ability to constantly succeed in throwing ever-increasing sums into the project against wide opposition. Former people of great influence such as his Chancellor of the Exchequer who were opposed to further extravagance were dishonored. Even natural obstacles could not stand in the way of the king's obsession.

Duc Louis de St. Simon described Versailles as: "A glum, meager place,

without view, no forest, no water, and even without firm foundation because the ground here consists of quicksand and morass, and inside there is a serious lack of fresh air." The king merely laughed at such criticism and had his soldiers reclaim the swamp, plant mature trees, and dig miles of ditches to provide water for both wells and fountains.

## A complete work of art

The completed work of art became what the garden historian Wilfried Hansmann described as: "The most tremendous edifice of all architecture and garden history of the Occident." The importance of the green surroundings to the palace for Louis is revealed in the instruction given to the garden designer André Le Nôtre to design a king's garden "such as the world has never seen before." From this point onwards the extension of the grounds surrounding the palace became the main priority above all other building work.

While Mansart was decorating the interior of the palace with marble, gold, and silver— the Sun King received messengers and envoys from every point of the compass while seated on a silver throne—and created a Hall of Mirrors in which the magnificence was multiplied, Le Nôtre was enhancing the garden with walkways, vistas, fountains, rills, ponds, garden sculpture, and an orangery. The culmination was the creation of the royal villas known as the Grand and Petit Trianons. Queen Marie Antoinette, for whom the Petit Trianon was built, described it as "the merriest message of Versailles."

*Versailles, seen from the gardens. The architect Jules Mansart was instructed to "build a palace of which the dimensions, design, and beauty would remain throughout the centuries as a testimony of the self-esteem of the most powerful king in Europe." Mansart furnished the interior with marble, gold (see Mars salon left with its gilt ceiling), and silver, while the famous garden designer André Le Nôtre created a garden with walkways, vistas, fountains, ponds, garden statuary, and an orangery as testimony to the power of "Le Roi Soleil."*

**49**

# Stone Age paintings in the caves of Lascaux

*Galloping horses, deer, ibex, and buffalo inhabit the rock walls, showing animals once commonplace*

Atlantic Ocean · EUROPE · FRANCE · Lascaux · Mediterranean

### ROUTE

Clermont-Ferrand–Perigueux to Le Jardin-St. Lazare (N89, then 6½ miles on D704 to Montignac)

### OPENING TIMES

Lascaux II: daily July–August 9.30 a.m.–7.30 p.m. Fewer visitors permitted in summer (advisable to pre-book well in advance)

### ALSO WORTH SEEING

Grottes de Lacave (28 miles SW), Grotte du Pech Merle (74½ miles SW)

In the French province of Dordogne, seventeen-year-old Marcel Ravidat and his three friends literally fell upon an amazing discovery. Looking for a place to bury a dead donkey, they were told by a woman farmer of an unusual hole beneath a fallen spruce. The tree seemed to be set well into the ground and so the boys took matches, and oil lamp, and a terrier named Robot and went in search of treasure. They found the hole close to the river Vezere and the terrier jumped in the hole followed by Marcel. Then, the ground beneath the three boys' feet gave way and swallowed them up. At the bottom of the hole the shocked friends saw the light of a match held by Marcel and heard him call to them to join him. So they continued further down into the cave, feeling their way along the walls of the dark tunnel until they reached a chamber about sixteen feet high. In the flickering light of the oil lamp they discovered something quite remarkable. A red horse was drawn on the cave wall between the horns of two bulls. This chamber has become known as the "Bull Chamber."

## Doll person

The abbot, Henri Breuil, the leading French expert on cave paintings, who was called in by the boys' teacher, immediately realized that this was a major discovery. The boys had stumbled across the largest collection of Paleolithic art that has ever been found. A pair of tunnels lead from this first small chamber that the boys discovered into larger areas with domed ceilings. The entire cave is around 460 feet long with walls with so many colorful drawings, such as depictions of animals, that they overlap. The abbot studied the galloping horses, deer with detailed antlers, fifty-foot-long bulls, ibex, and buffalo, most of which were painted in ochre, red, or black. Amid all these portrayals of animals there is only one of a human, but this is drawn as if by a child. Like a child's doll the figure is seen lying at the bottom, arms outstretched with a bird in

a branch drawn below it and a buffalo and running rhinoceros shown above in the same type of still life style. Could this be a hunting scene that is depicted?

Abbot Henri Breuil thought the paintings to be about eighteen thousand years old. His estimate proved to be fairly accurate. Modern research now places them at about fifteen thousand years ago. At this time most of present-day Germany lay beneath a sheet of ice while the south of France was savanna with only a few trees. Horses, buffalo, reindeer, and thick-skinned rhinoceros roamed the open grass land, and Stone Age hunters had learned how to kill them with spears

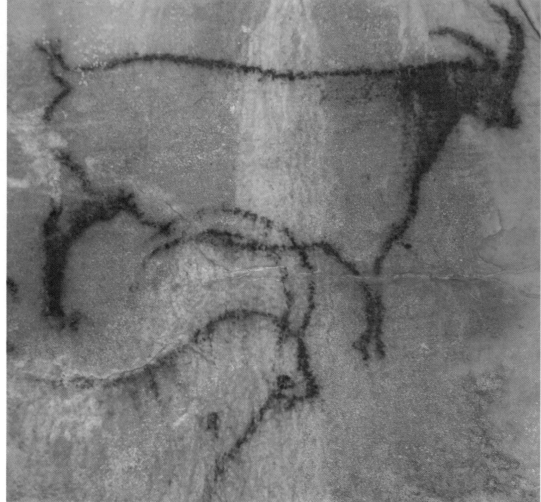

*20000 year old cave paintings - ibexes along with illustrations of footprints.*

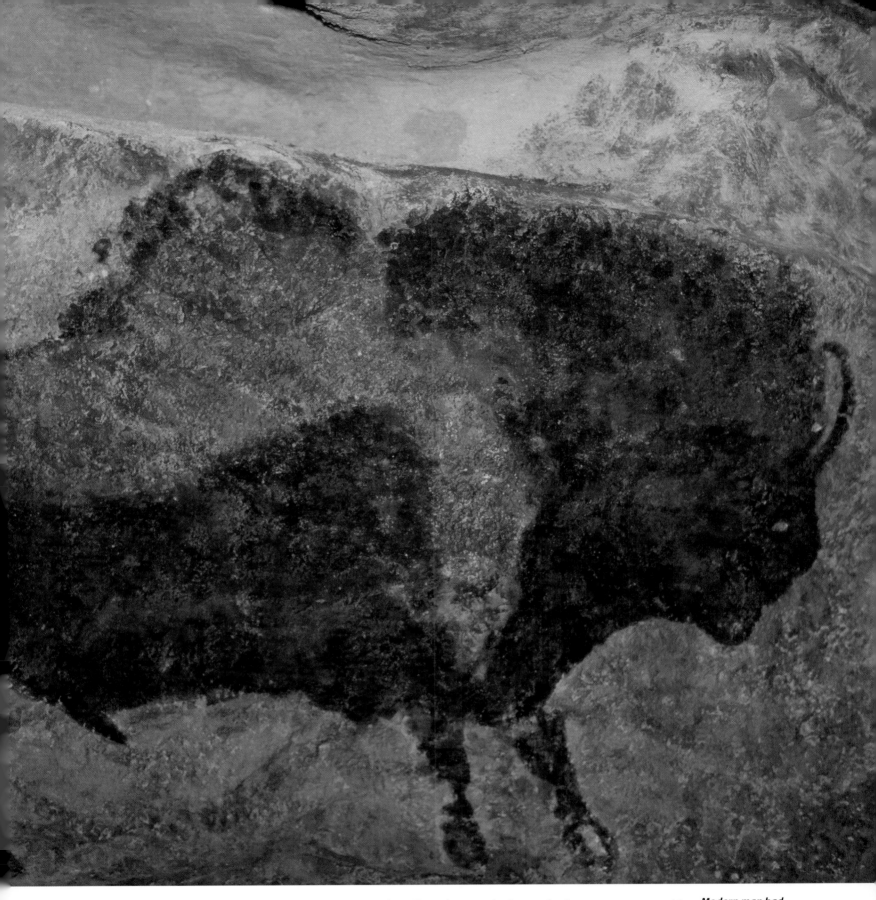

tipped with sharpened stones. The reason for the cave paintings remains a mystery and the subject of much debate. Did these budding Michelangelos want to portray their prowess at hunting, as many have suggested? If this is the case then why are there so few drawings of reindeer which were the principal prey? Perhaps the drawings have a mystical purpose of which we know nothing and the cave was used for rituals.

After the discovery at Lascaux, wall paintings were also discovered elsewhere, particularly in the valleys of the Vezere and throughout the Dordorgne, in the Perigord, along the Rhine, at the foot of the Pyrenees, and the Cantabrian Mountains. The most recent discovery was on the coat near Marseilles, where the cave is 118 feet under water. A discovery had been made at Altamira in Spain in 1879 but the authenticity of this was doubted for some time because it was felt that prehistoric man could not be capable of such creativity.

## Risk of colors fading

The discovery at Lascaux in the summer of 1940 was not made public until several years after the event because France had just been occupied by the Germans. The find was made known eight years later and people visited the cave in their hundreds. A road was built to make the cave more accessible and to protect the paintings from the vapor exhaled by the visitors, hermetically sealed doors were installed and a climate control system. But despite all this the colors of the paintings began to·fade. Paintings which had survived for thousands of years began to deteriorate rapidly. Today the 35,000 visitors each year have to be content with reproductions because the originals are no longer exposed to public gaze.

*Modern man had never before seen such a collection of art from the Stone Age as was revealed at the cave in Lascaux. Paintings of buffalo, giant bulls, horses, and cat-like predators adorn the walls of the cave in the Dordogne.*

# The divine art of Chartres Cathedral

*Notre Dame regarded as the supreme example of Gothic architecture*

Atlantic Ocean
EUROPE
• Chartres
FRANCE
Mediterranean

### ROUTE
Via A10/A11 for 52 miles SW of Paris

### ACCOMMODATIONS
Hotel Le Grand Monarque, Place Epars

### FOOD
Restaurant La Truie qui File, Place Poisonnerie

### ALSO WORTH SEEING
Church of St. Pierre, Musée des Beaux-Arts (Museum of Fine Art)

Medieval art achieved its zenith in the form of Gothic architecture. The Cathedral of Notre Dame (Our Lady) at Chartres in turn is regarded as the supreme example of Gothic architecture as a divine form of artistic expression. By the time of its building in the twelfth and thirteenth centuries all the building techniques established over the preceding centuries came together in a magnificent form that achieved superb optical effects and delightful proportions.

For the first time tall buttresses provided support and the slabs of walls were broken up and decorated with stained glass windows, the size of which had earlier been impossible. Chartres was the first cathedral to have three large rose windows, each of more than forty-two feet in height. These were points of concentration of this new divine form of art. For the first time too there were three huge naves decorated with many life size statues of earlier rulers and saints. All this created a different atmosphere for

the worshipper. Opulent jewels and expensive finery were replaced with colorful beams of light from the windows, which believers regarded as the "light of Christ."

### Pilgrimage to the "holy raiment"

The dimensions of the cathedral were a great novelty too. The vaulting above the nave for the first time soared to a height of more than one hundred feet. The great importance of Chartres was that it possessed the most important relic of the Virgin

Mary held in the western world, namely the "holy raiment" or blanket said to have been worn by Mary when Christ was born.

That Chartres Cathedral is so fine today is only in part due to this holy relic. In 1194 a fire almost totally destroyed the earlier church and the inhabitants of the small town were desperate because they were certain the holy relic had been destroyed in the fire. Cardinal Melior of Pisa, a papal legate who happened to be in Chartres at the time pleaded with the people of the town to rebuild their cathedral and when he repeated the request several days later the local bishop and his church council suddenly appeared bearing the holy raiment. A miracle had occurred in Chartres. The raiment had survived the fire in the church's crypt. Both clerics and citizenry pledged the

means to rebuild the cathedral over the coming three years.

This extraordinary commitment was described by the abbot Haimo of Chartres as "an example of nobility of soul," in a letter to fellow Christians in England. "When have you ever heard of lords, the mighty, those of honor and those of inflated wealth, noble men and women putting their proud and arrogant shoulders to the task, and bringing wine, corn, oil, lime, stones, wood, and other things required for the building of the church to Christ's place of refuge."

After only twenty-five years of building Chartres was once more proclaimed a place of pilgrimage to the Holy Virgin by Louis IX. There are more than 173 images of Mary in the windows and sculpture inside the cathedral.

It is not just for its medieval stained glass that Chartres retains the unity of the original work of art created here. The building is largely retained in its original condition and although much of the original paint has disappeared the sculptures remain undamaged.

*Chartres was the first cathedral to have three giant rose windows (left the window in the western facade) all 42 ft in diameter. Three giant naves are decorated with life-size sculpture of former rulers and saints (top). New building techniques allowed slender buttress supports and larger areas of window.*

# The rocky miracle of Mont-St.-Michel

*A stronghold of faith rises from the sea off the Normandy coast*

Atlantic Ocean

EUROPE

**Mont-St.-Michel**

FRANCE

Mediterranean

### ROUTE
From Paris: A11, A81 (211 miles) to Rennes then D173 for 43 miles N

### BEST TIMES
May–June (check tides)

### OPENING TIMES
Abbey: May–September 9.30 a.m.–6 p.m. otherwise 9.30 a.m.–4.15 p.m.

### ALSO WORTH SEEING
Coastal towns of St. Malo & Granville

*La Merveille or "the miracle" as the abbey was known when completed provides a superb view over this stronghold.*

Mont-St.-Michel can be seen from a long way off. The huge granite islet rises abruptly 525 feet out of the otherwise low terrain and is about one thousand yards from end to end. Sometimes it seems to float above the mist that often hugs the English Channel (or La Manche as it is known in France) at this part of the coast of Normandy. One million people come here to the border between Normandy and Brittany to see Le Mont-St.-Michel which was once described as "the miracle of the Occident." It is a castle and abbey with a shape, form, and location like none other: except that is its Cornish twin of St. Michael's Mount.

The building of the abbey started out with a vision. A tenth century manuscript relates that the archangel Michael came to Bishop Aubert of Avranches in a dream and set him the task to build a chapel on the highest point of the nearby Mont Tombe.

### A town of books

And hence the chapel was built and with the story about the archangel Michael, Mont-St.-Michel quickly became one of the most important places of pilgrimage. In 966, Richard I, who was also the Duke of Normandy, sent thirty Benedictine monks to the islet to start building an abbey on the rock. The monks and their workers had a major challenge ahead of them. The biggest problem was the pyramid shape of the slab of granite that forms the island. In order to build

the abbey as demanded to a length of more than three hundred feet it was necessary for them to build up foundations from the rock to provide the size of platform required. The crypt that this created served as a place for pilgrims to stay.

The work was accomplished and the Benedictine abbey was established and became very rich with the income from endowments of land and other donations. The monastery also acquired a certain intellectual charisma. During the period in which it flourished greatly, between 1154 and 1186, the Abbot Robert de Torigni established a great library so filled with manuscripts that the community was dubbed a "town of books."

In the Middle Ages, the only street on the rock was created,

known as *Grande Rue*, flanked then as today by countless shops, then serving the monks and the pilgrims, today meeting the tourists' demands for souvenirs. The road climbs upwards to the eleventh century Romanesque abbey church, which is one of the oldest surviving buildings in Normandy. The nave is of unusual form with only the central nave vaulted, following Norman tradition. The ruins of the monastery lie at the foot of the church but a visit still provides some insight into how the monks and pilgrims lived. The refectory and dormitory are still recognizable.

Part of the Romanesque structure was destroyed by fire in 1204 but a generous donation from French king Philippe Auguste—in settlement of obligations set forth in a treaty following war—more than met the cost of the repairs, which were carried out in Gothic style and completed in 1228. Following this rebuilding, the monastery was so grand and magnificent that it was known as *La Merveille* or "the miracle." The massive external buttresses are said to refer to the mightiness of The Holy One, the Almighty. It was said to be "the most prettily built thirteenth-century monastery between heaven and sea" from the room where alms were given, to the reception rooms where the abbot received guests of noble rank, the monk's refectory, the knights' hall with its finely arranged figures, right through to the clerestory.

During the One Hundred Years War between England and France (1337–1453) the monastic island was fortified into a stronghold but it continually declined. For a time after the French Revolution it served as a prison, until the entire rock was declared a national monument in 1873. The monastery used to be cut off twice each day by the high tide which rises here up to about forty-six feet. This happens less often these days since a causeway was built in 1880. However, plans are afoot to build a bridge or tunnel. The parking lot still floods at spring tides—that is big tides not just those in spring-time—so check the time and predicted height of the tide for your visit!

*The islet of Mont-St.-Michel rises 525 ft above the sea. The Gothic abbey is one of the most beautiful examples of monastic architecture of the 13th century. Sand banks have built-up against the causeway of 1880 so that the islet can now be reached during most tides.*

# Site of Stone Age rituals

*Stonehenge is Europe's most important prehistoric structure*

Atlantic
Ocean

GREAT
BRITAIN

Stonehenge
EUROPE

**ROUTE**

From London M3/A303 (88
miles) 10 miles N of
Salisbury (nearest station)

**OPENING TIMES**

Vary, check with Tourist
Information in UK

**BEST TIME**

Summer solstice, June 21
(Druid festival)

**ALSO WORTH SEEING**

Avebury Ring 15 miles N,
Europe's largest prehistoric
building

It is as if some race of titans has tried to build a temple from massive slabs of rock but not finished the job. The circle of great stones stands bleakly on the open hillside of the Salisbury Plain just ten miles north of Salisbury in the southern English county of Wiltshire. Many have wondered what the purpose of these stones is or sought their meaning. One thing though is certain, Stonehenge is Europe's most important prehistoric building.

Archaeologists now consider they know quite a lot about this apparently mysterious stone monument. The earliest construction on the site dates from the late Stone Age to early Bronze Age, while the main structure is dated between early Bronze Age and the

late Iron Age. It consists of four concentric rings of stones. The largest outer circle of the megalithic structure is about one hundred feet in diameter but beyond this there is a ring bank and further out a circular ditch some 340 feet across. The monument as it stands today was partially recreated in 1958, when several stones and their lintels that had fallen were put back into position. Stonehenge was comprehensively desecrated in Roman times and stands today largely as it probably did after that desecration. Evidence has been found of a much more complex structure than survives today.

## Sandstone for the ritual monument

About one thousand years after the initial construction at Stonehenge, presumably in the early Bronze Age, the first giant sandstone megaliths were hoisted into position to form a ring of rock pillars, or sarsen stones, about fifteen feet high that were capped with further such stones placed laterally as lintels so that they were butted up to each other. These stones weigh around twenty-eight tons each, and the type of rock used is not found locally so that the stones must have been transported to the site from some considerable distance. In addition to sandstone there is blue stone—spotted dolerite—and also specimens of rhyolite and of volcanic ash. The blue stones come from the

northern slopes of the Prescelly Mountains and the large "altar stone" is thought to come from Pembrokeshire, both in Wales.

### Astonishing feat of transport

Some of these stones appear to have been brought to Stonehenge from quarries more than 180 miles away. They probably rolled the stones on timber until they were able to move them by raft across the sea and perhaps also up the River Avon until they once were more transported over the ground on rollers. Great ingenuity must also have been used by the people who built this monument in order to lift the massive stones into position and then to cap them with massive stone lintels. The name Stonehenge refers to the "hanging stones" but archaeologists refer to all these Neolithic circular monuments as a *henge*.

There was no serious study of Stonehenge until the seventeenth century when the British antiquarian John Aubrey discovered fifty-six pits, now known as the "Aubrey holes," containing human bones and charcoal in the inner bank. Who these people were and why they were buried at what must clearly have been such an important site is shrouded in as much mystery as much else about Stonehenge.

It is believed that Stonehenge was built for ritual purposes. It is possible that Stone Age people paid homage to the sun, as did many early civilizations, possibly treating the sun as a god who created life. Computer models suggest the monument is capable of predicting the summer and winter solstices, the vernal and autumnal equinoxes, and eclipses of both the sun and moon and also acts as a calendar.

*Huge blocks of sandstone from Wales, weighing about 28 tons were used for part of Stonehenge's structure, placed upright as sarsen stones and capped with lintels.*

# Kings and Queens of England were crowned in Westminster Abbey

*Memorial tablets relate the history of an island race*

*Atlantic Ocean*

EUROPE

GREAT BRITAIN

**London**

## ROUTE
Westminster subway station (Circle/District Line)

## OPENING TIMES
Main entrance, nave and transept: 8 a.m.–6 p.m. (more limited times for access to the choir and royal tombs)

## FOOD
Ye Olde Cheshire Cheese, 145 Fleet Street (prominent pub of 1665)

## ALSO WORTH SEEING
St. Paul's Cathedral, British Museum, Victoria & Albert Museum

In 1700 a knight of the realm exclaimed: "Good God, I do not want to be buried in Westminster Abbey. They bury idiots there." Perhaps the culprit, Sir Godfrey Kneller, was a bit of a republican for apart from the handful of poets, philosophers, and scholars the Collegiate Church of St. Peter at Westminster, as the abbey is officially titled, is also the burial place of English monarchs. But even its role of burial place for the great and the good is dwarfed in significance by the abbey's close association with the throne itself. The coronation of every English king or queen since William the Conqueror crowned himself there at Christmas 1066 has taken place at Westminster Abbey.

## Built over five hundred years
When the English state split with Rome it kept the existing churches within the new Church of England. The abbey church was built and has survived under royal patronage to be one of the most beautiful of medieval churches.

A legend surrounds the origins of the abbey. The Anglo-Saxon king Sebert is said to have founded an abbey on the spot in the seventh century. It is certain that there was indeed a Benedictine abbey at what is now known as Westminster in the late tenth century for which Edward the Confessor (1042–1066) had an abbey church built. The name, that is also borne by a borough of London and the British parliament building (Westminster Palace), means nothing more than an abbey church, or minster, located to the west of the City of London–the old, historic heart of today's metropolis. Edward's church was inaugurated in December 1065 and eight days later the king died and was laid to rest in his new church.

Westminster Abbey as it stands today was largely fashioned in two phases. In 1245, Henry III wished to display his power and status by constructing a new royal church at Westminster to rival the great Gothic cathedral that was being built at Reims. The second major work was instigated one hundred years later by Richard II. His master builder was the architect of Canterbury Cathedral, Henry Yevele, who is largely responsible for the important adaptations in a style known as Early English Gothic.

Three hundred years later the outer stone cladding was renewed by Sir Christopher Wren who rebuilt much of the city of London after the Great Fire of London in 1666, and whose most important work is St. Paul's Cathedral in the city. A further one hundred years later—a building period therefore spanning five centuries—the twin Gothic towers were completed, that are such a key feature of the abbey.

In the usual manner, the basic form of the building is in the shape of a cross, 512 feet long by two hundred feet. The height above the nave at 115 feet is the highest in Britain. The abbey has largely retained its simplicity and remains in good condition in spite of a few minor changes and some restoration in the nineteenth century.

The vast majority of those who visit this house of God each year do not come for any religious purpose but for the mass of different memorials to "the great and the good," honoring members of the English aristocracy, major statesmen, scholars, and those from the arts. Some four hundred different memorials are reminders of our transitory time on earth but also shed some light on the history of the British.

## A magnificent nave
A French traveler and historian clearly disliked much of the abbey, London, and the English weather but managed a word of praise for the abbey's magnificent nave, along which kings and queens have trod in procession. In his diary for 1872, Hyppolite Taine observes: "Westminster Abbey: a beautiful nave. Curious Gothic architecture. It is the only kind suitable for this climate. It is spoiled by the jumble of forms and abundance of sentimental statues, but is quite in keeping with this depressing weather."

*Westminster Abbey was to rival Reims Cathedral. Its Early English Gothic style is the work of Henry Yevele who also built Canterbury Cathedral. Immediate left are the twin towers. Opposite page: the vaulted ceiling of the nave.*

# Scotland's Royal Mile

*The medieval street that links Holyrood Palace to Edinburgh Castle*

*Atlantic Ocean*

EUROPE

**Edinburgh**
GREAT
BRITAIN

### ROUTE
By air: direct to Prestwick (Glasgow) or via London to Edinburgh

### BEST TIMES
May–July, September–October

### OPENING TIMES
Castle (April–October): daily 9.30 a.m.–5 15p.m.; Holyrood House: check with Tourist Information as times vary due to royal state visits

### ALSO WORTH SEEING
Calton Hill (view point), Royal Botanical Garden

Daniel Defoe described Edinburgh's Royal Mile as perhaps the longest and most beautiful street in Britain, if not the world when he visited in 1706. Both the buildings and their inhabitants impressed him.

The name Royal Mile has a curious ring to it. Houses and people have been crowded into this part of the capital city since the sixteenth century. In 1558, the population of Edinburgh was eight thousand. A hundred years later it had grown to around sixty thousand—who all lived in or around the Royal Mile.

Edinburgh was the first European city to build apartment blocks, known there as tenements. In the seventeenth century, buildings of seven to eight floors were commonplace and ten to twelve floors not unheard of. The highest rise dwelling from this era was of fifteen storeys.

But the name Royal Mile relates to the property of the crown not the people. This is the street of the Scottish royalty that runs from Edinburgh Castle to the Palace of Holyrood House, where the present Queen spends time each summer. The Royal Mile consists of a number of streets: Castle Hill, Lawnmarket, High Street, and Canongate.

## A road steeped in history

The Royal Mile is a road that is steeped in the often bloody history of Scotland and of the British Isles, from the medieval castle on its hilltop that looks down upon the city to the Palace of Holyrood House at the other. It was here that the Catholic Scottish queen, Mary Stuart, who brought the influence of the French court to Edinburgh, was pursued with implacable hatred by the dark Protestant reformer John Knox, founder of the Church of Scotland. He was known by

the people as "Killjoy" somewhat appropriately. Knox lived a short distance away from Mary Queen of Scots, between the palace and Edinburgh's principal church of St. Giles—on the steps of which drunken Scots have been known to fight one another at Hogmanay (New Year's Eve)—and further up the street is the Tollbooth, court and prison where Mary Stuart's supporters, such as the Marquis of Montrose and the Duke of Atholl lost their heads. Mary herself was beheaded in England.

Other bloody deeds linked to the Royal Mile are the murder of Mary's secretary Rizzio by her jealous husband Lord Darnley and the infamous "Black Dinner" of 1440. The host, Sir William Crichton, served roast ox for his guests and then had them murdered. The unfortunate dinner guests were Crichton's rivals for Scottish power, the sixth Earl of Douglas and his brother.

Today this historic thoroughfare is overrun with tourists who often shuffle past places of great significance in blissful ignorance. The Palace of Holyrood House was originally the guest house of Holyrood Abbey, rebuilt in its present form in the seventeenth century for Charles II. Parts of Edinburgh Castle on the other hand date back to Viking times. Visitors today, whose imagination is caught by the tragic story of Mary Queen of Scots, press to see the small room in which she gave birth to her son who became James I of England and James VI of Scotland, uniting the English and Scottish crowns. Her claim to the English throne was barred because she was Catholic, but when Queen Elizabeth died without an heir Mary's son was the natural successor. Her son's name has adorned the authorized bibles of the Protestant church for centuries.

The Royal Mile has recently witnessed happier times when Queen Elizabeth II left Holyrood Palace to open the first Scottish Parliament since the eighteenth century.

*The Palace of Holyrood House was rebuilt for Charles II in the seventeenth century as a home for Scottish monarchs. Today is has largely become a focus of interest in the tragic story of Mary Queen of Scots. Mary's distant relative, Queen Elizabeth II, spends a little time here each year. The unicorn (far left) in the entrance hall is a blazon from the coat of arms of Mary Stuart. The historic apartment houses or tenements of the Royal Mile (left) are early examples of high-rise living.*

# Green hopes, icy white reality

*Greenland, the largest island in the world, retains a primeval icy nature*

**Greenland**

*Atlantic Ocean*

The indigenous people of Greenland call it Kalaallit Nunaat or "human hand" in their native Inuit (Eskimo) and yet there are few human hands on this island that is the world's largest. The population of this autonomous part of the Kingdom of Denmark is 57,000. Most of the island lies north of the Arctic Circle. The entirely inappropriate name of Greenland (Grønland in Danish) was given to the island more than a thousand years ago as a marketing trick by the rapacious Viking, Eric the Red, in order to attract colonists. He managed to persuade four hundred people to colonize the island, taking wives and children, equipment and cattle. Their Viking prows reached the shores in the summer of 986, landing at what is now Ericsfjord, close to Narssarssuarq where flights from the original mother country land. It was here that the first settlement in this inhospitable land was established.

From north to south the island is about 1,650 miles long but has a total of just over ten miles of paved road. More than four-fifths of Greenland is covered by permanent ice cap with a maximum depth of about eight thousand feet. When seen from the air Greenland mainly looks white and cold, like the North Pole. Standing on the ice cap one can see outcrops of basalt mountains breaking through the ice to reassure

one that this ice is founded on solid ground unlike the ice sheet at the North Pole.

The green land that Eric the Red promised is a thin strip of land at the coast and this is where Greenlanders live in small settlements. The coast, which is deeply indented with fjords, makes visiting a major undertaking. The only means of travel between the capital of Nuuk (Godthab) to the provincial town of Ivittuut is only

*Four-fifth of Greenland is covered by a layer of ice (3 km thick)*

possible by air or by sea. One fifth of the population of Greenland lives in Nuuk.

## From Eskimo to Inuit

Over time, the Viking population merged with the native Inuit peoples until there were no authentic Norsemen left. Soon after Greenland was rediscovered by Europeans, the Danes took possession of the island in 1721, ruling almost continuously for more than 250 years until 1979, when the colony became autonomous. Greenland has prospered since going its own way, with a freely elected parliament of twenty-seven members and a government with six ministries. The Royal Greenland Business Association, that had previously governed the island economy was replaced by the Kalaallit Nuerfiat enterprise. Greenland pulled out of the European Community following a referendum because of disputes over fishing quotas. Today Greenlanders are eagerly developing their own cultural identity. Because of this Greenlanders do not like themselves or their language to be termed Eskimo, rather Inuit, in

common with people of related ethnic origin in Canada, Alaska, and Siberia. They do welcome the benefits of western civilization in the form of hospitals, radio stations, and schools and they tolerate the American air bases that have existed there since the start of the Cold War. Life here is governed strictly by the time of year and though much of life is still largely traditional, such as hunting for seals in a kayak, modern vessels are used to fish for crab, trout, and cod. Enlightened animal rights activists have recognized the legitimacy of the traditional Inuit seal hunt. The principal source of income is derived from the commodity which the people of Greenland have in abundance but for which they have little use: icy wilderness. The sheer scale and magnificence of the landscape, astonishing geysers, and mountains of at least 13,000 feet lure increasing numbers of tourists to the island who want to breathe the pure Arctic air, see musk oxen, and Arctic foxes. They are also tempted into buying Inuit souvenirs made of rope and enjoying a Greenland *smörrebröd*. By the time these travelers have returned

home they will have learned the most important word used in Greenland: imaga meaning something like "maybe." This word is used widely, especially when weather conditions prevent flights back to the "civilized" world, as occurs often. This happens so frequently that all Greenland airports have a stopover hotel. The record delay is for Kangerlussuaq (Sandre Stromfjord)—which is rated as an airport usable in all conditions—where a group of tourists once had to wait three weeks before they could leave the island. The locals insist this kind of thing really only happens in winter.

*Enormous icebergs that have broken away from the northern coast of Greenland, close to the North Pole form a majestic backdrop to the huts of the native Inuit. The icebergs can be seen at closer quarters on boat trips through the fjords.*

# When Iceland's geysers boil and blow

*Hot springs are an astounding natural spectacle*

ICELAND
• Reykjavik
*Atlantic Ocean*

EUROPE

**ROUTE**

By air to Reykjavik

**BEST TIMES**

June–August

**ALSO WORTH SEEING**

Gulfoss Falls, Jökusárgljufur and Skaftafell Nature Reserves, Hot Spa at Hveravellir

Around sixty-five million years ago the earth's crust rent apart between Greenland and Scandinavia. Magma from the bowels of the earth flowed to the surface where it was cooled by the sea. As the process continued, mountains of basalt formed that grew higher and higher until about sixteen million years ago they emerged, hissing and steaming from the deep as volcanoes. Thus Iceland was born. The processes that gave birth to this island continues to the present day. The occupants of this volcanic island reap benefits from and face risks with their life above the cauldron.

## At the "hot spot"

The continents of the Americas and Eurasia have been drifting apart for millions of years by about an inch each year. Iceland was formed when a rift opened that allowed magma to emerge through the fault. This accounts for Iceland's fascinating geological history.

Iceland is still one of those "hot spots" in the world where large volumes of lava are spewed from the earth. In the case of Iceland one of the stranger factors is that this is mainly beneath the massive ice sheet of the Vatnajökull Glaciers covering 3,204 square miles, making them the largest expanse of ice within the European Community. This is not usually the place at which to witness Iceland's volcanoes erupting, but the danger is ever present and made apparent from time to time. When eruptions occur here large quantities of ice are melted. Some experts predict that much of the fertile southwestern part of Iceland will

eventually be flooded and force the population to evacuate.

Volcanic activity does have some benefits though. The heat of the earth's core there means that groundwater temperatures at a depth of just over 3,000 feet reach 536°F (280°C) and this provides energy for generating electricity, and is piped to homes and greenhouses for heating. This means that even the sidewalks are heated in the capital of Reykjavik to keep them free from ice in winter. The blue lagoon of cooled water at the Grindavik power station is used as naturally heated thermal baths for therapeutic purposes that permit comfortable outdoor bathing. The constant volcanic activity brings another benefit to the islanders: they attract tourists. Iceland's hot springs and geysers have brought an important cash crop of tourism to

land that is otherwise of no economic value.

The thermal springs of Haukadalur with its enormous geyser, about sixty or so miles east of the capital, is one of the most visited natural phenomena of Iceland, even if the springs do now seem to be less active. The geyser once spurted a jet of steam almost two hundred feet into the air every hour. This has been happening since 1294 but its performance is now less dependable.

## Hot springs at Strokkur

Tourists are more reliably catered to by the geyser at the hot springs at Strokkur which spouts about eighty feet into the air every ten minutes. After the brief shower of rain following this display the surface of the pool is calm except for a few wisps of steam on the surface. Then suddenly the water starts to boil and a large bubble of vapor forms until the moment when the bubble bursts as steam and hot water surges skywards once more. The water in the pool at this moment is 206.6°F (97°C). There are some thirty geysers in Iceland's interior but few are as attractive as Strokkur.

The blue springs of Hveravellir about 44 miles further north are also worth a visit, located between the glaciers of Hof and Langiökul, at a height of almost five hundred feet above sea level. The hot springs here bubble and fume but beware, the ground beneath your feet is brittle, especially where covered in yellow deposits of sulfur or white lime. The water here can cause severe burns.

*The thermal springs of Haukadalur with their main geyser of Strokkur are one of Iceland's main tourist attractions. At regular intervals Strokkur sends plumes of boiling water and steam high into the air. The pool of water then becomes calm again as if nothing had occurred, except for a few wisps of steam. Suddenly the water starts to boil and bubbles erupt from the depths, breaking through the boiling water to shoot eighty feet into the sky. This impressive show happens every ten minutes.*

# Where Swedish queens learned to dream

*Drottningholm Castle is the "Versailles of the north"*

Atlantic Ocean · SWEDEN · Stockholm · EUROPE

### ROUTE

By train to Brommaplan and then bus line 301/323 to Lovön Island; or by boat from Stockholm

### BEST TIMES

May–August

### OPENING TIMES

Summer: 11 a.m.–4.30 p.m.

### ALSO WORTH SEEING

The old town of Stockholm

Drottningholm, the "Versailles of the north" is something of a fairy-tale castle. Not just because this is considered the finest baroque palace in northern Europe but because it was the scene against which love stories were played out that caught the imagination of the people. The palace on the island of Lovön is also one of the few important places in history where women held sway. In

1662, Queen Hedwig Eleonora, widow of Carl Gustavus X, gave orders for a new palace to be built at Drottningholm, the Queen's island. This was to be built on precisely the same spot where exactly one hundred years earlier the Polish born Queen Caterina Jagel Ionica had resided. One hundred years after this, came yet another woman who ordered the expansion and renovation of the palace. This was Ulrike,

the sister of Frederick the Great and wife of the Swedish king Adolphus Frederick, who not only added an impressive new side wing but was also responsible for the splendor with which the many rooms were redecorated.

### Classicism in blue and gold

In 1771, Ulrike's son Gustavus III assumed the throne. He is known as the initiator of Sweden's "golden age,"

and the style of the era was also named after him: Gustavian—a French and Italian inspired classicism that was characterized by the use of blue and gold in decorating the houses of royalty and the aristocracy. The arts and sciences flourished under this monarch and theaters were added to the royal palaces, so that Gustav was also known as the "theater king."

### Bourgeois queen

Sweden was less fortunate with Gustav's descendants. The state imported the Napoleonic general Jean-Baptiste Bernadotte in 1810, made him dauphin, and then crowned him in 1818. His queen was a former love of Napoleon, Bernardine Eugénie Dési-

rée, daughter of a merchant known as Clary. It is her sad and moving story that is related in the novel *Désirée*.

The present lady of Drottningholm was also born a commoner. She was born in Germany as Sylvia Renate Sommerlath until she married the Swedish king Carl XVI Gustavus. She too had a former love and her story evokes great sympathy for the royal house in Sweden. Queen Sylvia, who lives in the south wing of Drottningholm, is more at home with the art and history of Sweden than many of her acquired countrymen and women. The palace's library is a favorite place for this cultural queen.

Drottningholm also has a room in full-blown rococo style by the

Swedish master Jean Eric Rehn created for Gustavus III, and parts of the gardens are in the English landscape style that contrasts with the formal beauty of the baroque French-style. These are further bequests to Drottningholm by that artistic monarch.

The palace's theater was inaugurated in 1766 and thirty of the original sets still exist. Performances of opera and ballet herald summer each year. The biographer of King Gustavus wrote: "Life was loved and lived in good taste," at "fairy-tale Drottningholm castle." Clearly, it was not only commoner queens Désirée and Sylvia who found their dreams of becoming queen come true.

*The front of the royal palace of Drottningholm looks out onto the gardens. It displays a happy blend of baroque and rococo. The castle's history is closely linked to the queens who have lived here. Queen Hedwig Eleonora had it built in 1662; Queen Ulrike had it expanded and redecorated; Queen Désirée tried to forget her native France here, and Queen Sylvia now organizes happy family parties here.*

# Moscow sparkles again

*Restorers now rule the Kremlin and Red Square*

**ROUTE**

Subway stations: Biblioteka Imeni Lenina and Borowizskaya (Kremlin), Plosjsjad Revoljoesji (Gum, Red Square)

**BEST TIMES**

May–June, September

**ACCOMMODATIONS**

Baltsjoeg Kempinski (luxury class) near Kremlin, Intourist (medium class) in city center

**ALSO WORTH SEEING**

Pushkin Museum, Trejakov Gallery, Kolomenskaye summer residence, Ostankino Castle

*Entrance to the Kremlin: the Gate of Resurrection. Deep religious belief has survived ideology.*

The eternal struggle in Russia between the church and state ended in favor of the church—at least so far as the architecture of Moscow is concerned. The golden crosses and domes of the Jesus the Savior Cathedral that were blown up on the orders of Stalin in 1932 once more dominate the view of the inner city. The cathedral has been rebuilt.

For hundreds of years the capital of the vast expanses of Russia was little more than a fortress or *kremlin* but the settlement kept expanding in a series of rings around the inner fortifications. Today in addition to this citadel with its defensive walls there are large avenues, a railway, the old city quarters, the Bolshoi Theater, the enormous cathedral of St. Basil, and Red Square.

## City behind walls

The Kremlin retained the basic form it acquired during the reign of Czar Ivan III in the late fifteenth century. The Russian word *kremlin* has an identical meaning to the English word *citadel*. This citadel has a triangular ground plan that covers about seventy-four acres on a hill

overlooking the Moskva or Moscow River. Ivan brought in architects from Italy and commissioned them to build palaces and churches around the Kremlin, but to Russian precepts. His successors later added chapels, churches, cloisters, an arsenal, several palaces, theaters, imperial mansions, and buildings for the administration of government. All these were within the Kremlin so that today the Kremlin has the appearance of an entire city within walls.

But the Moscow and Kremlin one sees today is a mere shadow of its former self, for the city had to be rebuilt after its brief occupation of thirty-nine days by Napoleon's Grande Armée in 1812.

Remains of the old city can still be found at the center of the rebuilt one. Red Square has stood alongside the Kremlin, at the heart of this settlement on the Moskva River since the early Middle Ages. People congregated here to hear the edicts of the czar or witness the execution of his enemies. And today the body of Lenin, founder of the Soviet Union, lies at the foot of the Kremlin wall, visible in a glass sarcophagus as an embalmed tourist attraction. Tourists come from all over the world to gaze at the impressive palaces that were built within the tall walls of the Kremlin.

When Moscow was rebuilt, theaters, museums, and even shops in the classical style were added. The

three huge galleried floors of the Gum department store were built on the perimeter of Red Square in 1856. There is also the somewhat pretentious delicatessen named Gastronome Number One, of 1910. The Bolshoi Theater opened its doors in 1856. Moscow's first subway or metro started running in 1935. Its opulent and palatial stations are a tourist attraction in their own right, heavily influenced by the German Bauhaus style of architecture. A classic example of this genre is the Soviet Laborers Club built in 1929.

At the present time the 850-year-old city is virtually the largest construction site in Europe. Reconstruction and restoration is mainly concentrated on churches and buildings that were destroyed or severely damaged under Communist rule. One of the men charged with the task of guardian to Russia's heritage, Victor Bulochnikov, says that the renaissance of the Russian state requires the restoration of its cultural heritage. It is expensive heritage for the cost runs into many millions in any currency.

*The Kremlin or citadel. What makes the Moscow Kremlin so important is that a major capital city grew up within its walls, complete with churches and palaces. The golden domed Archangel Cathedral (left, shows interior) is within the Kremlin, the Cathedral of St. Basil is just outside.*

# Beautiful St. Petersburg

*The city on the Neva is Russia's "window to the west"*

### ROUTE

Hermitage subway
Admiraleskaya; Tsarkoye Selo
(Pushkin); train from
Wetebsker station

### BEST TIME

June (long days)

### ALSO WORTH SEEING

Smolny Monastery, St. Isaac's
Cathedral, Peterhof palaces,
and Pavlosk

Of the major grand-style cosmopolitan cities of the world, St. Petersburg is the youngest of them all, more recent than New York for example. True, there are more recent cities such as Brasilia, but these have been built using modern construction techniques and town zoning. By contrast St. Petersburg is very much an eighteenth-century style city in which baroque and classical architecture dominates. Russia's "window on the west" was created by a mix of German, French, and Italian architects. Historians cannot agree if that description should be attributed to Peter the Great, the Italian writer Francesco Algarotti, or the Russian writer Pushkin.

St. Petersburg sprawls over more than forty islands and these are further subdivided by small rivulets and canals into about one hundred

smaller ones. At first sight it seems absurd to build a city on such a river delta, but this provided Peter the Great, who was constantly moving his place of residence, with additional security. Its modern virtue is that this has resulted in one of the finest cities in Europe, with ever changing vistas.

## Rastrelli's palaces

At the heart of the city is the baroque Winter Palace which Peter the Great's daughter Elizabeth had built for her by her favorite architect, Bartolomeo Rastrelli. The enormous palace was completed in eight years. It remains impressive with its 1,057 rooms, 1,945 windows, and 117 staircases. Rastrelli joined the court of Peter the Great when he was just sixteen. Once Peter's daughter Elizabeth became Czarina he came into his own. The Smolny

Monastery and five baroque palaces that he built in St. Petersburg led to his being dubbed Rastrelli the Magnificent.

The city on the river Neva owes its great beauty to Catherine the Great, who conscripted a great army of architects. Only one of the major palaces that she had built during her reign—the Taurist Palace—was built by a Russian architect, Ivan Starov. Catherine depended on foreigners for all the rest. The Hermitage and the art academy were built by the Frenchman Vallin de la Mothe, while the Italian Giacomo Quarenghi undertook the Hermitage Theater and the Academy of Science. The Czarina wrote: "Building is a sickness, just as dipsomania is." The best example of this "sickness" of hers is the Alexander Palace in Tsarskoye Selo, which experts consider is by far Giacomo Quarenghi's finest work for

St. Peterburg's finest church is that of The Savior, with its gold leaf embellished domes. Below is one of the many fascinating stairways in the Hermitage.

the empress. The colorful Catherine Palace, ornamented with golden domes, is from Elizabeth's reign. Catherine merely asked the Scottish architect Charles Cameron to "clear up and decorate the interior." The Scot did so with great enthusiasm and use of unusual materials for those days—malachite, bronze, agate, colored glass, and marble.

## Hermitage: a temple to art

The palaces and cathedrals that resulted from these imperial crazes for building provide a costly setting for the jewel in their midst: the new Hermitage. This building in the classical style was built between 1839 and 1852 and houses one of the largest art collections of the entire world. Each year more than three millions visitors admire a tiny portion of its works of art which includes many famous paintings.

# Novgorod, the cradle of Russia

*The St. Sophia Cathedral is an impressive display of former power*

Atlantic Ocean

**Novgorod**

RUSSIA

EUROPE

### ROUTE

By air to St. Petersburg and train to Novgorod

### BEST TIMES

June–August

### ACCOMMODATIONS

Beresta Palace Hotel, Intourist

### ALSO WORTH SEEING

Home of Dostoyevsky (Staraya Russ, Lake Ilmen)

Although the name of the city of Novgorod means "new city" it is actually as old as Russia itself. Founded in the tenth century, the name implies there must have been an earlier settlement on the site, which was perhaps established by the legendary Rurik in the ninth century. Novgorod is north of Lake Ilmen, about 119 miles from St. Petersburg. The city has long been divided by the Volkhov River which flows into Lake Ladoga, where it links with other waterways including one to the east.

It is these waterways to which Novgorod owes its economic position, which has made the city a powerful center of cultural richness for over five hundred years that is unique in Russia.

Vladimir I (The Holy) who reigned from 978–1015 was ruler of Novgorod before he gained control over all the Russian peoples and moved to Kiev to rule his wider realm. The freedom-loving people of Novgorod did not take kindly to being subjects of Kiev, but the wealthy mercantile city managed to retain a degree of autonomy from Russian authority. From 1136 the true power was in the hands of the major landowners or Boyars and their bourgeois government which appointed the governor. Novgorod by this time had achieved a status unique in Russia: a free republic known as Novgorodrodskaya.

The Boyar rule was checked though by the Russian alliance with the Orthodox church. In 988, Vladimir I had elevated Orthodox Christianity to the status of state religion. Conversion to Christianity was slow with the people of Novgorod, many of whom still worshipped the ancient Slavic god of thunder, Peroen, and it was also bloody. Eventually an archbishop was appointed to reside in the Novgorod kremlin who was also a representative of the general assembly.

### Mural by Theopanes

Novgorod's kremlin, known as Detines ("strong boy") is sited in the west of the city and the left bank of the Volkhov. Five onion-domed towers rise up above the sturdy walls of the citadel of limestone. This is the St. Sophia Cathedral, the finest and largest building within the citadel. It was built between 1045 and 1052 and has managed to withstand change and retain its simple and austere appearance. A number of characteristics of what was to later become recognized as a

"Novgorod style" are already evident in this early brick-built church: the enormous scale and dominance of powerful and heroic forms over quaint and poetic motifs.

The facade of the cathedral is not embellished. Little remains of the ancient murals of the interior. The oldest and most valuable icon, the eleventh century St. Peter and St. Paul icon, is now in the Novgorod museum with many other icons from Novgorod. These have long been greatly valued for their high artistic merit.

In the fifteenth century this city state had 150 churches and monasteries. Many of these were commissioned by families, mercantile associations, and the bourgeois, so that they are less ostentatious than buildings erected by royal decree. The city had buildings such as the Yuriev Monastery, capped with domes in the form of military helmets, the church of St. Peter and St. Paul in Kosjevniki, and the Christ the King Cathedral with its superb

frescoes that dominated the city for centuries. Byzantine artist Theophanes created murals in 1378 regarded as among the best of their age.

In 1570, terrible slaughter by Ivan the Terrible brought an end to Novgorod's political power. During World War II the Germans inflicted

considerable damage on both the population and to the city's churches and art treasures. Many of these monuments were carefully restored after the war, including the golden and silver domes of the churches of Novgorod, giving them back the old Russian charm.

*Gold embellishes the main dome and silver the lesser ones of the Cathedral of St. Sophia (top left). The principal churches of the city were built in 1045–1052 and retain their sober and austere appearance. The blue-gold onion domes of the smaller church (top right) is like a smaller version of the cathedral. The unusual 16th century wooden church dedicated to the Virgin Mary (left) stands in an open air folk museum.*

# City of the stones that speak

*The inner city of Krakow is the history of art in stone*

**ROUTE**

By air to Warsaw or Krakow

**ACCOMMODATIONS**

Hotel Francuski, Ull. Pjarska

**ALSO WORTH SEEING**

Auschwitz (Oswiecim) 31 miles W; Czestochowa (place of pilgrimage) 63 miles NW

One does not need to be a poet to call Krakow the city of the "stones that speak." For this city—the medieval heart of which was largely untouched by the destruction of World War II—contains a wealth of magnificent architecture in the form of patrician homes, palaces of the nobility, more than one hundred churches and cloisters, one of the oldest universities in the world, and the residence of Polish kings. Few places can boast such a collection of gems from the Middles Ages, through the Renaissance, to the baroque era. This is why Krakow was the first Euro-

pean city to be added to UNESCO'S list of world cultural heritage sites.

Krakow did not gain its charter as a city until 965 but was nevertheless already a well-known trading settlement on the Vistula River and an important center for Catholic missionaries. Krakow became a bishopric and then capital of the divided realm of the Piast dynasty that ruled Poland in 1039. The Piasts erected the Royal Wawel Castle and a cathedral on the nearby Wawel hill. Polish kings were crowned and buried at the cathedral until the eighteenth century.

In 1241 the city was invaded by the Tartars and razed to the ground, but under the Piast Duke and later King Boleslaw and his successor Casimir III, the city was rebuilt with great vigor. The new city was constructed in a checkerboard plan with the large Rynek square at its center as market place, and it developed into one of the leading cities of late medieval Europe. In 1364 the University of Krakow was founded, the first in Poland and one of the world's oldest. Nicholas Copernicus, the famous astronomer, studied here with thousands of other students. In the fifteenth century, the

Mary's Cathedral that features two hundred gilt carvings in lime wood. Stoss was engaged on this project for ten years. At thirty-six feet by forty-three feet, this is the largest Gothic altar in Europe and also the most important example of late Gothic altars.

## A city in decline

Krakow's golden age was from 1506 to 1572 when Kings Sigismund I and II invited Italian painters and architects to their court and commissioned them to rebuild the Royal Wawel Castle in the finest of Renaissance styles. With designs by the architect of the Tuscan court, Bartolomeo Berecci, the Sigismund chapel was created, which is the most important example of Renaissance architecture in Poland. An impressive collection of fine furniture and paintings, and the famous Flemish Arras tapestries can be visited by means of an Italianate arcade reaching three storeys high. The royal treasure chamber contains valuable examples of the goldsmith's art and royal regalia, such as the coronation sword, dating from 1320.

Krakow remained the center of Polish culture after the Polish king moved to Warsaw in 1596 but lost its significance. The ultimate horror was during the German occupation of 1939–1944, when the Nazi "governor general" Hans Frank took control. Krakow's large Jewish community of the Kazimierz district, which had contributed much to the city's history of art and culture, was deported to concentration camps and annihilated. It is fortunate that Nazi plans to explode mines beneath the city and eradicate it totally were foiled.

*The unequal towers of St. Mary's Cathedral soar above the patrician mansions of Rynek. Built in the 13th century, the Rynek Square was the trading center for textiles from throughout the world. This is still where the city comes to life, especially in the cool of the summer nights.*

university was attended by some 10,000 foreign students, which is an astonishing number for the times.

In 1439, Krakow joined the Hanseatic League, specializing as a trading center for textiles from throughout the world, and it became the leader in this activity. The Rynek Square still has a textile house and cloth halls more than three hundred feet long that are known as *Sukiennice*.

Flourishing trade made both the bourgeois and aristocratic Krakow patricians rich so that both classes built stately mansions close to the market place. The inner courtyards of many of these still survive. Generous patronage attracted both artists and artisans from Germany and Bohemia, including Veit Stoss from Nuremberg the principal sculptor of the late Middle Ages who created the tripartite altar for the St.

# The Belvedere Palace in Vienna

*Bureaucrats now rule where emperors once held court*

North Sea

EUROPE

AUSTRIA

Vienna

Mediterranean

### ROUTE

Nearest subway station is Herrengasse (U3)

### OPENING TIMES

Riding School and chapel closed July–August

### FOOD

Coffee houses, legendary Café Hawelka (Sacher Torte), Dortheergasse 6

### ALSO WORTH SEEING

Stephan Cathedral, Schön-brunn Palace, Hundertwasser Haus, The Prater (giant Ferris wheel) for the views

The Austrian emperor Leopold I complained he would rather live in a desert than his Belvedere Palace. The Viennese named him the "Turkish hare" after he fled the city during the Ottoman siege of 1683. The city was regained from the Turks by an alliance with the monarchs of Saxony, Bohemia, Bavaria, and Poland which restored the seat of the empire. When the Turks withdrew they left behind not only the secret of good coffee but also so many damaged buildings that on his return the Habsburg emperor created an

entirely new baroque city. Part of this grand architectural endeavor was Belvedere Palace.

The Belvedere Palace is a mixture of styles of different periods, now extending to 2,583,000 square feet if one includes the various buildings of the complex and the Belvedere Park that originate from the original thirteenth-century fortifications. The oldest portion of the Belvedere is the Schweizer Hof that was started by King Ottokar II of Bohemia. The name refers to the Swiss guard that Maria Theresa had billeted here.

### Extensive library

All that remains of the Gothic building of Ottakar is the apse of the palace chapel. From the Renaissance, the stables and Amalia wing survive. Baroque splendor is displayed in the chancellor's wing and the winter riding school where the gray Lippizaner horses of the Spanish Riding School and their riders now show off their prowess. The library, with its grand reception room, was designed by the leading baroque architect, Joseph Emanuel Fischer von Erlach.

Building continued until the start of the twentieth century because it

was deemed essential to reflect the importance of the empire. An Imperial forum was added as two wings alongside the main avenue but only one was completed. It bounds the Heindeplatz, named in memory of the successful Austro-Hungarian generals Prince Eugene and Grand Duke Carl. A curious but fine mixture of borrowed ideas and styles occurred at the behest of Habsburg rulers during Austrian history. They represent an astonishing labyrinth of power play, intrigue, and display of vanity.

### Chancellor's seat

Perhaps the grandest moment during these power games was the Congress of Vienna in 1814–1815 when the borders of Europe were redrawn following Napoleon's defeat. The feet of hundreds of diplomats, messengers, and chancellors scurrying across these floors will have added to their smooth sheen. The elite of European nobility were also present in the Austrian capital and they spent their time enjoying the city.

Perhaps less illustrious is the present day use of these buildings. Some five thousand bureaucrats now work in the Belvedere Palace in the Ministry of Foreign Affairs which occupies much of the space. The Austrian chancellor has his official chambers in the Leopold wing, where Maria Theresa and her son Joseph II once lived.

Despite this the Belvedere Palace is still a center of culture and science. Scientific institutes, the National Library, and an anthropology museum are all housed here. In addition, visitors to the Belvedere may take in the imperial silver collection or the Augustinian chapel, which contains silver urns holding the hearts of the Habsburg rulers from 1618 to 1878. However, the main attraction by far is the equestrian display of dressage as performed by the Spanish Riding School.

*The grounds of the Belvedere Palace extend to 2,583,000 square feet. (Left) The baroque domes of the old Belvedere Palace. (Above) Carriage ride through the Belvedere Park. Today the Belvedere is home to 5,000 bureaucrats of the Austrian government and several cultural and scientific institutes.*

*The Vienna Court Castle – from poor fortress to pompous residence*

# Benedictine monastery of Melk

*One of Europe's finest baroque buildings overlooks the Danube*

North Sea

EUROPE

AUSTRIA • **Melk**

Mediterranean

### ROUTE

A1, Melk exit or by boat along the Danube from Vienna or Krems

### OPENING TIMES

Daily May–September 9 a.m.–6 p.m. April and October until 5 p.m. Tours every hour

### FOOD

Castle restaurant in Lubberegg, Emmersdorf

Halfway between Vienna and Linz, rock outcrops rise up along the Danube which have always attracted the interest of those in power. Stone Age chieftains built their clan settlements there, the Romans used them for their forts, and the Hungarian tribes turned them into a buffer against Bavaria. This area is known as Medelike in Niebelungen song and flourished as Melk in the tenth century under the Duke of Bebenberg when it formed the Eastern Mark and cradle of Austria. Melk's enduring fame though is due to the Benedictine monks who built

one of the finest monasteries of Europe on this plateau.

It was in 1089 that Duke Leopold II founded a monastery within his stronghold at Melk and had a mausoleum built for St. Coleman, the Irish prince who got no further on his pilgrimage to Jerusalem than Stockerau, where he was tortured to death as a suspected spy. In the twelfth century, the Babenbergers donated their entire estate at Melk to the Benedictines who expanded the monastery, supported ecclesiastical reform, and made Melk into an important religious, clerical, and artistic center in Lower Austria.

In the fifteenth century, the abbey was one of the wealthiest in the Catholic church. During the Ottoman incursion of 1683, the fortified monastery, almost two hundred feet above the Danube, was beleaguered but not taken. The widely talented Benedictine, Berthold Dietmayer, was the abbot who had the former fortress and monastery demolished in 1700 and appointed the gifted Jacob Prandtauer of St. Pöltener to erect new cloisters on a grand scale. The rich and colorful form of high Austrian baroque was fashionable at this time with the royalty and

aristocracy along the Danube, but Prandtauer was determined to outdo all these previous efforts. He created a west front, facing toward the Danube, that rises up behind a terraced approach on the rocks, "like a huge organ sitting on a mountain," as it was later described. Two elegant towers complete the facade. The 1,050-foot-long monastery was completed in 1736, ten years after Prandtauer's death. The building is aligned along an east-west axis and it encloses a number of inner courtyards.

It is difficult to describe the abundant richness that the building displays to visitors. Artisans, sculptors, painters, and plasterers led by Prandtauer and his successors, created a work of baroque art that is impressive in its scale and the extent of the variation in its fantasy. The architectural forms are like individual

notes in music that together form chords, revealing a symphonic feast for the beholder.

One reaches the Prelate's Courtyard via the Benedictine Hall. The courtyard's seclusion is underscored by a marble fountain. The 210-foot-high dome of the monastery church surveys the entire monastery. A marble hall for festive receptions is a baroque masterpiece of spatial arrangement, and in the library, the goddess of reason exhorts humanity to emerge from barbarism with brightly colored ceiling frescos by Paul Troger.

A further surprise awaits the visitor in the basilica-like monastery church, with its vaulted ceiling, magnificent side columns, elegant clerestory and upper friezes, painting of architectural detail in gold, brown, green, and ochre, and the play of light beneath the cupola and on the

decorated chapel. The high altar is covered with generous golden swags and the lesser altar contains a sarcophagus with the remains of St. Coleman, the martyr of Stockerau.

The main hall of the monastery library is a spiritual and inspirational treasure house containing some 80,000 books and 2,000 ancient manuscripts, many of them superbly illuminated in the spirit of St. Benedict, who intended that "God should be adored in all things."

*The Benedictine monastery at Melk (left) was built anew between 1702 and 1736. It is built in Austrian high baroque and located on a rock outcrop above the Danube. It is one of the most exquisite of architectural masterpieces. The entire monastery, grouped around a series of inner courtyards, extends for 1,050 feet. From the entrance to the great Prelate's Courtyard (right) there is a fine view of the 210-ft.-high cupola of the monastery church.*

# Prague and the Charles Bridge

*Following history's traces: across the Moldau to the Hradcany*

## ROUTE

Closest subway (line A)
Starometska

## ALSO WORTH SEEING

The fortress of Hradcany with
St. Vitus Church, old town
hall, Tyn Church, Powder
Tower, Wencelas Square, old
Jewish cemetery

It is not often that a bridge marks the true center of a city. One such exception is the Charles Bridge that connects east and west Prague. From the Charles Bridge you can see the Hradcany and the Lesser Town on one side of the river and the inner Old Town and New Town on the other. Every road in Prague leads to the Charles Bridge as there is no other way to cross the Vltava (Moldau).

In 1357, Emperor Charles IV laid the foundation stone for the sandstone bridge that is 820 feet long, thirty-three feet wide, and supported by 126 arches. Its predecessor, the Judith bridge, had been damaged during a flood. The new crossing is modeled on the German bridge at Trier. The construction of the replacement bridge, that was to become world

famous, was entrusted to Peter Parler, a young man of twenty-seven, who later designed the St. Vitus Church in Prague which is a foremost example of Gothic architecture.

During the Thirty Years War much of the architectural detail of the bridge was heavily damaged by Swedish artillery—especially the sides of the bridge. Nevertheless the bridge remains a superb example of secular Gothic architecture and an artistic homage to its noble Bohemian patrons. In one of his poems Berthold Brecht begins: "Three emperors are interred in Prague..." as he writes of the fickle fate of history. Parler has captured the three kings in stone on the eastern side of the bridge tower in the inner city. Charles IV, Wencelas II The Holy, and Charles' son, Wencelas IV. Researchers were

astonished to discover the closeness of the likeness, and the bust of the emperor is particularly impressive. The pose of the bust is very imperial and examination of the skull has shown that even an injury gained through exercise has been reproduced.

## Collection of saints

The bridge is especially famous for its collection of thirty saints on its balustrades. Many of the patron saints have today been replaced with reproductions. Exhaust fumes from the city seem to be particularly harmful for saints. A special place was reserved for St. Nepomuk, a martyr who was leader of a counter-reformation movement during the Thirty Years War. To this day he is revered as the "true defender of the faith."

The fortress of Hradcany and the mighty St. Vitus Church of the 14th century form the impressive skyline of the Lesser Town of Prague. It can be reached via the Charles Bridge. In 1357, the Emperor Charles IV laid the foundation stone for this sandstone bridge that is 820 feet long, thirty-three feet wide, and supported by 126 arches. It is based on a German bridge at Trier. Peter Parler at age 27, was entrusted with the construction. He was later the architect of the fine Gothic St. Vitus Church.

Saints or heretics, kings or communists, the Charles Bridge has always been at the center of Prague's history. The Bohemian kings were crowned on this bridge, and the followers of John Huss massed on the side of the Lesser Town during the Hussite uprisings of 1420. In 1620, Friedrich von der Pfalz, the "winter king," fled across the bridge after losing the battle for the white mountain, where his Protestant army was defeated by Habsburg troops. In 1649, the students of Prague defended the old inner city against the advancing Swedish army and two hundred years later the struggle was for independence from Austria. Today only long streams of tourists, from every corner of the world, jostle with each other on the bridge. The Charles Bridge has become a place to promenade and a meeting place for artists and musicians, forming a great open-air theater.

# Dresden's merry Zwinger

*Once a place of pleasure, today a home for the arts*

*The pavilion is supported on columns and decorated with stucco (bottom right). The rounded arches inspired Gottfried Semper when he built the art gallery in 1847–1854, which also houses the armory of August the Strong (bottom left).*

For those with an understanding of German, the name of the Zwinger Palace in Dresden tends to mislead. This was a place where August the Strong, Elector of Saxony and King of Poland, held extravagant feasts. Yet a close study of the Zwinger's history reveals the name's origin. This was once the outer ward of fortifications. The sort of space where wild animals were often kept; hence, the name *zwinger* which means "cage" or "arena". The building in front of the Luna Bastion was significantly changed in 1700 and turned into a place for enjoyment of life.

## Built with sandstone from the Elbe

Even though the first new building on this site for August the Strong was a wooden amphitheater built specifically to celebrate the visit of August's cousin, King Friedrich IV of Denmark to Dresden in 1709, the name Zwinger was kept. The king's love of orange trees, which were such a costly status symbol at the time, prompted the Elector to build an orangery. The landscape architect Matthaeus Daniel Poppelmann created two bower galleries between 1710 and 1712, with one on each storey, where the sensitive orange trees could be nursed through the winter.

This though was merely the overture to the building activities with which August left his mark. The architect and sculptor Balthasar Permoser left his own strong imprint. He surrounded the natural dais of the Zwinger, where parties were held, with a series of baroque buildings that can stand comparison with examples of this style anywhere. Dresden's baroque is characterized by its lightness of touch and playfulness, while retaining symmetry that ensures the impression of seclusion in harmonious surroundings is maintained. The area that was enclosed according to Permoser's design measures 380 feet by 7,600 feet.

The pavilion, which was completed in 1718, is not just the most important building of the Zwinger Palace, it is also a high point in European architectural history. The elegant contours create an illusion of

motion and Permoser's busts of gods and heroes are woven into the Elbe sandstone like costly swags. The architecture strives to rise above the impressive central facade, rising upwards towards the figure of Hercules Saxonicus, bowed under the weight of the globe on his shoulders, that crests the pavilion's roof.

Building on the eastern side of the Zwinger was started by the master builder Poppelman in the same year, and he was pressed for time. The feast to end all feasts was planned for Dresden for September 1719 when the Elector and Prince Friedrich August, son and heir of August the Strong, married the Grand Duchess of Austria, Maria Joseph, daughter of the emperor. August the Strong had

two bowered galleries built at great haste on the eastern side in repetition of those on the west. Galleries had already been extended and a crown gate added in 1714 to mask the view of the moat of the stronghold. By these means three sides of the Zwinger were enclosed.

August the Strong died in 1733 and the Zwinger fell into neglect after his death. The days of great court feasting were over. The opulent ornamentation was no longer fashionable and it was even considered that they should be removed. As early as 1728 a pavilion was used to store the collections built up by the art-loving Electors and also a museum of porcelain that is only surpassed in art-historical

terms by the harem of the Topkapi palace in Istanbul.

The Zwinger Palace is still a center of the arts. From 1847 to 1854 an impressive art gallery was built by the architect Gottfried Semper, occupying space within the Zwinger next to the theater. In common with other buildings it was reduced to rubble in February 1945 by warfare. The entire complex of buildings has been restored to its former glory in a long running program of rebuilding and restoration. The gallery contains masterpieces such as those of Rembrandt, Dürer, and Rubens plus more than 350 works by Italian artists, including Raphael's "Sistine Madonna."

*The pavilion at the Zwinger Palace was completed in 1718 and is the most important of the Zwinger' buildings, an important monument of European architecture. Relief molding and sculpture are woven into the masonry like expensive swags.*

# Sans Souci, the palace in the vineyard

*Frederick achieved his dreams at Potsdam*

*North Sea*

**Potsdam**

GERMANY

EUROPE

*Mediterranean*

The name of the palace says it all really: *sans souci— without cares*. King Frederick II of Prussia gave the palace this name at the inaugural banquet on May Day 1747. Here Frederick, later known as Frederick the Great, could escape from his busy life and relax, leaving the strict discipline of the court at Potsdam, and dedicate himself, albeit briefly, to his hobbies of music and philosophical debate with scholars and writers.

Unfortunately for Frederick such opportunities were rare. Schloss Sans Souci soon became the actual seat of government for the Prussian king, even though it had been created as a vineyard château. Frederick loved country life though and was particularly fond of his summer residence, which was the fulfillment of a long-held dream.

As crown prince he had been through difficult times, in continuous conflict with his stern father, the soldier king Wilhelm Friedrich I.

The people were led to anticipate their new king as an artistically-inclined philosopher who would govern in the manner of the French Enlightenment when he assumed the throne in 1740, but he surprised them immediately after the coronation with his war-like power politics. Taking advantage of Habsburg weakness after Maria Theresa became empress, he had his army invade Silesia. Occupation of this province was the opening foray of the three wars against Austria at the end of which Prussia had gained the status of a major European power.

Construction of Sans Souci started during the War of the Austrian Succession. It was Frederick who personally led the Prussian army into battle. While in the field he was kept up-to-date on the progress of the building that he had commissioned his friend and architect Georg Wencelaus von Knobelsdorff to construct.

### Intimate and light

A vineyard was already established when von Knobelsdorff started to build a small château in April, 1745. At the reception area, where carriages pass by, a crescent-form colonnade was created to assure privacy. On the garden side, 132 elegant steps lead up to the château. Von Knobelsdorff succeeded in creating an intimate and light pastoral feeling with the soft yellow ochre of the building with its copper dome.

The small château only has twelve rooms and one of the most beautiful of them is the music room where concerts were given and in which the playful rococo decorations seem to anticipate Mozart's joyous music. Frederick gathered artists, philosophers, and scholars such as Voltaire around his "round table" in the marble hall with its sixteen paired columns and high gilt cupola.

## The gardens as counterpoint

The Architect von Knobelsdorff also laid out the first Sans Souci garden which incorporated such decorative elements as urns, sphinxes, and pavilions, with grottoes, fountains, springs, and temples for a sensual baroque counterpoint to the rigor of Prussian militarism.

The gardens cover about 740 acres and contain several buildings commissioned by Frederick. During his reign the gallery of statues, Neue Kammern guest house, the portal with an obelisk, and Chinese tea house were added in the palace garden. The final great building project was the new palace that was built between 1763 and 1769.

The grand gardens lead one to the magnificent palace, intended as a demonstration of Prussian might after their victory in the Seven Years War.

Frederick the Great never lived in the new Sans Souci palace, remaining faithful to the original building. When he died in 1786 he was buried in the garrison church of Potsdam.

However, an important stipulation in his will was not put into effect until 1991 when he was finally laid to rest in a sepulcher at a spot at Sans Souci which he said was the only place he could truly be "without cares."

*An impressive set of steps leads beyond the vineyard to the palace of Sans Souci. This summer residence of Frederick II was never intended to be a seat of government but a place of pleasing architecture. The many sculptures by Christian Glume impart elegant grace to the little palace. The main fountain spurts water 118 feet into the air but this was only achieved after installation of special equipment in 1842. Frederick gathered artists and philosophers at his "round table" in the Marble Hall (small photograph).*

# Chalk cliffs on the Isle of Rügen

*The King's Chair and the white cliffs have inspired painters and poets*

North Sea

EUROPE

**Rügen**

GERMANY

Mediterranean

**ROUTE**

By air to Berlin, train to Sasznits; on foot to the Stubbenkammer

**ACCOMMODATIONS**

Panorama Hotel Lohme (NW of the Stubbenkammer)

**FOOD**

Waldhalle (near Wissower Klinken)

**ALSO WORTH SEEING**

Vitt fishing village at Cape Arkona; Graznitz hunting lodge near Binz; Church of St. Mary in Bergen; Putbus

The landscape is bright blue from the reflection of the Baltic, shimmering green leaves on beech trees that overhang the chalk white cliffs of the coast. The chalk is sculpted with niches and deep channels. In places the cliffs are sheer, in others they slope towards the sea or form unusual contours and form small peaks. Some of these peaks bear names as if they were mountain tops.

The Stubbenkammer on the island of Rügen is one of the most attractive parts of the Baltic coastline. Poets and painters, like Caspar David Friedrich found inspiration here. The widely traveled scientist Wilhelm von Humboldt was moved to say: "Nowhere else does one encounter a simpler, more noble panorama."

## Protected nature reserve

The most famous bit of rock on the Stubbenkammer is the King's Chair, rising to a height of 384 feet. Some three to four hundred thousand visitors climb the steps to the small viewing platform that was built more than three hundred years ago. They are rewarded with a marvelous view of the chalk cliffs and the sea. To the south are the Wissower Klinken. Some say that Friedrich painted this view for his work *Chalk Cliffs of Rügen* but in reality it was a rock formation to the northwest of the King's Chair that the artist portrayed.

The Jasmund Nature Reserve was created in 1990 to protect this coastline. Its 7,400 or so acres includes almost 5,000 acres of forest,

left as much as possible in its natural state, about 1,230 acres of the Baltic, and a similar amount of chalk cliff, marsh, and grassland.

There are a number of places between Sasznits and the King's Chair at which it is possible to leave the road and climb down steep steps to the beach. Walking along the beach is not easy because of the rocky terrain, but the cliffs attain their full majesty when viewed from this angle and the bands of flint that run along the cliffs like strings of pearls can only be viewed from down there.

The phenomenon of the bands of flint are caused by small organisms that became trapped in mud. The cliffs too are organic in origin.

Around eighty million years ago in the Mesozoic era, the atmosphere of the earth warmed up causing the glaciers and ice caps to melt, flooding the whole of northern Europe. The sea was filled with starfish, mussels, coral polyps, algae, and plankton. It is their chalky scales, skeletons, and shells deposited on the sea bed when they died that combined with other sediments that formed these chalk cliffs up to 1,600 feet high.

During the next period of the earth's history in the Tertiary period, the sea withdrew to the extent that the present day Baltic became dry land. Around 800,000 to one million years ago (during the Pleistocene) glaciers almost 3,300 feet thick pushed south from the coast of Scandinavia on three occasions to shape the landscape of Rügen, but not the cliffs themselves.

These have resulted from movements in the earth's crust during the Pleistocene when layers of chalk split and lifted or dropped, obstructing the advance of the glaciers which then deposited the boulders of granite they had carried from mountains in Scandinavia—some as much as 21,200 cubic feet in volume and weighing up to 1,800 tons.

When the glaciers withdrew the changes that occurred in the ensuing 100,000 years were not solely wrought by the rise and fall of the sea. Humans too have intervened in this landscape. From the mid nineteenth century Rügen chalk was a prized commodity that has been incorporated in paint, china, and toothpaste.

*A superb panorama opens up from the steep cliff top of the Baltic and Wissower Klinken (above). Huge boulders and fallen trees make a stroll along the beach arduous (left). It is only possible at the very brim of the cliff to gain a true impression of the majesty of these cliffs, formed from billions of skeletons, scales, and shells of minute organisms over millions of years.*

# Jewel of the Hanseatic League

*Lübeck is a wealth of medieval merchants' houses*

North Sea • Lübeck GERMANY EUROPE Mediterranean

### ROUTE

By air to Hamburg, train to Lübeck. The Holstentor is a 5-minute walk from station. The old town is inaccessible to cars.

### ACCOMODATIONS/FOOD

Historical guest house Schiffersgesellschaft, Breite Strasse 2

### ALSO WORTH SEEING

Travemunde, (Lubeck's seaside resort), Ratzeburg (12 miles S) for its churches, Möln (19 miles S)

*The Holstentor, symbol of Lübeck, was built as part of 13th-century fortifications. Sited across the Trave, it protected the entrance to the city. In its present form it dates from the 15th century.*

It was almost certainly not out of humility that the good burgers of Lübeck were inspired to erect seven great church spires that rise above their city. No other town in northern Europe was so fashioned by its citizenry as this ancient metropolis on the coast of the Baltic. Nowhere else has developed building in brick in the Gothic style into such a fine art form as this city on the river Trave.

The origins of Lübeck though are indeed humble. The stronghold of Liubice that was damaged in 1138 was of little significance, but this was changed by the new standards set by Henry the Lion, Duke of Saxony and Bavaria. He founded a town of the same name on an island surrounded by the Trave and Wakenitz. Fifteen years later he personally laid the foundation stone for the first large church. Soon, Lübeck merchants were prominent in trade throughout the Baltic, using shallow-drafted but seaworthy craft, they brought salt, textiles, beer, and wine to Visby, Novgorod, and Bergen and returned with lumber, hides, ore, tar, and wax.

### Respect for the city's elders

From 1226 on, the free imperial city of Lübeck was directly subject to the German emperor, and when Charles IV visited in 1375 with a large entourage, he addressed the city's elders with considerable respect, calling them the Lords of Lübeck. In the late fourteenth century the city on the Trave reached the zenith of its influence, when it was as powerful as Venice and as magnificent as Florence. It took on the leadership of the Hanseatic League. This alliance of mercantile trading cities offered protection from attacks on

land or at sea and was the most important trading alliance of the Middle Ages. Ultimately two hundred trading towns joined the League. Lübeck served as the seat of the League's assembly so that the city had a major role in the economic politics of the entire Baltic region.

But Lübeck also became a beautiful city of fine architecture. Most of the other members of the Hanseatic League modeled themselves on Lübeck's magnificent churches and town hall. In 1276 the city elders only permitted building with brick and this prevented the fires that destroyed many other medieval cities. As a result Lübeck became and is a treasure house of architecture in northern Europe.

When the Hanseatic League declined, Lübeck lost its hegemony but the really serious economic crisis for the city was its occupation by Napoleon's army from 1811 to 1813. The darkest era of all though for this jewel of the Hanseatic League came during World War II when Allied bombers dropped more than three hundred tons of bombs on the town on March 28, 1942, turning the city into a cauldron for thirty-two hours. Five of the seven church spires were severely damaged and one in five homes was reduced to ash.

With a fanaticism that can only be explained in terms of the city's history, the citizens have rebuilt the old inner city, retaining the old structures. More than eight hundred

buildings have been designated as monuments. UNESCO placed the city on its list of world heritage sites "in virtue of its exceptionally great cultural value."

Surveying the city from the vantage point of the tower of the St. Peter's Church, one can see the checkerboard grid pattern of the old Hanseatic city. The church, with its twin spires rising like mountain peaks, vies with the wide towers of St. Mary's, which in turn compete with the Town Hall. This palatial hall with its glazed tiles, Renaissance canopy, and baroque reception chambers is still the heart of this self-conscious city.

*View of the church spires which tower above this ancient city. Tall merchants' houses border the river as they did in the Middles Ages when the city flourished. The warehouse (bottom) is renowned for its stepped gable. It is now a restaurant.*

# Cathedrals of commerce

*The fine warehouses of Hamburg's trading past*

North Sea
**Hamburg**
GERMANY
EUROPE
Mediterranean

**ROUTE**

Direct flight or via Frankfurt; Subway line 1 (Mesberg) or line 2 (Baumwall)

**VISITING HOURS**

Warehouse Museum, Hot Spice Museum, German Toll Museum: all 10 a.m.–5 p.m. City tours: Sundays 11 a.m.

The vast array of warehouses of the free port of Hamburg is regarded as a great architectural achievement. Most of the buildings date from the late nineteenth century. Hamburg Docks has the largest collection of old warehouses anywhere in the world. Their facades are so finely decorated that some have called them cathedrals of commerce. They reflect the pride of the merchants who owned them.

All this began with a financial crisis. The German chancellor Otto von Bismarck had pressed the Hamburg senate from 1879 onward to join the German duty association, but the "pepperbags" as the Hamburg merchants were deridingly called were strongly opposed. Hamburg levied no duty which did

away with bothersome controls and had helped trade to flourish, with the city on the Elbe second only to London as a major European port. Free trade ensured the city's wealth. Eventually a compromise was found that took account of Hamburg's privileged position. Goods could be handled, stored, and transshipped within a "free port zone" without payment of duty. Only when goods were delivered to a German recipient would they become liable for duty.

**Relocation of 30,000 people**

The old weavers' quarter of the port was earmarked for the new free port. This location had the advantage of canals that crossed this residential area and both the port and city were close at hand. The population of 30,000 people who lived in the

quarter were relocated and the new collection of warehouses sprang up between 1882 and 1888. This was later extended with an additional 323,000 square feet. Forty-two different architects were responsible for the new warehouses, which from the outset were designed with intentional grandeur. The entrance to the free port was very grand in scale with ornately decorated bridges with motifs from the Middle Ages crossing the 246-foot-wide canal. Inside the complex itself there was a pervading odor of amber and myrrh.

All the warehouses were built according to the same well-proven concept. Resting on heavy piles, the foundations and cellars carried four to five storeys. Extremely thick walls kept both the heat of summer and winter frost at bay. Almost

everything that could be traded was stored in these warehouses: coffee, tea, hides, ivory, and spices were unloaded with the same ease as tapestries, nuts, and French wines. Each warehouse was built so that it could be reached both from the waterfront and from the street. Hoists suspended from beams lifted goods that were pulled in through hatches in the walls.

## Embellished facades

In addition to their desire for technical efficiency, the merchants of Hamburg also set great store by the appearance of their warehouses. At that time brick Gothic was gaining popularity and so the otherwise severe brownstone facades were embellished with decorative towers, balconies, and stepped gables. Hamburg was wealthy enough to permit such artistic luxury. The copper roofs were punctuated with towers and pinnacles. Romanesque arches supported windows, and steel fire escapes added detail to the walls in the form of Italianate balconies.

After the end of the nineteenth century a less forced style was more fashionable and the later warehouses exhibit less exuberance. Despite this the verdigris copper roofs and glazed roof tiles remain the abiding image of these unique cathedrals of commerce.

These warehouses are largely still used in the original manner but modern handling methods for shipping will cause profound changes. It is not impossible to imagine that in the future these warehouse will see the area returned to residential use once more.

*The largest collection of warehouses in the world. The warehouses of the port of Hamburg still serve commerce. The brick buildings date from 1882–1888 and they were decorated as if serving a less down-to-earth function. Attention to detail vitalizes the otherwise functional structures. The aerial photograph gives an impression of the scale of the area. The interior view of a warehouse gives an impression of atmosphere.*

# Wattenmeer National Parks

*Unique environment created by the tides of the North Sea coast*

North Sea

**Waddenzee**

GERMANY

EUROPE

Mediterranean

**ROUTE**

By train from Hamburg to Westerland

**BEST TIMES**

May–September

**ALSO WORTH SEEING**

Walking on the Wattenmeer between Föhr and Amrum; seal crèche at Frederiksoog

Many holiday-makers on their first visit to the North Sea coast ran enthusiastically towards the sea only to find it was not there. Instead they were confronted with miles of grayish mud flats. Known in German as Wattenmeer and Dutch as Waddenzee, the wat or wad merely means shallows or mud flats. The pull of the moon that causes the tides to ebb and flood sees this area along the coast of Friesland (Dutch and German) flooded at high tide and dry at low tide. Because the area is so flat the tide ebbs a very long way. This is an extremely important environment for all manner of species but especially for birds. A large part of the German Wattenmeer is protected as the Lower Saxony, Hamburg, and Schleswig-Holstein National Parks.

The special environment of these areas is not solely restricted to the shallows and mud flats themselves. The dunes, beaches, and islands are also an important part of this unique natural world.

The Schleswig-Holstein part of the Wattenmeer was declared a national park in 1985 covering an area from the German-Danish border to the mouth of the Elbe.

### Mud flats, sand banks, and mixed flats

The flats are not one homogenous type of mud/sand mixture but vary depending in part on certain conditions. The more sheltered an area is, such as in the lee of an island, the flatter it will be and the greater is also the surface area covered at high tide. Water will also ebb away less quickly. In such places a more glutinous type of mud-flat occurs. Where the current is stronger, one finds larger sand banks and in between these two sets of conditions

*Although the Wattenmeer mud seems devoid of life it is home to countless species.*

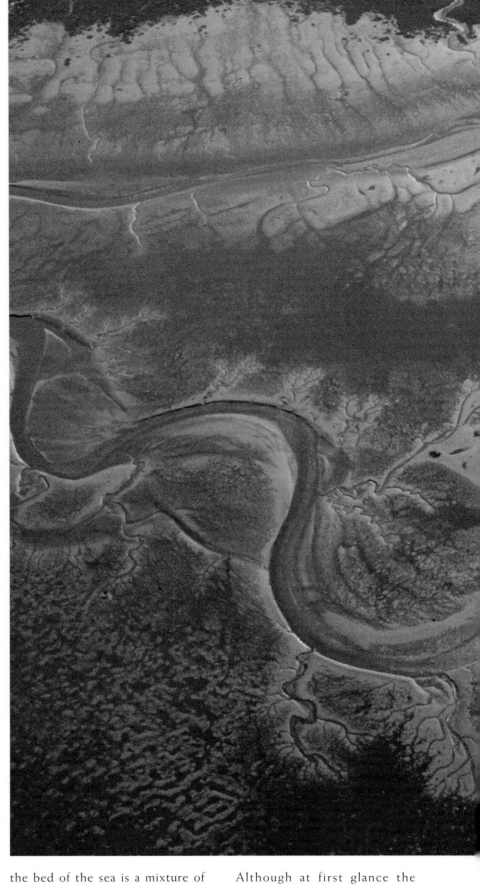

the bed of the sea is a mixture of mud and sand. In addition to the tide there are other factors which affect the formation of the flats and banks. These were formed off the coast of Denmark through thousands of years of silting up with the deposit of sediment. In North Friesland great expanses of reed beds and marshland formed where there was shelter of sand dunes. When the sea level rose at the end of the last Ice Age these areas were flooded and covered with fertile soil. In places where the land was only flooded occasionally— during the big spring tides—sandy beaches and salt flats formed. Certain types of hardy plants took root there, depending on the distance from the sea.

Although at first glance the Wattenmeer does not appear very hospitable and rather devoid of life, nothing could be further from the truth. Two thousand different species of animals live on these flats. The flats are teaming with life and at low water it is even possible to hear the activities of the myriad collection of worms, snails, mussels, and crabs searching for food. This is a land of plenty for these creatures. On average there are over six million algae per square inch here. Worms and crabs in turn are prey for countless other creatures of the Wattenmeer, from fish to seals.

One of the most popular tourist activities on the Wattenmeer are the trips to the sand banks where seals

haul themselves out or breed and the areas where millions of gulls, terns, oyster-catchers, eider ducks, and geese congregate. Special protection areas are designated to guard these birds from disturbance. Fishing is permitted in the National Parks and is the cause of constant conflict between the fishermen and environmentalists.

The government says that the protection of nature has to be balanced with economic interests but the principal threat to the Wattenmeer is from pollution by oil slicks from North Sea shipping.

*A kind of system can be detected from the air: larger channels and smaller ones drain the Wattenmeer. Where water flows slowly mud-flats are formed, where it floods and ebbs quickly sand banks are created. These are the preferred haul-out spots for seals.*

# Mother of all churches

*Cologne Cathedral is one of Germany's most important religious buildings*

**The Cologne Cathedral and the Wallraf-Rtichartz Museum/ Museum Ludwig (left)**

Cologne Cathedral is the symbol of Cologne and perhaps the architectural monument of Germany that is best-known world wide. In the Middle Ages it was already being described as "the mother of all churches." From the mid-nineteenth century it was elevated to a kind of national shrine. When the final act of construction took place in 1880, with the placing of a cross on the south tower, it was 632 years since the foundation stone had been laid.

The first Gothic cathedral was already in existence in France when the government in Cologne decided to replace their old cathedral dating from the fourth century with a new building. The laying of the foundation stone was delayed though because of the transfer of the Shrine of the Three Magi—said to contain the remains of the three kings who visited the infant Jesus—from Mailand to Cologne. This turned Cologne into one of the best-known places of pilgrimage in the west.

## No building for 250 years

The master builder Gerhard and his successor Arnold took the cathedral at Amiens as their model for the choir and tripartite transept. The five-part nave was based upon a predecessor of Cologne Cathedral of the twelfth century. In September 1322, Archbishop Heinz von Virneburg was able to consecrate the choir even though the rest of the building was far from complete. A wooden partition closed off the nave to the west and masons were busy constructing a south tower. According to the thirteen-foot-long plans which still exist, the tower was

to be proportional to the overall length of the cathedral: 492 feet high to the length of 1,640 feet. On the north side from 1410 onward work was underway on the transept which was provided with magnificent stained glass in 1508. The typical Gothic flying buttresses were for the first time extensively embellished.

But building ceased in 1560. Some argue this was because of the spirit of the times. A more pragmatic age began in which people were more inclined to consider their earthly life than look toward heaven, and they were more interested in exploring and conquering the earth, with less time for church buildings on such a grand scale. At this time about ninety percent of the planned cathedral was available for services and a provisional wooden roof enclosed the interior above the arcades.

Cologne Cathedral continued with a shadowy existence until the nineteenth century. During the French Revolution it even served as a fodder store for the French cavalry and was then promoted to the humble role of diocesan church. In 1815, when Cologne became Prussian territory, all Germans hoped construction work would start again. King Frederick IV did advocate the establishment of a national shrine and in 1842 he laid the foundation stone for the front of the south transept. Under the leadership of Zwirner and Voigtel the cathedral was now completed in thirty-eight years. The two final master builders took the medieval plans and elevation drawings as their starting point. Their work is a masterpiece of late Romantic architecture, showing

both care and historical awareness. Zwirner improved on the plans with a southern transept that is a masterpiece of Neo-Gothic architecture.

The most impressive of all though is undoubtedly the cathedral's west front. The north tower at 516 feet four inches is just 2½ inches higher than its southern neighbor. When one enters the cathedral there is an overview of the slender lofty heights of the central nave, 390 feet long. Among Cologne Cathedral's most significant art treasures is the Gero Cross. This tenth-century crucifix is one of the oldest in the west.

The Shrine of the Three Magi was eventually sited behind the main altar after World War II when the damage to the interior was repaired. The shrine, which was made in the twelfth century, is regarded by experts as one of the most significant pieces of goldsmith's art from the Middle Ages.

Cologne Cathedral is still a construction site today because pollution is harmful to the materials from which it is built. Residents of Cologne have come to terms with the constant restoration and scaffolding. For, they say, when the cathedral is complete, the world will end.

North Sea

**Cologne** EUROPE
GERMANY

Mediterranean

**ROUTE**

By air to Cologne, via Frankfurt; or by regular trains to the Köln Dom station

**OPENING TIMES**

Daily 6.30 a.m.–7 p.m.

**FOOD**

Früh am Dom (traditional brewery) Am Hof 12–14

**ALSO WORTH SEEING**

Archbishop's Diocesan Museum, Wallraf-Richartz Museum, Romanesque churches, city hall (rathaus)

*The twin spires of Cologne Cathedral soar majestically. The northern tower is 516 ft 4 in, just 2½ in higher than its neighbor. The facade is the largest of all Christian churches. Flying buttresses (top right) are customary for Gothic architecture. Of the three portals, only the St. Peter portal on the south is medieval. The other two and their sculpture are from the 19th century. The statue of St. Christopher (bottom) adorns the nave.*

**ROUTE**

From Munich A95/E5 to Oberau, B23 then signs for Wies

**OPENING TIMES**

Daily May–September 8 a.m.–7 p.m. Closes 5 p.m. in winter

**ALSO WORTH SEEING**

Rococo Church of St. John the Baptist, Steingaden; Hohenschwangau, Neuschwanstein, and Linderhof castles near Fuessen

# Bavaria's rococo jewel: the Wieskirche

*The pilgrims church that is a magnificent example of full-blown German glorification*

It all started with a miracle in June of 1718 when a local farm girl, Maria Lory placed a wooden statue in her room and prayed before it. The statue depicts Christ being scourged. This Scourged Savior was carried through the Upper Bavarian village of Steingaden during processions on Good Friday but no-one had noticed anything special about it before. Soon though the farm girl from the meadows reported miraculous cures and the flagellated figure of Christ was said to shed tears.

The message spread to the devout and soon so many pilgrims came that the abbot of Steingaden, Hyazinth Gassner, decided to build a fitting sanctuary for the miraculous statue. The work began in 1745 and was completed nine years later. When the church was dedicated it was one of the finest examples of Bavarian high rococo style, standing in a pastoral and gently sloping landscape at the foot of the Alps.

## Divine view of heaven

Abbot Gassner was not to witness the realization of his dream, for he died soon after construction of the church began, but the work was continued under his successor, Abbot Marian Mayer, apparently without begrudging the cost. Initially eight thousand marks were reserved for the building costs, but the actual cost eventually ran to 180,000 marks. Under pressure from the elector of Bavaria, Max II, abbot Mayer surrendered his office but was permitted to continue supervision of the building of the church through to its completion. The builder was Dominikus Zimmerman, while his brother, Johann Baptist, was responsible for the frescos and stucco work. Both had already established their names before this masterpiece was created.

Dominikus Zimmerman's concept for the pilgrimage church was as an oval central form with more sober outer walls. An adjacent choir was to display the miraculous Scourged Savior statue. This was customary practice for places of pilgrimage at the time, enabling people to file past the object of veneration. The master builder gave special consideration to the harmonious relationship between forms and the interplay of color and light. Twenty tall windows flood the interior with light.

Eight pairs of columns support the great expanse of vaulted ceiling that is surrounded with detailed plaster work. The ceiling represents the divine heaven and it acts as a setting for a precious gem. The ceiling frescos are in the form of a trompe l'oeil, yielding a series of surprises for the viewer. At the center of heaven is Christ the Savior, seated on a rainbow—symbolizing a link between man and God— offering his divine grace to humankind.

Angels float through the heaven in a manner that is both joyful and inspiring. The Day of Judgment has not yet arrived, the throne of the judge of the world is vacant and the gate to paradise is closed. The message repeatedly impressed on pilgrims is that those who live by faith and in humility will experience the Savior's grace.

Because of the unrestricted view, it is possible from the main nave of the Wies church to look at its sacred heart, the twin altars and gracious image of the Scourged Christ. Reliefs and moldings together with allegorical frescos in confusing proliferation seem to form a rhythm through the space. Where Johann Baptist Zimmerman created color harmony with use of white, blue, and gold in the main nave, he has added the warm red glow of marble columns beside the statue of grace. This symbolizes Christ's blood shed for us, for our salvation.

The magnificent Wieskirche was only rediscovered and recognized as the great work of art that it is in the 1920s. Since that time it has become not just a renewed place of pilgrimage but a major tourist attraction. Although the frescos have survived superbly, the church needed extensive restoration between 1985 and 1990. The breath of so many tourists had affected the colors.

The master builder Dominikus Zimmerman kept the exterior of the Wieskirche relatively simple. Inside, it is one of the most elaborate examples of high Bavarian rococo. Tall windows flood the colorful frescos and the ceiling trompe l'oeil— that depicts heaven— with bright light.

# Schloss Neuschwanstein – monument to a romantic

*Kini's dream castle is like some backdrop for a Wagner opera*

North Sea

EUROPE
GERMANY

**Castle Neuschwanstein**

Mediterranean

### ROUTE

From Fuessen take B17 direction Augsburg, right to Hohenschwangau. Short walk from parking lot to castle

### OPENING TIMES

Neuschwanstein and Hohenschwangau: daily, April–September 8.30 a.m.–5.30 p.m.; October–May 10 a.m.–4 p.m.

### ALSO WORTH SEEING

Hohenschwangau and Linderhof castles, Wieskirche

*Sets for Wagner operas and the Wartburg in the Thuringia Forest inspired the romantically inclined King Ludwig II to build his castle at Neuschwanstein. The fantasy castle cost many millions but pulls in millions in tourist revenue each year. The king's writing room is shown in the main photo (right).*

Wagner's *Das Rheingold* carries a love ode for the castle of Neuschwanstein built by the fellow romantic and friend, King Ludwig II (known as "Kini" or the "only true friend").

"As I saw it in my dreams/ as my will had meant it to be/ beautiful it stands for all to see/ this marvelous edifice." Nowhere is the exalted, almost mystical friendship between Richard Wagner and King Ludwig more palpable than at Schloss Neuschwanstein, perched atop its peak in the Allgau Mountains. It is a German manifestation of the archetypal fairy-tale castle.

We owe this castle's creation to the fact that king and composer were soul mates. Sets for Wagner's operas *Lohengrin* and *Tannhauser* and memories of the Wartburg in the Thuringia Forest were the inspiration for the fantasy castle.

### Ludwig's bequest: castles and debts

This "other Wartburg" was built between 1859 and 1892 by architects Eduard Riedel, Georg Dollmann, and Julius Hofmann. Ludwig did not live in his dream castle until May 1884, but the disillusioned king moved to Schloss Berg on Lake Starnberg on June 12, 1885, where he died the very next day under inexplicable circumstances, in a tragedy worthy of a Wagner opera.

The king, who loved the arts, left behind him numerous magnificent castles, country houses, countless art treasures, and a debt of fourteen million gold marks. The 300,000 marks in stipend that the king received annually from the German chancellor Bismarck had not been sufficient for Ludwig's extravagant ways.

Today though the objects of Ludwig's beautiful legacy are a veritable gold mine bringing millions of tourists to Bavaria who spend a lot of money. Probably the most popular tourist attraction of them all is Schloss Neuschwanstein.

### The gods will avenge themselves

The main part of the castle is a four-storey palace with official and personnel quarters on the ground floor. The sumptuous royal chambers are entered through the almost two-hundred-foot-high main tower. It is difficult to know which way to look first, with the superb murals that depict medieval scenes of chivalry—as do virtually all the paintings in the castle. The romanticism in the Sängersalle is almost oppressive. This is the most impressive space in the entire castle, a very fine hall that surpasses even the beauty of that other hall which inspired it—the Sängersalle of the Wartburg in Thuringia, where festivals of singing were held, inspiring Wagner for his opera *Tannhauser*.

The king wrote to the composer of his plans for this hall: "It is one of the finest halls you will see, holy and unapproachable. You will also find there things that remind you of *Tannhauser* and *Lohengrin*, and the hall is more beautiful in every respect than Hohenschwangau, which is yearly sullied by my mother's prose. They will avenge themselves, those dishonored Gods, and sojourn on high with us, in rarefied air."

The king departed from the Wagnerian model in one detail only, in the design for his throne room. This reception room in Byzantine style, focuses its attention on a large Byzantine imperial crown with 139 steps leading to a portal where the king's throne, made of gold and ivory, was to have stood. The mysterious death of the king prevented this from happening.

# History in manuscript

*The monastic library of St. Gallen brings the Middle Ages to life*

**ROUTE**

N1 Zurich–Bodensee/Lake Constance (62 miles NE of Zurich); From Konstanz via Roschdach to Sankt Gallen (27 miles)

**OPENING TIMES**

Cathedral: Monday–Friday 9 am.–6 p.m.; Cloister library: Monday–Saturday 9 a.m.–12 a.m. and 2 p.m.–5 p.m., Sunday 10.30 a.m.–12 p.m. (June–August open Sundays 2 p.m.–4 p.m.)

**ALSO WORTH SEEING**

Historical museum, Fabric museum, Lake Constance/ Bodensee cruises

No reading room in Switzerland is as fine and few libraries elsewhere in the world can rival that of St. Gallen for its precious collection. The origins of the monastic library date back to 612 when the Irish monk and missionary Gallus established a hermit's cell in the mountain valley of Steinach, south of Lake Constance. One hundred years later a monastery was established there under Benedictine rule and a settlement grew up around the monastery that eventually became St. Gallen, the principal town of eastern Switzerland.

Over time the monastery acquired both religious significance and political power, so buildings were added or rebuilt as the monastery was extended. The library of the cloisters and monastery church date from 1755–1766, and it is these buildings which have achieved world renown.

In the interior of the monastery church, the worldly magnificence of baroque architecture is consecrated to the worship of God, and bright green rococo stucco covers walls that would otherwise be white. The choir stalls, organ pipes, and confessional are of gilded walnut. The ceiling paintings and screening of the choir compete in opulence.

### God's reading room

The church pales into insignificance though alongside the library which contains some two thousand medieval manuscripts, with an emphasis on the eras of the Carolingians and Ottonians. Most of these manuscripts were not acquired by collecting but created by the monks of the monastery themselves. When one adds to this 1,700 of the earliest printed books, and a further 100,000 books, mainly of the baroque era, you have a near perfect reference library for medieval studies.

In spite of this great mass of literature, the two-storey library does not seem oppressive or stuffy in any way. This is due to the way the architect Peter Thumb has furnished the library with the help of his son and a team of talented craftsmen. Abundant light is provided by thirty-four windows that illuminate the magnificent painted ceiling with their motifs from ecclesiastical history, the rich plaster moldings, elegant galleries, and tastefully patterned hardwood flooring. Since the monastery was secularized in 1805, many of the valuable manuscripts are kept in the manuscript hall in decorative bookcases that hide the supporting arches.

In addition to the Notker Labeo Psalter of the tenth century or a copy of the *Nibelungenlied* of the thirteenth century, the monastery library of St. Gallen contains the first known book in the German language. The Codex Abrogans dates from 770 and is a Latin–German dictionary. To spread the Gospel among the German people, the missionary monks, who were largely Irish, had first to learn German.

A document from about 820 is considered very important by many scholars. It contains the construction drawings for a monastery. It is not entirely certain if these yellowing sheets were studied by Abbot Gozbert as the actual plans for St. Gallen or an ideal form of Carolingian cloister. In any event, the four parchments that are sewn together constitute a unique insight into early medieval Christian architecture. The work sheds light on the entire Benedictine experience with such early buildings. Precise explanations in Latin answer questions about the purposes of some of the inner spaces of these buildings. Such precise detail showing the pulpit in the refectory from which scripture would be read aloud during meals is not overlooked. The library offers medieval scholars a fascinating glimpse into life in their chosen era of study. The library means even more than this for some visitors. It is summed up by a text above the entrance to the library in classical Greek, that names the library "the soul's utopia."

*Magnificent ceiling paintings, elegant galleries, and a finely-patterned hardwood floor make the manuscript hall a fitting home for a collection of unique manuscripts and books.*

# Mountain romance on the Glacier Express

*Legendary Swiss railway from St. Moritz to Zermatt*

North Sea

EUROPE

SWITZERLAND

● Glacier Express

Mediterranean

### ROUTE

Bernina Express from Chur to
St. Moritz; to Zermatt SBB via
Berne and Brig. No cars in
Zermatt. The Mattertal
accessible only to Tasch

### BEST TIME

Great interest all year round
so book well in advance

### ALSO WORTH SEEING

Zermatt Schwarzseekleine
cable car; Matterhorn
(Europe's highest mountain),
mountain station at 12,532
feet

Eight hours on the world-famous Glacier Express train from St. Moritz, at an altitude of 5,823 feet across mountains and through valleys to Zermatt, 181 miles away, at a height above sea level of 3,494 feet. Eight hours of traveling from one worldly resort to another in a class-A carriage. Most people who make the journey do not do so to get from A to B but for the ride itself. For the route offers literally breathtaking scenery of the Swiss Alps as it crosses the Upper Alpine Pass at an altitude of 6,670 feet for the most romantic of high Alpine railway journeys.

## The world's slowest express train

The Glacier Express has been running for more than half a century in a tremendous triumph of Swiss engineering against Alpine challenges. The first train ran from St. Moritz to Zermatt hauled by a steam locomotive on June 20, 1939, following years of bridge and tunnel building under difficult conditions. It took until 1982 before engineers felt

they had made the mountain track safe enough to use in winter. The luxury saloon-style panoramic cars have been part of the train since 1993. This comfortable train represents an investment of twenty-five million Swiss Francs.

The Glacier Express does not really exist, a railway expert from Berne tells us. It is really three different trains or rather these days three different companies who operate the same train. They maintain their independence by changing the locomotives. Once

passengers had to change trains too. The Rhiatic Railway starts the journey in St. Moritz and the Furka–Oberalp Railway takes over in Disentis. From Visp to Zermatt the train is operated by the Zermatt Railway. Tourists today are happy to find they can buy one through ticket.

Such rationalization is profitable, for tourists from throughout the world buy tickets for the train ride across the Swiss Alps and past glaciers. Seats have to be booked months in advance. There are up to four trains each day in addition to the Glacier Express with its Italian Pinanfarina-designed observation car with large expanses of glass, that was specially developed for the high-level Alpine track.

The journey begins in St. Moritz. Climbing at about thirty-seven miles per hour, the train passes through Engadin on its way up to the Albula tunnel. Later at the tunnel where the train must reverse between Preda, at 5,879 feet and Bergun at 4,514 feet, you have some appreciation of Swiss tunnel building. The Landwater viaduct further on near Filisur is also a marvel of expert civil engineering

from the early 1900s. Just before Filisur, the Lenzerhorn soars to a height of 9,514 feet. Once the train has left the fortifications and castles on the outskirts of Domlesch behind it is time to be seated at the wooden dining tables. Red and white wines are served in special Glacier Express glasses with special stems designed for stability during the climb. They make popular souvenirs. Then the panorama of the 11,762-foot-high Galenstock opens up.

Once the train has negotiated the narrow gorge of the Upper Rhine and crossed the steep high Alpine pass, it passes a waterfall at Fruka before diving into the nine-mile-long Furka tunnel. Emerging once more into the open air, passengers soon see the Weisshorn and the Monte-Rosa range of the Matterhorn region. The Matterhorn itself is not visible until the last moment, shortly before Zermatt station is entered. Perhaps jaded from all that scenery the traveler alights after eight hours on the train at altitudes of up to 6,561 feet, having traveled 181 miles, crossed 291 bridges, and passed through ninety tunnels.

*The piece de resistance at the end of an astonishing luxury train ride: the Matterhorn. On its way from St. Moritz to Zermatt the red Glacier Express overcomes 6,500-foot-high mountain passes, deep gorges, expanses of white glacier, and passes numerous places of importance such as Disentis Abbey (below). This exciting journey through the mountains was made possible by Swiss engineering that created such spectacular structures as the Saliser Viaduct and the elegant Landwater Viaduct (below, far left)*

# A Portuguese dream

*Batalha monastery is a monument of medieval art*

Only dreams of past glory remain of the power once achieved by the Portuguese under Henry the Navigator in the fifteenth century, but every stone still stands of the chapel he built at Batalha monastery, which remains one of the greatest works of medieval monastic architecture.

## Memorial of battle

The name *Batalha* in Portuguese means battle, and it was a battle that led to the founding of the monastery. Close by is the battlefield of Aljubarroto, on which the Portuguese gained independence from the King Juan of Castile in 1385 under the leadership of John I, father of Henry the Navigator. Grateful for the victory, John I founded the monastery of Santa Maria da Vitoria. The very scale of the building in the heart of the town of Batalha is noble, extending 584 feet by 450 feet, paying opulent homage to the assistance of the Holy Mother and also an impressive place of worship for the new royal house of Aviz of which John I was the founder. The styles of the monastery buildings range from high Gothic to Manuelist and also Renaissance. Six important architects and their followers have had a hand in creating the buildings which were commissioned by six different kings.

King John I ordered the Dominicans to start the monastery in 1388, and they engaged the Portuguese architect Afonso Domingues, who worked on the project until 1402. Domingues created the greater part of the imposing structure, including the nave and choir with its beautiful stained glass, the richly ornamented portal and grand cloistered cross passage, known as the "Claustro real."

## Portuguese Gothic

The other Gothic sections were the work of the French church architect Ouguete. He created the magnificent Founder's Chapel (*Capela do Fundador*) of 1430, which is a particularly fine masterpiece of Portuguese Gothic. It varies from the mainstream Gothic just as the earlier Portuguese Romanesque architecture had done.

## Manuelist style

The individualist artistic approach of the Portuguese achieved a high point under King Dom Manuel I (1469–1521), who was known by the Portuguese as "The Fortunate." Proud of the way the Portuguese seafarers, explorers, and scientists were opening up the world *"abertura du mondo"* and entirely preoccupied with what they brought back with them from unknown lands, the spendthrift monarch decreed that much should be built so that the kingdom's new wealth could be preserved in stone.

Heedless of the stylistic norms of the time, his architects became estranged from Gothic and brought in exotic additions of their own, including vernacular elements. These "Portuguese barbarians" hereby managed to create a particular style of their own, now famous, which is known as Manuelist, after their exuberant king.

The monastery of Batalha also absorbed this style. The Gothic transept was adorned in the Manuelist manner with ornamental filigree forms of exaggerated scale, with slender columns. As if flowers rather than stone, the vaulted arches were to open and close, allowing sunlight to penetrate like the dappled sun beneath trees. The Manuelist style turned the *Claustro Real* into one of the finest cloisters in the world. The fountains at the northwest corner are considered by many experts to be "a pearl of medieval masonry." And the 49-foot-high portal to the *Capelas Imperfeitas* or unfinished chapel is regarded as the finest example of Manuelism.

Unfortunately Dom Manuel I lost interest in Batalha and cared more for buildings he himself had founded, such as the monastery at Belem but his successors returned to the building of the monastery dedicated to the great Portuguese victor over the Spanish. The monastery has withstood the passage of time and remains a Gothic masterpiece, enhanced by the best of Manuelism.

*Filigree ornamentation and slender pillars: Manuelism triumphs at Batalha. The fantastic and arabesque style arose under King Dom Juan I (1496–1521). The superb fountain (below) with its three tiers is regarded as "a pearl of medieval masonry."*

# Gaudi's sermon in stone

*Spanish architect bequeathed his life's work of the Sagrada Familia to Barcelona*

*The spires of the Sagrada Familia tower into the Catalan sky.*

It was to be "a sermon in stone" and a testimony to his Catholic faith but most of all the cathedral was to be his greatest creation. The architect Antonio Gaudi gave more than forty years of his life to his dream of a cathedral for the twentieth century. When he died in 1926, just short of seventy-four, he left behind him a giant building site. Only the north front of the cathedral had been constructed and of the planned eighteen spires just one had been completed. The Church of the Sagrada Familia (Holy Family) is still unfinished, and tools and cranes continue to clutter the site. In spite of this though the *corpus* has become one of the world's best known religious structures and an emblem for Barcelona, and a symbol also for artistic individualism that scorns purely economic considerations.

The final years of this brilliant architect's life were spent living on the site, worrying about dwindling funds from sponsors. So far the church has been entirely funded by donations. In the turbulent 1920s interest in religious buildings diminished and Gaudi's architectural style was deemed *passé*, with a stern functionalism in fashion. When the Spanish Civil War broke out in 1936, ten year's after Gaudi's death, work on the cathedral was terminated. The famous son of Catalonia was branded an enemy of the people and anarchists set fire to the subterranean sepulcher in which his remains were interred, and plundered his studio. Few of his sketches, plans, and models survived.

Building was finally started again in 1952. The few remaining drawings were used to determine the floor plan and beyond this, efforts were made to empathize as closely as possible with Gaudi's own imagination. Such an approach was entirely in keeping with Gaudi's own philosophy. He had never worked from an overall grand plan, with concepts developing as the project progressed. How the finished building would look he could only describe in lyrical terms. "My model is a tree. It has branches, and branches bear leaves. And every part grows in harmony...This tree needs no assistance from outside. Of themselves, all things are in harmony. All things are in balance."

## Master of Moderism

Around 1900 a "return to the roots" or to the forms of nature was celebrated in the style known as Modernism. This style was seeking similar goals as Jugendstil in Germany, Art Nouveau in France, and Modern Style in the English-speaking world. Modernism took root in Catalonia. In Barcelona's Quadrat d'Or alone there are twenty-seven houses by different architects all in the style of *Modernismo*. Three of them are by Gaudi who was undoubtedly the most important interpreter, architect, and designer of this style, that developed a character of its own with symbolic ornamentation and expressive style of construction.

For Gaudi, humankind is part of nature, and dwellings should be shelters; spaces, not a succession of cubes but should have flowing lines without angles or sharp corners. He was particularly taken with traditional materials and had them painted in many colors. The Sagrada too was meant to be entirely painted.

The east front, with its theme of the "redemption of humanity" was to be light and friendly, while the west front that reflected martyrdom was to be dark in tone. Of the eighteen spires, sixteen were reserved for the apostles and evangelists and the other two for the Mother and Son. This symbolism did not prevent Gaudi from using modern technology. Gaudi's houses incorporate elevators, underground car parking, and removable walls as a matter of course. He experimented with air conditioning, designed door handles, heating equipment, lighting, and stairway balconies.

The Sagrada Familia is currently a hive of activity with considerable work under way, rather in the manner of churches in the Middle Ages. The eighteen spires reach toward the sky, while sculpture for the north portals have been created by Josep Gubriachs. Gaudi's dream is gradually being fulfilled but as completion approaches there are misgivings. After all part of the plan's magnificence lay in Gaudi's dream not being achievable.

**ROUTE**

Subway station Sagrada Familia; Casa Mila: subway station Diagonal; Parc Guell, bus 24, 25

**BEST TIMES**

May–June, September–October

**ALSO WORTH SEEING**

St. Eulalia cathedral, Picasso Museum, Barri Gotic (inner city Gothic quarter), modern architecture Passeig de Gracia, Rambles promenade, Parc Guell

*Casa Battlo, a house of 1877, was entirely rebuilt by Antoni Gaudi in 1905 in his characteristic sculptural style. The fin de siecle architect paid attention to the smallest detail. Even the roofs and stairway balconies were rebuilt. The Casa Mila (bottom) is like a giant sculpture which people live in. This was Gaudi's final secular work.*

# Palace, monastery, and mausoleum

*El Escorial is magnificent but austere and forbidding*

### ROUTE

From Madrid: NV1/M505 39 miles NW. Coaches and trains from Madrid stations Atocha, Chamartin, Nucvos Ministerios, Principe Pio

### OPENING TIMES

April 15–October 15: 10 a.m.–6.30 p.m., rest of year 10 a.m.–6 p.m. Siesta 1.30 p.m.–3 p.m.

### ACCOMMODATIONS

Hotel Victoria Palace in San Lorenzo de El Escorial

### ALSO WORTH SEEING

Valle de los Caidos (valley of the fallen), Segovia (cathedral, aqueduct), Alcàzar

*Viewed from above by floodlight The Escorial sheds some of its severe asceticism. Large numbers are attracted by the valuable collection of paintings, especially those of El Greco.*

The monumental building known as the Escorial is El Real Monasterio de San Lorenzo del Escorial. The royal monastery of St. Laurence happens to be located outside of the small town of Escorial. This is not some grand display of vainglorious power, nor does it reflect the dreams and fantasies of a narcissistic ruler. The sublime is worshipped at El Escorial. Surrounded by untamed nature, the monumental parallelogram has a western and main front of roughly 680 feet by 530 feet with sixteen inner courtyards, fifteen cross passageways, eighty-six stairways, and eighty-eight fountains. Residents could look down from two thousand windows but it was impossible for anyone to look in.

The founding charter records that King Philip II founded the monastery in honor of St. Laurence, for it was on this saint's day in 1557 that an important battle was won against the French. The other reason for the building's construction is more human. It was one of Charles V's final wishes for a church to be created in which he and his kin could be entombed.

Philip was happy to meet this wish but as the most powerful man of his day he also wanted to erect a monument to his secular and spiritual power.

The king personally sought a fitting place with religious zeal, seeking advice from geologists, men of medicine, and philosophers. He finally found the spot a day's journey from his new capital at Madrid, in the Sierra de Guaderrama, where there was a plateau which met his needs. The unattractive name of the nearby community of El Escorial (Snail Hill) came to be applied to the building itself at its 3,461-foot-high location. There was an abandoned mine nearby. From this point to the top, there is firm ground again, and mountains loom threateningly over the site. In the distance one catches a glimpse of the capital from which Philip II reigned. This misanthropic king, who seldom traveled and rarely consulted with any one, ruled the world by decrees written on "two inch paper."

He undertook the supervision of the project himself, engaging the architect Bautista de Toledo from Naples, who died in 1567, four years after work began. His assistant Juan Herrera took over, and managed to complete the enormous building in a period of twenty-one years. The multi-purpose structure combines a

monastery, palace , and seminary for priests within one building. Philip monitored the progress on the mountain plateau from a spot still known as Silla de Felipe II. Modern visitors too get the best view of El Escorial from this vantage point.

## Between Renaissance and baroque

Viewed at close quarters one can see a building constructed of cold gray granite-like stone, perfectly cut and jointed from massive blocks. This style with its clearly defined lines is characteristic of the Renaissance, but Europe was already succumbing at this time to baroque and there is evidence of this here too. Not the customary ornate baroque but *desornamentado*, or without embellishment and playful forms. The architect consciously avoided all forms of decoration. This type of baroque style later took its name from El Escorial, estilo scoralense. No ostentation was to be displayed here either. Some abhor this *"barbaridad de piedras,"* (barbarity in stone) while others admire its sense of purpose. In any event, it accurately reflects the character of its founder: stern, forbidding, absolute in power, and deeply religious. It is not accidental that St. Peter's in Rome was the first model proposed for El Escorial, since Philip primarily saw himself as a servant of God. But this was no humble servant. "We, the King, proclaim: live near to God. We, the King, proclaim royal order, which is divine order." The wing of El Escorial to which the ruler of the great Spanish Empire retired and eventually died, was of extreme and stern simplicity: a tiled study/bed-room with a window overlooking the high altar.

*Behind the 675-foot facade is hidden a palace, a monastery, church, library, and royal tomb. Philip II had this somber monument of the Habsburg rule built to fulfill a vow. El Escorial is certainly "Worthy of a man of who chose a wilderness as his capital and a tomb for his palace," as Alexander Dumas put it about this great complex of buildings.*

# Moorish Cordoba

*The Mezquita was once the largest mosque in the Occident*

D eath and destruction lay behind him, in front of him lay the fertile plains of the Rio Gualdalquivir, and at a bend of the river, at the foot of the Sierras, lay the town of his dreams. It had once been the Romans' provincial capital, was the diocesan center, and birthplace of the last of the Visigoth kings. Now Cordoba was his, his flight was ended. He would found his own dynasty as Abdr-ar Rahman I.

The Persian Abbasids had exterminated all his relatives in Damascus. As the sole survivor of the Omaijad clan, this twenty-year-old had managed to escape the bloodbath. The young prince hid in Egypt, was discovered, and then found refuge among the Berbers in the Atlas Mountains, where his mother had been born. She had been abducted and sold as a concubine to the Caliph. Since she was not a wife, her son was not admitted to the close circle of pretenders to the throne. Now though, he was the last member of the Omaijad clan alive.

### Symbol of early Islam

Accompanied by a group of militant Berbers, the crown prince departed for Spain in September 755. Forty-five years earlier the North African warlord Tarik had conquered the south of the country with just seven thousand men and had driven the Visigoths north in spite of their determined resistance. The Moors, who had come to Spain as nomads, took root in Spain, cultivated the land and created their own culture. Their style and taste spread to other parts of Islam and even to the Christian world.

Abdr-ar Rahman I, the young man who had fled Damascus and Africa, was their pioneer. He founded the independent emirate of Cordoba and

*An example of Moorish art: the western front of the mosque.*

purchased land from the Christians on which a Roman temple had once stood, and where there was a Visigoth basilica at the time. It was here that his Mezquita was built, the largest mosque in the Occident, built in the manner of North African mosques. Under the leadership of his dynasty, Cordoba became an important center of the arts and sciences, highly prosperous and elegant. Even the Christian nun Roswitha von Gandersheid wrote enthusiastically about the capital: "The illuminating star of the world shines over the west, Cordoba!" Within the city's wall lived 800,000 people. There were 130,000 houses, eighty schools where lessons were free, 900 bathing houses, one

hundred hospitals and libraries, and three hundred mosques.

The Mezquita was unique and remains so. Like no other structure in Europe, it is a symbol of the spiritual vigor of early Islam. Although quite unprepossessing from the outside, the interior has an ethereal kind of beauty. This is wholly in keeping with Islamic traditions. Luxury should be intimate and private, not ostentatious for public display as in the European manner. Those desiring to enter the mosque must first pass through an orange grove (Patio de los naranjos), walk beneath citrus trees, palms, cypresses, gnarled olive trees, and disappear beneath a mass of columns of an arcade—865 in all—supporting

an endless row of horseshoe arches that support a second row of arches like some mythical labyrinth. At the outer edge of the Mezquita, facing Mecca, there is the holiest of places, an octagonal prayer niche with a Byzantine mosaic with Arabic inscriptions between pink and blue columns.

Amid all this oriental flavor there is a cathedral. This "barbarian" intrusion dates from the sixteenth century, but there is no doubt that this church saved the superb masterpiece of Abdr-ar Rahman, for without it, fundamentalist Christians would long since have demolished the mosque.

*Three generations created this forest of masonry. Many of the 856 columns and their capitals originated from the diocesan church of the Visigoths and some date back to Roman times. They were adopted by the master builder of the caliphs. Plants were an important part of Moorish architecture, intended to create a unity between the structure and nature.*

# Spain's Moorish palace

*The Alhambra is one of the best examples of secular Islamic architecture*

**ROUTE**

Flight to Granada via
Barcelona or Madrid

**OPENING TIMES**

Daily 9 p.m.–10 p.m. but
9.30 a.m.–5.45 p.m. in
winter

**BEST TIMES**

May, Holy Week (Semanta
Santa), fall (Midsummer
temperatures of 104°F (40°C)

**ACCOMMODATIONS**

Parador Real de la Alhambra
(on the Alhambra site)

**ALSO WORTH SEEING**

Cathedral of Santa Maria de
la Encaración

Granada is one of the finest examples of a multi-cultural society. Muslims, Christians, and Jews lived together in peace in the small kingdom of Granada for 250 years. Eventually, under Isabella of Castile, Christian fundamentalists ousted the Moors in 1492 and prohibited freedom of worship.

The Alhambra Palace rises up in front of the snow-capped mountains of the Sierra Nevada like a memory of a lost dream. This building ranks alongside the Taj Mahal in terms of secular Islamic architecture. The fragrance of the flowers, the coolness of the marble, the gurgling water in the fountains and rills all transport visitors back to the oriental style of life in Spain, to a rich Moorish heritage which flourished in Andalusia in the thirteenth and fourteenth centuries.

The Calat Alhambra or red castle crests one of the foothills of the mountain range which rise at their eastern end to a summit of 11,483 feet. To the west, at the foot of the mountains, lies Granada. The Alhambra's outward appearance owes much to the fortified wall which encloses the hill. The Moorish palace is found behind this wall. From below one first sees the Alcazaba, the oldest section of the Alhambra, jutting out above the city like the prow of a ship.

## Home of the Nasrite kings

This home of the Nasrite kings is the only Moorish palace in the west. Its system of defensive walls and towers encloses separate buildings and a series of pavilions and courtyards. Various sources of diffused light penetrate into every corner of these spaces. The plants on the outside of the buildings are continued inside by decorative moldings in stucco. Cooling water from fountains flows through the living quarters. This creates a unity between nature and the man-made structure. Standing at the back of one of the inner hallways the landscape is seen as a series of images framed by richly ornamented window casements. Conversely when viewed from outside the architecture acts as a setting for the fountains, flowering jasmine, and cypresses. Gardens have always been special for the Moors. They remind them of the quiet pleasures promised by the Koran as a reward for devotion. Perhaps this is why the Christian conquerors changed them beyond recognition. High above the Alhambra though there is El Generalife, a building with the most exciting and delightful Arabian gardens to be found in Spain.

Decorative exteriors are not part of the Moorish tradition. Ornamental display of wealth is something reserved for the intimacy of inner parts of the building. Hence the sober simplicity outside contrasts starkly with the overwhelming beauty within. Inside the palace both the floor and apparently weightless columns are of marble while the ceilings are decorated with coffers and woodcarvings.

The palace itself falls into three areas: the Mexuar Palace was originally reserved for administrative and judicial matters, the Myrtle Court, with its magnificent pool in which the columns are reflected, was favored for official audiences. At the center beneath the Tower of Comares is the Ambassadors' Hall where the sultan sat enthroned in a room with windows down to the floor. The Lion Court and adjacent buildings were reserved for the sultan's private life and for his family and harem. At its center are twelve lions supporting a fountain of white marble bearing an inscription which seems the essence of Moorish architecture: "Let your eyes mingle with the flowing and the still water and marble, and we know not which of them guides you."

Amid this oriental magnificence is the palace that the Holy Roman emperor and Habsburg monarch Charles V built on this plateau in astonishing harmony. The fine detail of the Arab buildings contrast strongly with the powerful forms of massive masonry of 206 feet in length. In 1526, Pedrom Machuca, a student of Michelangelo, designed this example of high Renaissance architecture but sadly the work was never completed and Charles V never lived there.

*The interior of the palace is richly adorned with stalactite arches, colonnades, and elaborate stucco ornaments. In the Lions Court twelve of the beasts support the marble fountain (left). High above the Alhambra the colorful and delightfully fragrant gardens of El Generalife are cooled by water in the most beautiful Arab garden on Spanish soil.*

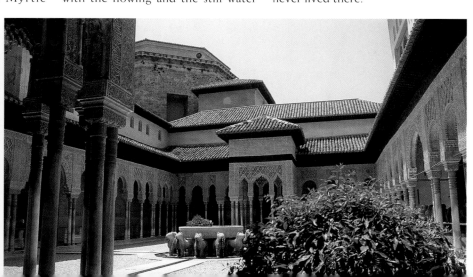

# Doric columns in Segesta

*A temple to the Elimi's gods where sheep graze on Sicily*

The inhabitants of Segesta in Sicily are recorded in ancient history primarily as the implacable enemies of neighboring Selimunte, a trading town. Various treaties with the rulers on the mainland were interspersed with bloody wars. Eventually only remnants of the town remained and the ruins of the Doric temple of Segesta.

Around three thousand years ago the Elimi lived in the limestone hills of Calatafimi in northwest Sicily. Legend has it that they had fled the burning Troy, led by the Homeric hero Aeneas, whose sons or cousins founded Rome. The refugees selected the mountain of Monte Barbaro

for their fortified settlement of Segesta from where their look-outs could keep an eye on the entire area and the Gulf of Castellemare. It was there that the first homes and public buildings were erected, and perhaps a few small temples.

## Following the Greek way

Most of the town in the mountains is now nothing but ruins and much of it still has to be excavated by archaeologists. Remains of fortifications and a few derelict watchtowers suggest the place was protected by a double wall. The Elimi theater is relatively well preserved and its seats hewn from rock offer a view to the Mediterranean.

The colonists built their first grander temple around the sixth century BC, behind the walls of their stronghold. Its outer wall measures 272 feet by 154 feet but it is unknown to which particular gods the Elimi offered their sacrifices. A century later construction was begun on the famous Elimi temple on the western side of Segesta. Its classic Doric styling is reminiscent of Grecian temples although these builders were not Greeks. It is assumed a Greek architect played an important role in the project.

The temple dominates the hilly landscape today as far as the road to Trápani, and although it was never finished, the temple still appears a

model of perfection. The superstructure in the form of a Doric metope frieze is supported on thirty-six Doric columns that taper slightly towards their capitals. There is no sign of an entranceway or an altar and is thought likely work had to be suspended before completion.

The Elimi and the Greeks maintained close cultural relations. This is apparent from various sections of wall that have been uncovered in the ruins of Segesta, with inscriptions dating from the fifth century BC. The lettering is Greek but the language is not.

Segesta's decline began around the fifth century BC when a series of border feuds occurred with their neighbors of Selimunt. In 409 BC, the Elimi, aided by the Carthaginians, attacked Selimunt, razed it to the ground, and killed more than sixteen thousand inhabitants. The following year an allied force from Syracuse recaptured Selimunt but it soon fell

again to Carthage and never regained its former glory. All that remains in evidence are a number of reconstructed temples.

For a long time the people of Segesta were dependent on the Carthaginian town of Panormos (Palermo) until it became Roman. Ultimately the city was severely damaged by the Vandals and other marauding tribes. The survivors fled, and the city deteriorated rapidly. Only the impressive Doric columns remain as a memory of the Elimi.

In recent years the theater of Segesta has once again seen performances. Classic dramas are enacted every other year in this third century BC amphitheater.

# Pompeii emerges from its entombment

*A city frozen in 79 AD and preserved beneath volcanic lava*

The catastrophe that overcame the Bay of Naples started in the morning of August 24, 79 AD. A noise like a tremendous thunderclap rolled down Mt. Vesuvius. The entire top of the mountain had blown apart and was venting a dark cloud and spewing forth fire. Soon a storm of rock and ash descended from the darkened sky and a surge of molten lava headed from the flanks of the volcano towards the valley.

The first place to be overcome was the small seaside resort of Herculaneum. A torrent of muddy water, earth, and lave surged through the homes, suffocating man and beast, and ultimately covering the town beneath a sixty-five-foot-thick layer that turned to rock. The 100,000 or so citizens of Pompeii on the southeastern flank of the volcano seemed to be more fortunate. Only a continuous drizzle of ash fell there and the fiery lava flow headed in a different direction.

Those on the paved streets of the city took shelter in their villas, shops, temples, and bath houses but wherever they hid they were caught in a death trap. The drizzle of ash soon changed to small volcanic rocks, mixed with larger chunks of pumice. The stench of sulfur pervaded the entire city, reaching to every corner in which people sheltered, suffocating every breathing creature.

Two days later the smoke and dust clouds cleared and the sun shone brightly above the Bay of Naples, but Pompeii had vanished. The once wealthy provincial city was covered by a gray mass. The city had repaired the damage from the previous eruption a few years earlier but now its entombed population were soon covered by new grass and forgotten.

### Treasure hunters discover civilization

Time passed. More than fifteen centuries later, treasure seekers started to take an interest in the buried city. A few statues were found at the site of Herculaneum but the mass of rock covering the site was difficult to

penetrate. Matters were more favorable at Pompeii for it was buried beneath a more fragile covering of ash, small volcanic stones, and pumice.

In 1748, during the first archaeological excavation that had been commissioned by royalty, the diggers chanced upon an astonishingly well-preserved Pompeiian villa with walls covered with murals. Marble and bronze statues of their gods were recovered and a market hall for selling produce and wine was uncovered.

The most pitiful findings relate to the people whose lives were abruptly ended by the eruption and its poisonous cloud of sulfur. One group that had been surprised by sudden death were gathered for a funeral meal. Others had fled, laden with their most treasured possessions but been overtaken by the poison lurking everywhere.

Other finds reflect a sensuous life style which authorities long kept under wraps. A sign was found in the shape of a penis, pointing to a brothel. A mosaic in the Casa del Fauna depicts a satyr engaged in love play with a naked nymph. Discoveries included a sculpture more than 160 feet high, that was painted red, of a vigorously erect phallus. It is clear that such erotic art was an important part of their Bacchus cult, while scholars suggest that representations of penises on the outside walls of their homes were intended to ward off the evil eye.

After 250 years of increasingly more methodical excavation, Pompeii has risen again from the ashes of Mt. Vesuvius like a phoenix, to provide us with a unique insight into city life around the time of Christ.

*One of the main streets buried in 79 AD by the volcanic eruption. Cart tracks are worn into the paved street. The main walls of the houses were left standing and murals like that at the bottom left were preserved. People became mummified where they died, as the family shown at the bottom right.*

# Residence of the Pope

*The Vatican contains more art treasures than any other building in the world*

**ROUTE**

Bus line 64 to Piazza San Pietro (St. Peter's Square), subway line A to Otttaviano Station (about 300 yards N of Vatican)

**BEST TIMES**

Easter, April–June, September–October

**OPENING TIMES**

St. Peter's: daily 7 a.m.–7 p.m., winter to 6 p.m. Public audiences with the Pope on Wednesday, usually at 11 a.m. Requests to the Prefetturia della Casa Ponificia, Tuesdays 9 a.m.–1 p.m.

When the Roman emperor Constantine the Great embraced Christianity in the fourth century, he also established the basis for the political power of the Roman Catholic church, headed by the Pope. Constantine gave the Lateran Palace to the Christians as a residence which still belongs to the Vatican. This was where the Popes lived until 1308. Constantine also established the palace church of San Giovanni in Laterano. To this day it is the papal cathedral and the highest ranking church of Catholicism.

It was not until 1377 that the papal palace of the Vatican was developed on the hill on the right bank of the Tiber known as the Mons Vaticano. Construction of the Sistine Chapel began in 1473. The papal residence was built in the sixteenth century, designed by Raphael. At this time one of the most historically significant popes, Julius II, started collecting and exhibiting works of art, laying the foundation of today's treasury of Vatican art that is of inestimable value.

## More than a thousand different rooms of every size

Art now became wholly associated with these holy places. The Sistine Chapel is richly decorated with the work of Sandro Boticelli and Pietro Perugino. From 1508 to 1512, Michaelangelo created the famous paintings depicting the story of creation which have recently been superbly restored. In 1541, *The Last Judgement* on the altar wall was completed. At present the Vatican, with its thousand plus rooms and a library of about 60,000 manuscripts, houses more art treasures than any other building in the world.

Surrounded by this beauty, the pope lives in and rules the world's smallest state or *Stato della Città del Vaticano*, the fragmentary remains of what was once a vast Roman Catholic empire. The Vatican City measures a mere 108 acres, with St. Peter's Square at its heart, and a population of about one thousand. In the Lateran charter, Italy guaranteed the independence of this church state which has its own "army" —the Swiss Guard—a mint, railway station, radio station broadcasting in thirty-five languages, and its own daily newspaper, the *Osservatore Romano*.

At the very center of this minuscule state is St. Peter's Square and the eponymous church, first built in 326 on the grave of Peter the apostle.

In the early sixteenth century, the artistic Pope Julius II had an enormous new basilica built to replace the original. It was designed by Bramante. St. Peter's can hold 60,000 people in its 15,708 square yards of space and took 120 years to build (1506–1626) before this enormous basilica was completed.

The 433-foot-high dome was designed by Michaelangelo. The basilica was regarded as a miracle of architecture. The most famous artists of the day contributed to both the church and its surroundings. The colonnaded crescent which encloses the forecourt, its columns, pylons, and life-size sculptures of various saints is by Giovanni Lorenzo Bernini, who also designed the installation of the eighty-two-foot-high Egyptian needle at the center of St. Peter's Square and the canopy

above St. Peter's altar. Michaelangelo's *Pieta* appears in the right-hand side nave of the church. At the entrance to the principal nave, one is reminded that this is where Pope Leo III baptized Charlemagne and crowned him as Holy Roman emperor. The church's need for buildings has vastly outgrown the tiny Vatican state and there are palaces to be found elsewhere in Rome plus three patriarchal basilicas and the pope's summer residence at Castle Gandolfo.

*St. Peter's Square and the administrative buildings of the Vatican State. Bernini, who designed the square's colonnades, also arranged the 82 ft-high-needle in the center of the square. The Vatican's greatest treasures are 60,000 manuscripts, housed in the beautiful Bibliotheca Palatine (below view of library and mural).*

**ROUTE**

International flights to Peretola airport, Highway A3 and A11. Restricted access for vehicles to the inner city

**OPENING TIMES**

Uffizi: Tuesday–Saturday 9 a.m.–7 p.m.; Sunday to 2 p.m. Closed Mondays

**ACCOMMODATIONS**

Porta Rossa, Via Porta Rossa 19 (central, one of Italy's oldest hotels)

# Florence: cradle of the Renaissance

*Under the Medici the capital of Tuscany reached sublime cultural heights*

Human beauty soon fades, but art endures, wrote the Tuscan poet Francesco Petrarch (1304-1374). No other city impresses us with this wisdom so strongly as Florence. Its astonishing richness of truly great architecture, sculpture, paintings, manuscripts, bronzes, and masterpieces of the goldsmith's art is simply incredible.

Here, on the banks of the Arno River, surrounded by green hills, an Etruscan settlement existed as early as 200 BC. As a Roman colony one hundred years later, the still small town was named Florentia, suggesting it was blossoming. Changing fortunes brought a succession of rulers to Florence until its citizens deprived the nobility of all their privileges in the thirteenth century and established the first citizen's republic, in which the bourgeois and well-intentioned merchants held sway. Ultimately though, the Medici family drew all power unto themselves.

The Medici were merchants and bankers who brought great commercial prominence to the city. However it was their role as patrons of the arts that led to an incomparable blossoming of creativity. Through their patronage, some of the Tuscan capital's most important buildings came into being, the first public library in Europe opened its doors, science and the arts were advanced, and great works of art collected. Great minds were able to develop in Florence, like those of Brunelleschi, the painter and sculptor Michaelangelo, and the universal genius Leonardo da Vinci.

One of the most attractive routes through Florence of the Middle Ages and Renaissance leads from the south bank of the Arno across the old bridge known as the Ponte Vecchio. This spanned the river in 1342 and by the sixteenth century goldsmiths had established their workshops and shops on either side of the bridge. Pedestrians jostled shoulder to shoulder among the continuous line of precious objects for sale. Just one corner of the bridge was not built upon, and this provides a view of the warren of alleyways, palaces, churches, and towers of the inner city.

The octagonal baptistery that was once the Cathedral of John the Baptist has stood here since the eleventh century, with its green and white marble and bronze doors that are heavily encrusted with reliefs. Immediately below the baptistery the 351-foot-high dome by Brunelleschi of the Santa Maria del Fiore reaches skywards. This church was completed in the fifteenth century.

## Collection of masterpieces

One day's sightseeing is not sufficient to see the inner city of Florence. One must take time to look properly at the San Lorenzo Church built by Brunelleschi and embellished with sculpture by his contemporaries Michaelangelo and Donatello. There are Renaissance palaces to be admired such as the Palazzo Medici-Ricardo with its inner courtyard, and the crenellated fortified tower of Palazzo Vecchio, complete with its murals, painted ceilings, grand halls, and sculpture.

In the famous Uffizi Gallery the visitor can admire one of the most significant collections of paintings anywhere in the world, with ancient sculpture displayed alongside masterpieces by the leading European artists. And within the Palazzo Pitti, built in the fifteenth century to a Brunelleschi design, there is the Palatini Gallery with works by Titian, Rubens, Raphael, and many other masters from the Medici collection.

The French poet Guy de Maupassant took special pleasure in gazing upon Titian's naked *Venus*, but after many visits to the museum he was "exhausted from looking, as a hunter of the hunt." And his very sensitive German colleague Rainer Maria Rilke reported after touring Florence: "Wandering through the network of quaint alleys I had to tear myself away. I could take no more."

*Three images of Florence: painted ceilings in the Venus Hall (below) of the Palazzo Pitti, which holds one of the largest art collections in the city; the rich facade of the Santa Maria del Fiore (consecrated 1467) with 269-ft campanile of the 13th century; and the Ponte Vecchio, which has spanned the Arno since 1342. Goldsmiths built their studios and shops on the bridge.*

# Venice: "La Serenissima"

*The merchants' city maintains time-worn splendor*

North Sea

EUROPE

Venice

ITALY

Mediterranean

**ROUTE**

International flights, bus transfer to Piazzale Roma

**BEST TIMES**

Carnival (just before Lent), May–June, September

**FOOD**

Café Florian, Piazza San Marco

**ALSO WORTH SEEING**

Murano (island of glassblowers), Chioggia island city

When the Huns captured and devastated Padua and Aquilia in 452, the population fled to the 120 small islands in the Venice lagoon. Hence the jewel of Mediterranean cities or *Serenissima* was founded by fugitives. The next marauders were the Lombards who caused the inhabitants to draw closer together and to place themselves under the protection of the Byzantine lords of Ravenna. The people of Venice did manage to re-tain sufficient independence though to develop their own political structure. In 697, twelve tribunes of the islands elected the first doge. This city became the first republic of Upper Italy. The system was maintained for 1,100 years until Na-poleon occupied Venice in 1797 and forced the final doge to step down.

Napoleon brought an end to one of the most developed systems of government in Europe which had been tried and tested long before the rise of the great monarchies and empires. In 811, the doge moved from the island of Malamocco to Rialto Island, which was easier to defend. With the endless stream of relics of St. Mark, Rialto Island became the power center of the city in the lagoon. The lion of St. Mark has been the emblem of Venice ever since. Trade privileges, daring diplomacy, and accomplished seamen combined to make the republic a center of east–west trade. The wealth amassed by Venice is reflect-ed today in the many patrician palaces, rare art treasures housed and exhibited in the city's museums, and the extravagant feasts that Venice has celebrated through the ages. The great masked ball of carnival in Venice is a constant theme in art, literature, film, and music.

*Ponte dei Sospiri – Bridge of Sighs (named after the sighing ("sospiri") of the condemned en route to their execution) – connects the Palazzo Ducale to the former prisons. One prominent prisoner who walked this bridge was Giacomo Casanova, who managed to escape from the death cell in 1756.*

*Venice is flooded 100 times each year. St. Mark's Square is then under water. The celebration of Carnival lifts the spirit of the lagoon on sad wintry days.*

Today it is not a human enemy that threatens Venice. The piles on which the city stands are being eaten away by pollution which can be detected in the unpleasant smell from the 150 canals that is noticeable when crossing the four hundred brick bridges.

Fortunately steps have been taken to protect this site of importance to our world heritage. The numbers of tourists is to be restricted. This will provide some relief for the decaying glory of this unique city. Those responsible for protecting the city are based in the very heart of the maritime republic, close to St. Mark's Square (Piazza San Marco). They have particular concern about the Doge's Palace, with its ornamental colonnade, and buildings designed by the man who re-discovered the classical style of architecture, Andrea Palladio. Among his Palladian masterpieces are the Church of the Redeemer (*Il Redentore*) on the Guidecca, and Santa Maria della Presentazione. There are also villas by Palladio on the mainland.

*The legendary romantic Venetian gondolas seen in front of the Doge's Palace. In the distance is church of Santa Maria della Salute.*

# The magnificent "salon of Milan"

*The Galleria puts mere malls in the shade*

The city fathers of Milan wanted to find a suitable manner to develop land adjoining their cathedral. In1860, they resolved to hold a competition for ideas to resolve the problem which was won by Giuseppe Mengoni of Bologna.

Work started in March 1865. Mengoni's design was for an enormous glass-covered arcade or atrium topped by a curved dome such as the world had only previously seen at St. Peter's in Rome. This was to fill the space

between the cathedral square and the Piazza della Scala. Milan's Galleria Vittorio Emanuele has a 147-foot-high dome of glass and steel, modeled precisely on the dome of St. Peter's in Rome. The architect intended his new building to be something of a temple for the bourgeoisie as well as a covered shopping mall.

## Dedicated to the King

The five-storey structure is impressive for its monumental scale alone. Laid out in the form of a

cross, one axis is 643 feet and the other 344 feet. At the center where the axes intersect is a domed octagon of 118 feet in diameter. Mengoni had artists portray people from the arts, sciences, and industry of national importance in a kind of hall of fame, rather than a collection of latter day saints. The mosaic of the superb marble floor represents the *Stemma* of the royal house of Savoy and the coats of arms of the Italian provinces.

Mengoni specifically regarded his commission as an incarnation of

Italian national consciousness following the proclamation of a unified Italy in 1861. His patriotic project was intended specifically to honor the one man who was so closely associated with the unification of Italy: King Vittoria Emanuele II. Built by two thousand workers in the space of one and a half years, the gallery was dedicated to the king, who opened it on September 15, 1867. Something was still felt to be lacking from the area around the cathedral and so a triumphal arch was decided upon. Ten years later, the architect Mengoni fell to his death from the scaffolding on the arch during its construction but he had known the success of the Galleria before his death. The Milanese adore the Galleria and call it the *Salotto di Milano* or "Salon of Milan." The marble pavement and its artistic mosaic, the

famous shops, restaurants, and bars were the background for the daily bustle of vigorous political and communal life.

Well-dressed men and women (as perhaps only the Milanese know how to dress) dined at the luxurious Savini restaurant, promenaded and visited the shops, cutting the *bella figura* so important to Milanese life. Debating fraternities met at Biffi, the large, spacious bar, with an army of staff, who reserved one corner just for them. The small bar of Gaspare Campari, close to the exit towards the cathedral, was also very popular. He served a very special aperitif bearing his name that was eventually to achieve world renown.

The Galleria is no longer the center of Milanese intellectual and social circles but still reflects Milanese life. It is a stage in which everyone is a performer and part of the audience,

whether the distinguished business-man on his way to a deal, a back-packer enjoying a picnic on the marble floor, or just a tourist with jaw-dropping awe photographing the architecture of the Galleria and its shops . The Galleria still looks much as it did a century ago. The damage done by allied bombing during the war has long since been repaired.

Restaurant Savini still exists as does the Café Camparino with its famous buffets, where the composers Verdi and Puccini were habitués. The Biffi café is also still there but now much smaller. Biffi had to sell out part of its space to a fast-food chain because of financial difficulties.

*The cross axes of the Galleria intersect at the octagon. The Galleria is impressive both for its monumental scale and the richness of its design detail. Architect Giuseppe Mengoni decorated the floor and walls with emblems of the modern united Italy. He regarded its opening in 1867 as an incarnation of Italian national consciousness.*

*The shrine in the Rila mountains is a Bulgarian masterpiece, with colonnades and painted pergolas surrounding the inner courtyard.*

# Rila monastery: Bulgaria's holiest shrine

*Here rest the remains of a devout man and the heart of a czar*

The holiest national shrine of Bulgaria is found at an altitude of more than three thousand feet. The Rila monastery rises from the rocky plateau like a fortress, with high outer walls and a Medieval watchtower. The dome of the church is decorated with blue adorned by golden crosses. The Bulgarian adherence to western Christianity is indicated here by the use of white and black marble. Bulgaria's most famous and devout monk is interred here, and their royal family offer prayers from time to time before a family mausoleum.

The monastery's origins date back to the middle of the ninth century. Bulgarians had embraced the Christian faith under Czar Boris I and around 900 a devout villager from Skrino journeyed to the Rila Mountains, around sixty miles from Sofia, to seek solitude in order to strengthen his faith. The hermit lived there for twelve years, praying and fasting in a cave next to the site of the future monastery. Mountain dwellers called him Ivan Rilski or Ivan of Rila, and before long pilgrims came to the country from different parts of the country to be taught by this devout man.

### Masterpiece of "rebirth"

In the years that followed, brethren in faith established a small monastery on the rocky plateau. Their founder, Ivan Rilski, established rule for monastic life. By the time of his death aged 70, on August 18, 946, his fame had spread to the extent that Czar Peter had his remains interred in the cathedral at Sofia. Later they were returned to the monastery at Rila so that his final resting place was close to the cave where he had lived for much of his life.

The monastery was repeatedly plundered and in the fourteenth century much of the building was carried away by an avalanche. The monks who survived rebuilt the monastery in the form of a fortress with a rectangular row of almost windowless buildings surrounding an inner courtyard. During the course of the next five hundred years of Ottoman rule though these defensive walls were unable to withstand repeated attacks by plunderers, and the monastery was put to the torch three times. An Ottoman decree which stipulated that no Christian church was to be larger than a farmhouse prevented any effort to restore the monastery.

In its present form the monastery dates from the time of Bulgarian national rebirth in the nineteenth century. Between 1816 and 1870, architects, sculptors, woodcarvers, silversmiths, and painters were eager to be part of the rebuilding of this national shrine incorporating Ivan Rilski's tomb and the crenallated medieval watchtower. They all sought to create a masterpiece of Bulgarian architecture. Today's monastery has outer walls seventy-eight feet high, enclosing an irregular shaped inner courtyard of over 3,500 square yards. It contains colonnaded arcades, painted pergolas, and wooden galleries. A medieval appearance has been combined with Bulgarian vernacular forms.

The main feature of the huge monastery is its church. Here artists used rich colors and copious gold leaf to depict important scenes from Bulgarian national history on the frontage beneath the dome. The beauty of the church's interior is enhanced by a golden wall behind the altar with icons depicting saints, superb woodcarvings, and a richly ornamental ceremonial cross.

The monastery church is brightly lit by daylight and the burning of thousands of candles. After a strange odyssey, the heart of the Bulgarian czar Boris II has finally been laid to rest here too. The czar's remains, from which the heart was removed as was customary, was entombed at the monastery in 1943 but three years later the new Communist rulers transferred it to the royal villa at Vranja. This second resting place was destroyed in 1956 and the body was considered to be lost too. Only the heart remained, which had been embalmed and escaped the attention of the Communist government in the medical department of the University of Sofia.

The family of the late czar now live in Spain. They arranged for the heart to be returned to the church of the Rila monastery, which is now accessible to them once more.

North Sea

EUROPE

BULGARIA

**Rila Monastery**

Mediterranean

### ROUTE

International flights to Sofia. 62 miles S of capital on E79. Daily flights to Rila via Sofia and from Varna

### BEST TIMES

May–June, September–October

### ALSO WORTH SEEING

Sofia: Alexander Nevski Cathedral, Ethnographic Museum, National Historical Museum

# Monasteries perched on pinnacles

*Greek monks found solitude on the peaks of the Metéora*

In Greek, *metéoros* means "raised up." And this is precisely how we find the monasteries in the Metéora Mountains of Greece. Monks built their refuges atop pinnacles of rock that tower up to a thousand feet above the Pinios River. When dusk covers the valley as the sun has almost disappeared, or when the morning mist still hovers over the peaks, the monasteries appear to be floating amid veils of white gossamer.

Hermits were drawn to the mountain peaks northwest of Thessalia as early as the ninth century. The caves at the foot of these mountains provided adequate shelter and made it possible to meditate without being disturbed. Using ladders, some of them climbed to crevices in the sandstone higher up, cast away the ladder, and fasted and sought the presence of God through self-castigation and ecstasy.

Serbian incursions into Byzantine Thessalia in the fourteenth century prompted the construction of the first settlements and monasteries in virtually inaccessible places on rocky ledges and mountain peaks. The monks used ropes or lashed ladders together to carry the materials up to the site, and later they hauled both men and materials up in nets or large baskets.

## No admission to woman

One of the first monasteries in the Metéora Mountains was that of Agios Stéfanos (St. Stephen), established in 1332 by the Byzantine emperor Andronicus III. After Thessalia was conquered by the Serbs in 1340, who were also Orthodox Christians like the monks, building activities grew apace. Abbot Athanasius, named after Mt. Athos and nine fellow believers, started in 1356 to build a monastery on the highest pinnacle of *Platos Lithos* or the "Broad Stone." The most prominent monk of this community was the Serbian heir-apparent to the throne, John. In common with the others he had to obey a very strict regime, particularly the injunction forbidding woman to the cloisters. If a woman offered food, it could not be accepted, even if starvation was the result.

During the long period of Ottoman rule, which began in 1420, large and small monasteries continued to be added to the pinnacles. In 1438 monks built the small monastery of Hagai Triada on a narrow ledge of rock with sheer drops. The building of red sandstone against the dark rock is a pleasing

sight. The monastery and its fresco decorated chapel is reached by means of a steep flight of steps hewn from the rock. This is the route used by thieves in 1979, when they stole a number of priceless icons.

By the sixteenth century there were twenty-six monasteries on the Metéora Mountains. The Turks levied high taxes and appropriated land to resettle refugees of Greek origin from Asia Minor. Eventually this weakened the economic position so much that many of the monasteries were abandoned and became derelict. During the nineteenth century, only seven of them were still inhabited. Monastic life halted almost completely during World War II because Thessalia became a battlefield, firstly through the advance and then retreat of German troops and then through the civil war between the Communists and anti-Communists.

In the mid 1960s, monks started to live again in those monasteries that had not been damaged beyond repair. In the meantime one of them is now exclusively reserved for nuns. The abbots of these monasteries have accepted tourism as a major source of income and easier means of reaching the monasteries have been created to facilitate this.

The abbots no longer shun or debar female visitors, but women are expected to wear skirts that cover their legs.

North Sea

EUROPE

GREECE

**Metéora Monasteries**
*Mediterranean*

**ROUTE**
E75 to Larisa, N6 to Kalampáka (237 miles NW of Athens/125 miles SW of Thessalonika)

**BEST TIMES**
May–June, September–October

**ACCOMMODATION**
Hotel Amalia, Kalampáka (2 miles from monastery)

**ALSO WORTH SEEING**
Témbli valley 62 miles E, mountain village of Makrinitsa, 75 E in Pilion Mountains

*Monks once more live in mountain-top monasteries such as Russanú (left) and Haga Triada (right). Tourists can visit.*

# The Acropolis–Athens' holy mountain

*The Parthenon was once a treasury and then a powder magazine*

North Sea

EUROPE

GREECE

**Athens**

Mediterranean

### ROUTE

By air to Athens. Ten minute walk from central Sindagma Square

### BEST TIMES

May–June, September–October. Severe air pollution in midsummer

### ALSO WORTH SEEING

National Archaeological Museum, the inner city of Plaka, view from Likavitos Hill

The Acropolis or "high city" of Athens is situated on a limestone outcrop 512 feet high. This formed a natural stronghold, complete with its own wells. The Mycenaean kings settled here in the early thirteenth century BC and were the first to build a palace on the hill associated with the goddess Athena, daughter of Zeus, surrounding it with an enormous wall.

When the Mycenaean monarchy was abolished the palace became a temple during the seventh century BC. The first major new buildings on the site—the old Parthenon or temple of Athena and the pre-Parthenon—were started in the sixth century BC. A century later the buildings of the Acropolis took the form we know today.

Athens was frequently conquered and subject to different rule and during the Middle Ages it became a fortress once again. The Acropolis

knew Catalan and Frankish dukes and regents as residents and the Turks too, until in 1687 a Luneburg artillery officer brought this to an end. Serving in the army of Doge Morosini of Venice, who were beleaguering the Turks in occupation of the Acropolis, he landed a direct

hit on their powder magazine and blew up the Parthenon.

After this severe damage the Parthenon became a source for souvenir hunters on the grand tour. The British diplomat Lord Elgin ran a booming business in artifacts from his base in Constantinople. This

Scottish lord purchased large parts of the fallen buildings, parts of which went in 1809 to the British Museum in London where they are known as the "Elgin Marbles." Until her death, the famous Greek actress Melina Mercouri pleaded with Britain for their return as Greek minister of culture. Greece continues to press the British, who produce evidence of their "legitimate purchase."

## Goddess of gold and ivory

The entire area of the Acropolis was declared an archaeological monument as early as 1854, but it was not until 1977 that an archaeological reconstruction of the structures on the site began. Since that time each of the buildings of the Acropolis has been reconstructed. Those parts that are missing were carefully recreated in marble and fixed into place with stainless steel pins. It is an expensive effort to restore the most important collection of historical monuments in Europe.

The Parthenon is the primary image of the Acropolis. This ruin, surrounded by columns, is the finest building from ancient civilizations still existing. Today's Parthenon or Temple of Athena was completed in 438 BC as a place to house the treasure chests of the Attica Sea League and from the former Athena temple within the stronghold of the Acropolis. An almost forty-foot-high statue of the goddess Athena in gold and ivory cost more than the building itself. Its gold alone weighed more than a ton. In the fifth century BC this priceless Athena disappeared somewhere in Constantinople. Smaller marble copies are now in the National Archaeological Museum in Athens. In the sixth century the Parthenon served as a church for the Athenians, and in the thirteenth century, the Holy Roman emperor dedicated it to Catholicism. In 1640, the Ottomans turned the classical edifice into a mosque.

Whoever ruled Athens, and no matter how badly the Parthenon suffered in terms of plundering, fire, or war, the Greeks continued to regard the Acropolis with its Parthenon as the home of the goddess Athena.

No other ancient building was as well furnished with sculpture and reliefs as the Parthenon and no other ancient building was dedicated to just the one goddess. The achievements of the goddess Athena were depicted on the front wall in a deep relief of more than eleven feet in height and ninety-three feet wide. The frieze that surrounded the Parthenon was 525 feet long, portraying the Pan-Athenian procession that was central to the Athena cult. This procession paid homage to the goddess who watched over the city for more than three thousand years.

*The Parthenon rises from the Acropolis which sits high above Athens. Lesser temples of Nike (bottom left) and the Erechtheion with its group of caryatids (below). These are within that part of the monuments being restored since 1977 under archaeological supervision.*

# The awe-inspiring Hagia Sophia

*For a thousand years it was the largest church of Christendom*

ASIA

**Istanbul**
TURKEY

Indian Ocean

**ROUTE**

Hagia Sophia and the Topkapi Palace are next to Sirkeci Station

**OPENING TIMES**

Hagia Sophia: Tuesday–Sunday 9.30 a.m.–5 p.m.; Topkapi Palace: Wednesday–Monday 9.30 a.m.–5 p.m.

**ALSO WORTH SEEING**

Archaeological museum, Blue Mosque (Sultan Ahmed Mosque), the great bazaar

It all started with arson. Early in 532 a rebellious mass set fire to certain Byzantine buildings in Constantinople, including the large cathedral or "Megale ekklesia." Within a matter of weeks the Byzantine emperor Justinian I had masons start building a new church on the ruins of the old one. It was to surpass anything else Justinian had previously ordained. The new cathedral of his realm was completed within five years. The emperor named it Hagia Sophia or the Church of the Holy Wisdom.

The master builders Anthemios of Tralle and Isidoros of Milete created one of the most impressive sacred buildings the world has ever known. Never before had a dome of such dimensions been constructed, purely on the basis of mathematical calculation. To the believers coming to worship, it seemed as if the dome was floating above them. With a rather squat appearance from outside, the interior of the Hagia Sophia is flooded with light from the many windows, making its interior a beautiful and most perfect spatial

arrangement in the history of architecture. "Praise God who found me worthy to complete this task," Emperor Justinian declared on the day of dedication, as he led the procession entering the high-vaulted nave.

A thousand years passed by before the Hagia Sophia was surpassed by the building of St. Peter's in Rome. Michaelangelo, who supervised its construction, devised even greater and higher domes. At about this time the Hagia Sophia, with its golden mosaics and artistic

marble arches, was lost to Christendom when the Ottoman empire conquered Constantinople in 1435. The city became Istanbul and the cathedral was turned into a mosque, known as the Ayasolya Camii. Four minarets were added around the dome, and inside the church, plaques were added citing passages from the Koran in golden script.

It was Kemal Ataturk, the founder of the modern Turkey, who prohibited Islamic use of the building in 1934 and opened it as a museum.

### Blue mosque as counterpoint

A short distance from the Hagia Sophia is the Blue Mosque which provides visitors to Istanbul with an opportunity to compare this early example of Christian architecture with later Muslim efforts. Just across

the Sultan Ahmed Park is the equally impressive domed structure of the Blue Mosque or Sultan Ahmed Camii. Sultan Ahmed was keen to surpass the greatness of the nearby unique Christian church, so he had the most famous Ottoman building erected in the early seventeenth century. The main dome of the Blue Mosque is actually slightly smaller than that of the Hagia Sophia but the exterior is certainly comparable and perhaps more harmonious. It is the only mosque in Istanbul with six minarets instead of the customary four. The interior is entirely decorated with tiles, predominantly of blue.

Another major tourist attraction close at hand is the nearby Topkapi Palace in the large park of the former sultan. At the time Constantinople was captured, most of the buildings here were constructed of wood.

These were mainly pavilions which looked like a city of tents. When these buildings burnt down, as eventually they did, they were replaced by brick structures, and so gradually, an exciting row of palaces, domed halls, pavilions, courts, and minarets filled the view.

The Topkapi Palace today is primarily a rich collection of the riches from the Ottoman empire. Distributed through the various buildings, the collection includes weapons, porcelain, tapestries, miniatures and other paintings, antique clocks, calligraphy, and religious items, such as the tools used for circumcision. The harem is a realm of its own, with a dozen rooms, including those for the Nubian eunuch slaves, the court of the favorites, and the chambers in which the sultan would spend his time with them.

*The Byzantine emperor Justinian erected the Hagia Sophia in the sixth century on the ruins of Constantinople's earlier cathedral. It was the principal church of his realm and a brilliant architectural creation. Under Ottoman rule the church became a mosque in 1453 and gained four minarets. The golden mosaic (top right) recalls the Christian origins of the building.*

ASIA

Taj-Mahal
INDIA

Indian Ocean

## ROUTE

Internal flight to Agra. By
train from Delhi (125 miles/2
hours); coach tours to Taj
Mahal

## BEST TIMES

November–February

## ACCOMMODATIONS

Hotel Taj View (luxury hotel
with best view of the Taj
Mahal)

## ALSO WORTH SEEING

Fort Agra, mausoleum of
Itimad-ud-Daulah

# Mausoleum for a beloved wife

*The Taj Mahal is famous as India's most beautiful building*

It is not just the architectural
beauty of the Taj Mahal that
enthralls people but the
moving story of its creation.
Probably one of the best-known of
all beautiful buildings, its enchanting
elegance in white marble rises
majestically out of the plain of Agra.
Its 236-foot-high structure seems so
insubstantial that it has an ethereal
quality. One large dome, echoed by
seven smaller ones in a reflection of
the female form are in turn reflected
in a plain ribbon of still water for an
image of perfect harmony.

The Taj Mahal's origin is a story
worthy of the imagination of a
romantic poet and legend has
embellished the tale. The Muslim

Mogul emperor Shah Jahan and his
favorite wife Arjumand Banu Begum,
whom he called Mumtaz-i-Mahal,
"the pearl of the palace," are at the
center of the story. The great Mogul
was still a prince when he took a wife
at the start of the seventeenth
century. She was the beautiful
fifteen-year-old daughter of a high
official.

The ruler, who governed the
country from 1628 to 1658 added
her to his harem but left no doubt
that all his adoration was directed at
Mumtaz. It was she who sat beside
him on formal occasions, and who
accompanied him on his campaigns,
and with whom he discussed matters
of state.

## Lamentation in stone

The favorite wife produced eight
sons and six daughters for her lord
and master. Soon after giving birth to
her fourteenth child she died. Many
moving stories are recounted of the
Mogul emperor's grief, both as
written by the court chronicler and
suitably embellished in reworking by
other writers.

It is said the emperor's dark mane
of hair turned instantly gray at his
wife's deathbed. Following her death
he instituted a two year period of
mourning. It was forbidden to feast,
listen to music, wear jewelry, or
perfume.

To express his sorrow "in stone"
the grief-stricken husband promised

to erect a Taj Mahal or crown of a palace for his deceased wife. The emperor recruited architects, engineers, sculptors, and calligraphers from Persia, the Ottoman Empire, and the city of Samarkand. These people were put to the task of expressing his ideas for a mausoleum in the form of a mosque with four minarets.

To decorate the interior, a Venetian artist was commissioned, who also designed the sarcophagus that was placed above the sepulcher. A goldsmith from Bordeaux fashioned the silver entrance gate. It took 20,000 laborers twenty-two years to complete the building and to surround it with a Persian garden with ponds and rills. Its almost forty-five acres certainly meet the requirement for a "crown of a palace," presenting the eye with a vision of harmony that is truly a work of art.

The Taj Mahal remains the most beautiful and impressive example of Indo-Islamic architecture erected by the Mogul emperors during the sixteenth and seventeenth centuries. India has declared the shrine a national monument while the rest of the world views it as a magical example of Indian architecture.

*The Mogul emperor Shah Jahan built the Taj Mahal as a mausoleum and expression of grief for his favorite wife, Arjumand Banu Begum, also known as Mumtaz-i-Mahal ("pearl of the palace"). She died in childbirth. An army of 20,000 laborers needed 22 years to complete the superb edifice and its gardens. Later Mogul emperors were also entombed there. For the interior decoration, artists were commissioned from Samarkand, Venice, Persia, Turkey, and France.*

# Home of the gods

*Mount Everest is the world's highest mountain*

Tibetans says that the world's highest mountain is best recognized by its "prayer flag." This is the name they give to the veil of ice crystals that swirl around the summit of Mount Everest on most days. Without its veil it is difficult to identify this famous giant among the eight thousand or so other peaks on the borders of the Hindu kingdom of Nepal and the ancient land of Tibet. It appears from a series of surveys of recent years with highly accurate satellite equipment that Mt. Everest is getting taller and also moving. Its current height is 29,035 feet, an increase of seven feet over the height recognized for the past forty-five years.

Long before westerners became aware of the mountain the people of Tibet worshipped the "goddess-mother" or Chomolungma as the holy abode of the goddess Tseringma. The people of Nepal, who have declared their part of the mountain as a reserve, call it Sagarmatha "whose top reaches the heavens." Its western name is derived from a British artillery officer and geodetic surveyor, Sir George Everest, who discovered in the mid nineteenth century that the peak which he listed as XV was higher than any other in the Himalayas.

Scientific expeditions experienced great problems finding the highest mountain peak of the world among the snowcaps of the eastern Himalayas, calculated by trigonometry. Early in the twentieth century Western encyclopedias still confused Everest with the Nepalese peak of Gaurisanker. This confusion arose through reports of the German explorer Hermann von Schlagenweit, who when journeying through Nepal mistook Gaurisanker—a mere slip of a hill at 23, 441 feet—perhaps because he was unaware of the "prayer flag".

## Assaults on the top

British and Swiss climbers did find the right mountain the 1920s but failed to reach the top. After numerous failed attempts had been made, it finally fell to the New Zealander Edmund (now Sir Edmund) Hillary and his Nepalese Sherpa, Tensing Norgay to reach the top on May 29, 1953. They hoisted three small flags on Everest representing the colors of

Great Britain, Nepal, and the United Nations.

In the decade that followed, more than one hundred other climbers reached the summit of Everest, and in 1978, Reinhold Messner of South Tyrol and his partner Peter Habeler were the first to make the climb without oxygen. Two years later Messner repeated this alone.

Although everybody was climbing the same mountain, the precise altitude has not necessarily been agreed. The first measurements in the nineteenth century calculated the height as 29,002 feet and later a height was calculated of 29,160 feet but this was widely contested. Since 1954 the height stood officially at 29,028 feet, and Everest was even deposed in 1987 as the world's tallest mountain by a U.S. satellite survey by Prof. George Wallerstein which found that K2 was thirty-six feet higher than Everest.

The old ranking was restored a few months later by the Italian Prof. Ardito Desio who calculated with a number of satellite measurements that K2 was 28,267 feet and Mt. Everest 29,107 feet, but this did not last long either. Scientists have now discovered that Mt. Everest grows by about seven inches each year. At this rate the mountain will grow to 32,808 feet 6,300 years from now.

*On their way to the top of Mt. Everest (above), climbers were constantly battered by heavy snowstorms. The first successful ascent of this giant on the borders of Nepal and Tibet was on May 29, 1953 when the New Zealander (now Sir) Edmund Hillary and his Sherpa, Tensing Norgay reached the summit. Reinhold Messner from South Tyrol and his partner Peter Habeler were the first to climb Everest without oxygen in 1978. The smaller photograph shows Everest by evening sunlight. The Tibetans call the mountain Chomolungma, the "goddess-mother."*

# India's Seven Pagodas

*The Temples of Mahabalipuram on India's Coromandel coast*

ASIA

INDIA
**Mahabalipuram**

*Indian Ocean*

**ROUTE**

Direct international flights to
Madras or via Bombay
(Mumbai); coach from
Madras to Mahabalipuram
(37 miles)

**BEST TIMES**

February–March

**ACCOMMODATIONS**

Temple Bay Ashok Beach
Resort

The small town of
Mahabalipuram, which
makes its living from
fishing off southern India's
Coromandel coast, may appear
somewhat sleepy at first but it does
invite a journey back in time. Its
history goes back to the fourth to
ninth centuries when this was a
religious center with ample gods to
worship. There was Shiva, the god of
destruction and procreation, Vishnu,
preserver of the universe, and his
beautiful wife Lakshimi, goddess of
beauty and fortune.

Not far from the beaches of the
Bay of Bengal, where tourists tan
themselves, to the south of
Mahabalipuram, great peaks of
granite soar above the green trees.
Almost all of these apparent rock

formations prove to be Hindu
pagodas and sculptural works of art
of considerable beauty.

The Pallava kings, the mighty
rulers of southern India, built their
temples here. The stories carved in
rock greatly enhance this temple to
the Hindu gods and provide them
with mythical events.

**Heavenly chariot**

The oldest of the temples of
Mahabalipuram are within caves such
as Vahara. Its walls have reliefs
depicting the various good
incarnations of Vishnu. As a wild
boar he battles a snake-headed
demon who would cast the earth into
the abyss of the world's oceans. One
entire wall is filled with the fifth of
Vishnu's manifestations as the dwarf

Vanana who suddenly changes into a
giant with one foot resting on the
earth, the other in heaven, thereby
liberating humankind from the
beast's reign of terror.

Impressive further development
of early Hindu architecture is
exemplified by the nearby cave
temples of the five Rathas or
heavenly chariots. These temples
have ornamental animals that are
each carved from rock by
generations of different sculptors.
The Pallava rulers had these rock
carvings made in the fashion of the
wooden processional chariots and
shrines on which Hindu deities are
borne by crowds of the faithful
during festivals. These were the first
free-standing stone temples of
southern India.

Hindus still visit the eighty-eight foot-long relief cut into a rock slope to a height of twenty-three feet, which depicts the source of the River Ganges, which Hindus believe sows seed in both the earth and the human mind.

The famous pagoda on the beach is not carved from a single piece of granite but built of pieces of stone which have been cut and dressed to shape. It dates from the seventh century and rises up picturesquely from the surrounding surf. The pagoda is surrounded by sculptures of bulls, representing Shriva's mount, Nandi. The pagoda is built from rectangular elements placed one on top of the other so that they taper to a point at the top. When Mahabalipuram still had a harbor, this pagoda also acted as an orientation point for sailors and a fire was lit on it at night. Today the shore is illuminated by the lights of restaurants and small hotels.

*Heat, wind, and salty air have badly eroded the pagoda on the beach (7th century, top left). It is the best known pagoda of Mahabalipuram. Rock walls and caves near the town are also decorated with carved figures from Hindu mythology (top right). A heavenly chariot or Ratha was carved from a single piece of rock for the small pagoda shown left.*

# Thousand and one nights in Lahore

*Art, architecture, and the cities too flourished under the Mogul emperors*

ASIA

**Lahore**
PAKISTAN

*Indian Ocean*

**ROUTE**
By air to Lahore

**BEST TIMES**
November–February

**ACCOMMODATIONS**
Holiday Inn

**ALSO WORTH SEEING**
Fort Lahore, Jehangir Mausoleum, Wazir Khan Mosque, Maryam Mosque, Shalimar Gardens

No matter which old gate, mosque, palace, or mausoleum you pause in front of, the people who live in Lahore will be able to tell you its story. The entire inner city, enclosed by a dilapidated wall, is like a stage set in brick for a tale from the *Thousand and One Nights*. The Muslim faith flourished more exuberantly in Lahore than anywhere else in Pakistan. Lahore sits on the Ravi River in the fertile Punjab, or "land of the five rivers."

## Comfortable stronghold

The Muslim conquerors hoisted the green flag of their prophet in Lahore at the end of the tenth century. The mighty sultan Mahmud of Ghazni incorporated the city into his realm from the Punjab to Samarkand. Five hundred years later the powerful Mogul warlords enclosed this area

within a wall with twelve towers and built a town within the fortifications which already existed, complete with inner courts, palaces, bath houses, and the "pearl mosque" with its three domes. As with the Taj Mahal in

India, Lahore brought together the best of Mogul architecture and art. Beneath the long since disappeared Sha-Buri gate at the main entrance there was an inscription in Arabic: "The likes of this have never been

*Colourful frescoes cover the walls of the Wazir Khan mosque from 1643.*

140

seen and shall never be seen again." Gates of huge proportions were needed to allow the Mogul emperors to enter upon an elephant. The massively strong steps allowed an elephant to ascend to the famous Shish Mahal or "Mirror Palace" which reflects the artistic interior a thousand fold. On the walls mosaics of colored mirror shards produce a pleasing motif. Larger mirrors reflect gilded ornaments, while gems set in marble form enchanting floral patterns.

## Enticing gardens of Shalimar

The "mirror palace" was the home of the ruler's wife. The Grand Mogul himself had a place of his own, complete with the "court of the harem maidens," and the "house of dreams" with the emperor's bedroom. Banquets were held in the "hall of forty columns." The residents of Lahore were also very active sportsmen as can be seen from tiles and murals. The best horsemen played polo, which originated in Central Asia. Other contests involved elephants, camels, and bulls.

In addition to the stronghold, the Moguls left mausoleums and buildings used for receiving visitors, plus the Badshahi Mosque, which is the finest religious building in Lahore. It was built of red sandstone in the late seventeenth century and set in its inner courtyard with minarets at each corner. It can accommodate 60,000 Muslims for prayer. The gate and the form of the three white domes echo the Taj Mahal. In common with that famous mausoleum, this mosque is also raised up on a plinth to emphasize its beauty.

Outside the city of three million people are the wonderful Shalimar Gardens with their green, flowering, and gurgling oriental park landscape, created in 1641–1642 on three terraces. Among the marvels of garden landscaping are a water basin of almost two hundred feet with 412 fountains, beautiful islets, bathing areas, superb pavilions, and marble walkways. The Moguls and higher nobility spent the hottest part of summer in the adjacent palaces and guest houses.

*The courtyard of the 17th-century Badshahi mosque (top left) can accommodate 60,000 at prayer. The Shalimar Gardens (top right) and the miniature mosque (bottom right) are among the finest examples of Islamic architecture.*

141

# The palace of the Dalai Lama

*Lhasa was home to Tibet's divine leaders*

CHINA(TIBET)
• **Lhasa**

*Indian Ocean*

**ROUTE**

Internal Chinese flights from Beijing and Chengdu or by air from Katmandu

**BEST TIMES**

October–December

**ACCOMMODATIONS**

Holiday Inn

**ALSO WORTH SEEING**

Monasteries at Sera, Ganden, and Drepung

Amid the mountain range known as the "house of snow" there is the "land of the calling deer" and its capital "the seat of the gods" in the valley of "happy rivers" that reflect the "palace of enlightenment." The names of these places are poetic when translated into English. We are talking of the Himalayas, Tibet (once known as Boyul), its capital Lhasa, the reflecting waters of the Kyichu River, and the Potala Palace.

Set at an altitude of 12,083 feet, the "seat of the gods" was one of the most isolated places in the world until the twentieth century, reachable only by difficult pilgrimage and

caravan trails, and no strangers were permitted. In the final years of the nineteenth century the Swedish explorer of Asia Sven Hedin was not even permitted to glance at the objective of his Tibetan expedition from a distance. China, which occupied the mountain country in 1951, has also refused to grant visas to foreigners wishing to visit the "autonomous region" of Tibet.

## Center of the world

For the inhabitants of Lhasa, the town has the same significance as Rome for many Christians and Mecca for Muslims. For this is the holy Jokhang Monastery of their

spiritual and temporal leaders with its statue of Srongtsan Gampo, who introduced Buddhism into Tibet in the seventh century. The later Lamaism is a form of Buddhism with the addition of elements of Shivaism and the native shamanism. The divine ruler, the Dalai Lama, is believed to be a reincarnation of Buddha.

The twin spiritual and temporal leadership roles were first assumed in the seventeenth century by the fifth Dalai Lama, Lobsang Gyatso. This high priest built a kind of Tibetan Vatican on the Marpori or red mountain that skirts Lhasa, founded on the remains of the "Castle of

Immortality" of their leader Song-sten Gampos. The fortress-like Potala Palace has since been extended by Lobsang Gyatso's successors. Until 1959, when the fourteenth Dalai Lama fled to the west to escape the Chinese, the Potala served as a monastic retreat, seat of government, and administrative center of Tibet's spiritual and temporal leaders.

## Monastery as museum

When mist spreads out across the mountains, the Potala appears to hover above Lhasa to approaching visitors. Its architecture reaches upwards to the heavens, with walls that taper and angular towers. Most of the facade is a bright white honeycomb, although some of the upper layers are red. This is the red palace and former residence of the Dalai Lama. The building is now a

fine museum of Tibetan art with depictions of their deities, painted mantra scrolls, and incense vessels and other treasures of the Lamas romantically lit by oil lamps.

The Lamaist priests made certain in the past that noone entered, on pain of death. Today one might encounter more tourists than Tibetans in the course of the thirteen levels of the building. And instead of the chanting of mantras one hears the loud voices of guides as they drone their standard patter in English. The Potala contains one thousand rooms, supported by 15,000 columns, has 10,000 individual shrines, and 200,000 devout statues. Below, part of the cellar floor is of the reddish brown rock of the Marpori peak. The oldest wall of the over 1,300-foot-wide complex is thought to be that surrounding the "nuptial chamber" of Srongtsan

Gampo. The upper floor of the Potala contains the former private chambers of the self-exiled four-teenth Dalai Lama, who to the discomfiture of the government in Beijing does not let up in his struggle to regain Tibetan independence.

Communist ideology and the traditionally-minded and nationalist Tibetans do not gel well with each other. The historic center of Lhasa has seen many demonstrations against their occupiers. Under the suspicious eye of the Chinese police an almost endless procession encircles the main Jokhang Buddhist temple and its Buddha. Monks in colorful robes, sunburned nomads, and beggars in rags continue to chant their mantras as they did in the days of their spiritual leaders. The principal mantra is *o mani padme h'um* "O lotus jewel, amen."

*Until the Dalai Lama fled the Potala Palace from the Chinese, this monastic retreat at 12,083 feet was also the seat of government of Tibet's spiritual and temporal rulers.*

# The Great Wall of China

*The one man-made structure that can be seen from space*

Surely the biggest ever construction project ever undertaken, demanding the efforts of the greatest numbers of laborers, has to be the 4,075-mile-long Great Wall of China. U.S. astronauts on the moon revealed that the only impression they could see of man on our planet with the naked eye was the Great Wall. Even in those places where the wall has crumbled it resembles, in the words of the French writer André Malraux: "A still extant prehistoric dragon winding its body over the hills."

It is wrong to think of the wall as a continuous Chinese bulwark against the rest of the world. Its essential purpose was to ward off attacks from the north. Apart from the main defense line extending 2,156 miles from the steppes of Turkestan to the shores of the Yellow Sea, there are numerous walls parallel to the outer boundary wall or protecting specific locations. When viewed from the moon it looks like a giant scrawl.

### Protection from marauders

The first sections of the wall were built in the north of China, long before our calendar began. These were meant to defend the peasants on the fertile plains of Central China against frequent incursions by nomadic tribes who frequently invaded from the north in search of pasture for their cattle. The truly stupendous work of the Great Wall was started in the third century BC during the reign of Shih Huang Ti, the first Chinese emperor. Legend has it that the emperor was advised by one of his wizards to have a man by the name of Wan executed at the foot of the wall in order to assure its completion.

It is certainly true that the wall's construction, which continued well

into the seventeenth century, cost the lives of hundreds of thousands. The work traversed mountains and valleys. Building materials had to be transported in searing heat and freezing cold. Hewn stones weighing twenty pounds each had to be transported along with the many smaller pieces of stone used as infill for the up to thirty feet high and twenty-six-foot-wide wall. It is said that in the days of the first emperor some 300,000 soldiers and 500,000 peasants sentenced to forced hard labor toiled at the project. In later times some 1,800,000 farmers worked alongside convicts.

But even this enormous army of laborers could not have succeeded without the ingenuity and organizational talent of the men leading the project, most of whom were military officers. If no natural stone was locally available, then bricks were made locally. Where there was clay this was used and through the Gobi desert the coolies filled the wall with sand, pebbles, twigs of tamarisk trees, and rushes. Where the wall crossed rapidly flowing white water or river deltas great care and skill were required.

A watchtower was placed every three to six hundred feet, amounting to almost 20,000 of them along the entire length of the wall. Smoke signals or flags would warn other garrisons along the wall of the

enemy's approach so that soldiers could be moved into position. They could move much more quickly on paved roads than the enemy. Garrisons at strategic locations increased the protection of the boundary but the enemy could not always be repulsed. In spite of the wall, the fearsome Mongolian warlord Genghis Khan and his horsemen successfully invaded China in 1211.

The largest defense system in the world, which took about two thousand years to create, is mainly kept in good condition. It has repeatedly safeguarded the peace for China and become a symbol of national unity. The wall has inspired poets too, like Ho Chifang, who in a work of 1934 has a traveler utter the words: "The Wall is like a column of galloping horses that, just as they reared their necks and neighed, turned to stone."

If the wall was supposed to ward off strangers it now achieves precisely the opposite. As China's principal tourist attraction it draws enormous numbers of visitors. The section northwest of Beijing in particular becomes crowded with the kinds of crowds of people once reserved for Broadway in New York, the Champs-Elysées in Paris, or the Kurfürstendamm in Berlin.

*Crossing mountains, deserts, and cereal fields, the 4,075 mile long Great Wall of China snakes its way across the country to protect it against attack from the north. Chinese emperors employed up to 1,800,000 peasants at a time in forced labor. Hundreds of thousands of them did not survive the ordeal.*

# A glimpse of the Forbidden City

*Beijing's old imperial palace opens its gates*

ASIA

CHINA **Beijing**

*Indian Ocean*

### ROUTE

International flight or 6-day journey on the Trans-Siberian railway. Emperor's Palace/Tienamen Square subway station Quiamen

### BEST TIMES

September–October

### ALSO WORTH SEEING

Heavenly Temple, Lama Temple, Confucian Temple, Summer Palace, Beihai Park

The people of Beijing used to marvel at the "purple city" hidden from them behind a forty-foot wall where their emperor lived. All they saw on a sunny day were the elegant purple tiled roofs. A Chinese person without either a job in the palace or an invitation was allowed no closer view. The emperor considered himself the self-evident center of the earth, and those who did not give his haven a wide berth could expect a savage beating. It is from these times that the foreigners gave the name "The Forbidden City" to the area of the palace.

### Home to twenty-four rulers of the Ming dynasty

The palace compound that is rich in treasures of art was begun in the fifteenth century. The emperors of the Ming dynasty moved their seat of government from Nanking to the new capital of Beijing. A hundred thousand craftsmen and a million coolie slaves were engaged in the task. The 178-acre site reserved for the emperor was to accommodate the imperial palace, housing for the royal entourage, and formal halls for official functions. Most of these early wooden structures were eventually burned to the ground, and when

rebuilt, great changes were made, so that the current architecture of The Forbidden City mainly dates from the eighteenth century.

Twenty-four emperors lived in the palace before it was finally opened up to the public following Mao Zedong's Communist victory. Endless crowds of sightseers now shuffle through the Noon Gate to enter the palace compound where they enter the famed Hall of the Highest Harmony, a huge wooden building from the seventeenth century which is held together with wooden pegs rather than nails. The inside of the hall is 115 feet high and

the roof is supported by twenty-four pillars of hardwood, half of which are gilded. At the center of the hall is the imperial throne which is also gilded, on a dais of rosewood, with a dragon suspended above it from the ceiling. From here the emperor, as the self-styled "heavenly son," issued commands and decrees to his courtiers who had to prostrate themselves.

A second imperial throne is located in the adjacent Hall of Perfect Harmony, albeit somewhat less ostentatiously furnished. This served the rulers of the Middle Kingdom as a place for rest and meditation. A third Guardian of Harmony hall between heaven and earth was used for audiences and banquets. Today the People' Republic exhibits its archaeological treasures there.

## Symbol of power

Quite apart from those items shown in this exhibition, there are more works of art on show in the Forbidden City than anyone can take in on a single visit. The interior has priceless room partitions and engravings, large statues of animals from Chinese mythology in stone and bronze—turtles and cranes to symbolize long life and lions representing imperial power. A particularly fierce lion raises a paw—the emperor will crush those who disobey.

There are 9,000 different rooms within the palace compound. New residences alone were needed for the countless eunuchs and concubines across the years. The emperors were by tradition permitted three wives, six other favorites, and seventy-two concubines, but this was not enough

for some of the emperors. China experts have discovered that some of these "sons of heaven" retained up to an unimaginable 2,000 concubines. To prove their status, the women wore golden chains engraved with their date and place of birth.

These ornaments can also be seen in the no longer forbidden Forbidden City. Sometimes such human touches attract more interest than the valuable works of art.

*Thousands of woodcarvers, painters, and gilding experts, 100,000 other craftsmen, and a million slaves built the Forbidden City, Beijing's Imperial Palace. At left a beautifully decorated dome and above the Gate of Divine Courage or northern exit.*

# China's clay army

*A terra-cotta army guards the tomb of the first emperor*

ASIA

CHINA

**Xian**

*Indian Ocean*

**ROUTE**

Flight from Beijing or Hong Kong to Xian

**BEST TIME**

September

**ALSO WORTH SEEING**

Huaqing Hot Springs, Wild Goose Pagoda and large mosque in Xian

The shaft of the new well was quickly sunk for the members of a Chinese communal farm...but instead of water they found the fired earthenware heads of life-sized soldiers. The well diggers in the maize field between the Li Mountain and the Wei River, close to the northeastern provincial capital of Xian were replaced by archaeologists whose excavations turned a surprise into a sensation. They unearthed a complete army of life-size terra-cotta warriors, standing row upon row beneath the maize field.

That was in 1974, and today further battalions of this subterranean army are still being uncovered. This army, which stands

to attention as if on parade, guards the tomb of China's first emperor, Shih Huang Ti. In the third century BC the first emperor, who had conferred the title on himself, had a gigantic mausoleum built for his burial. History recalls him as a man who successfully united a divided land into a single realm, ordered the building of the Great Wall, reformed writing and legislation, but also burned down libraries and buried learned men alive because of his displeasure with them.

## Monument to excess

Chronologists say that about three decades before his death, Emperor Shih Huang Ti had 700,000 forced laborers from all over the country

build a palatial subterranean mausoleum for him. A copper sarcophagus was made for the emperor and his treasure-filled sepulcher was protected against robbers by crossbows that were loosed automatically. When the emperor died, his son and heir buried him together with his childless concubines. Finally he buried alive all those who knew of the buried treasure.

Slaves heaped a mound of earth more than 160 feet high over the imperial grave and planted it with cypresses and spruce. It was close to this hill that the well diggers made their astonishing discovery in 1974. Subsequent excavations in the ensuing decades suggest the

emperor wanted a representation in clay of his entire army buried with him. To the east of the hill more than eight thousand terra-cotta soldiers have been unearthed, and it is probable that further ranks of warriors are standing to attention to the north, west, and south of the burial mound.

The entire area of the current archaeological dig is covered. The warriors are arranged in columns of four, forming parallel corridors which the archaeologist call shard spots. Some figures lead horses and wagons and thanks to the extraordinary attention to detail of the soldier's uniforms it is possible to assign them to their units.

There are infantry, spear throwers, archers with both longbows and crossbows, cavalry leading their steeds, charioteers, officers, and a six-foot-tall general who stands out above them all, wearing a well-modeled scarf and three ornaments on his breast plate.

## No two faces the same

Thousands of skilled sculptors and dozens of potteries must have been pressed into service to produce the thousands of figures. The bodies may have been mass produced but the heads and many of the hands were separately modeled and attached later. Those who made the warriors were careful to copy hairstyles. There are twenty-four different types of mustaches and a rich variety of different headdresses.

Far more astonishing though is the often lively and widely different facial expressions on the faces of the terra-cotta warriors. One gets an impression that men from every tribe in the realm modeled for the statues. There are broad Mongolian faces, men with exceptionally high foreheads, or with pronounced noses. The faces of the officers are highly individual and the terra-cotta horses are also of great artistic merit. With their mouths usually open, nostrils flared, and ears pricked, these give a strong impression of untamed power.

The question remains what secrets still lie in the emperor's tomb itself beneath the burial mound? So far the Chinese have been terrified of disturbing the death rest of the first emperor, his concubines, and his unfortunate servants, who were buried alive.

*The first emperor of China Shih Huang Ti ordered the building of the Great Wall of China in the 3rd century BC and the building of a mausoleum for himself close to the northeastern provincial capital of Xian. Since 1974, archaeologists have unearthed 8,000 life-size terra-cotta warriors (top left) who were buried with him for symbolic protection. The soldiers all have individual expressions on their life-like faces (above).*

# The holy peak of Mount Fuji

*Japan's highest mountain is a place of pilgrimage and rich traditions*

ASIA

JAPAN
**Fujiyama**

*Pacific Ocean*

### ROUTE
Odakyu railway from Tokyo to Yumoto, mountain railway to Hakone-Tozan

### BEST TIMES
October–December

### ALSO WORTH SEEING
Sulfur caves, Lake Ashi

Mount Fuji is the most frequent motif found in Japanese landscape art. Supremely understated watercolor drawings use a few diagonal lines sweeping upwards, a brief stroke with a flat brush and downward line to reveal the contours to portray this object of awe and veneration. The symmetrical beauty of Mount Fuji and its height of 12,389 feet which is unsurpassed in Japan have made Fujisan or Fujiyama an emblem of Japan and an object of veneration.

Although the peak of Mt. Fuji is snow-capped, it is a volcano which erupts from time to time. The main crater is 500–650 feet deep with a diameter of almost two thousand feet. There are smaller craters of over two hundred feet in diameter around the rim of the volcano. During Mt. Fuji's last eruption of

1707–1708, a layer of ash 4½ inches thick descended on the then city of Edo fifty-six miles away. That city today is Tokyo.

The volcano inspires more than painted drawings. The mountain is

an important muse too for Japanese poets. The form of its contours are praised in song, as is its summit, which is often shrouded in cloud. Poets speak of the magical landscape below the peak including primeval

forests and the five lakes that mirror the mountain's image. This nature was threatened by the constant spread of human settlement but is now protected as the Fuji-Hakone-Isu National Park.

## Image of purity

Just as Mt. Olympus was for the Greeks, Mt. Fuji historically has had an aura of divinity. Could the gods find a more fitting place to dwell than on this mighty throne? The mountain is revered too by Japan's most important religion, Shintoism, which fuses the veneration of both ancestors and nature. It is an age-old tradition to climb the mountain in pilgrimage, wearing white gloves and sandals made of straw.

Japanese Buddhists also revere Fujisan. In the thirteenth century the Buddhist samurai and guru Nichiren called upon his faithful to create "a sanctuary of true Buddhism" at the foot of Mt. Fuji. The Soka Gakke Society responded to this call in the 1960s and built the Sho-Hondo

temples. Their modern concrete structures, said to be the largest Buddhist temples in the world, are located in the temple district of Taisekiji where they are elevated to ensure a good view of the revered mountain.

Singing Shinto pilgrims and other devout travelers who scale Mt. Fuji on its steeply inclined paths are in the minority, for it is a popular pastime in Japan to climb the mountain at least once, preferably more often, in your lifetime. Some summer weekends see entire families complete with children, upwards of 30,000 people scrambling up the peak, armed with picnic baskets. The total number of annual visitors to the mountain is estimated at half a million.

Unlike the Shinto pilgrims who start their climb from the foot of the 12,389-foot-high mountain, the crowds reach the top by easier means. Buses carry people to a parking place at a height of 7,545 feet from where the summit can be

reached in a mere five to seven hours of walking.

*A chain of devout pilgrims carrying lanterns (right) pass Shinto shrines (bottom left) on their way to the top of Fujisan, which rises to a height of 12,389 feet above the lakes of the Fuji-Hakone-Usu National Park.*

# Old imperial city of Kyoto

*Shinto shrines and temples amid a treasure-trove of Japanese culture*

The year 794 is very significant in Japanese history for in that year the inhabitants of the Japanese islands created a new capital and seat of government for the new Emperor (*Tenno*) Kammu, with help from Korean immigrants. At first this city was known as Heianko but it later gained fame as the cultural and religious center of Japan under the name of Kyoto.

The new imperial city was modeled on Chinese examples in a grid of slightly more then three miles by just under three miles. Absolute symmetry was observed in the erection of the various districts. Each new street and alley within the walls and moat of the city was at right angles to those it intersected but this rigidity was quickly softened by the richness of form and color of traditional Japanese architecture which unfolded there during many centuries to make Kyoto one of the most fascinating places to visit in Japan.

## Roofs that protect against demons

The imperial family moved from Nara to their new residence in the year the new capital was founded. The emperor's palace and the first temples were much influenced by Chinese-Buddhist architecture. This meant that elegant roofs were preferred which are upswept at their ends so that any demons sliding down the roof will be swept upwards and not fall to earth. The Tenno's palace was at first sited in the north of the new city but later was relocated to the northeast. It burned down completely in 1228 and was eventually rebuilt in its former splendor in 1856. Together with the Nijo Palace, it recalls the glorious times for the emperor of the feudal ages.

Central Kyoto—now a city of more than 1,500,000 people—still bears the imprint of its medieval temples and palaces.

The oldest surviving sacred building is the Tshionin Temple of

the Jodo sect which dates from the thirteenth century, although its impressive gate is an addition of five centuries later.

Buddhism was imported from China and adapted to Japanese thinking. It finds expression in Kyoto's architecture, such as the thirteenth-century Sanjusangendo Temple and the highly artistic Nishi-Honganji and Hagashi-Honganji Temples.

## The cult of simplicity

The style of traditional Japanese tea ceremonies is associated with simplicity in design of living spaces that reached a high point in the imperial villa at Katsura near Kyoto. The basic design module used for all the rooms is the size of sleeping mats when spread on the floor. The smaller rooms can hold four mats while the larger ones accommodate multiples of four. There is also a platform in the house for looking at the moon.

Further impressive examples of Japanese arts can be found in the gardens of the imperial city. Influenced by Zen, the miniature landscapes of traditional Japanese rock gardens originated here. These are not gardens designed to stroll through but to be interpreted like paintings or other works of art. The fourteenth-century Kinkakuji and fifteenth-century Ginkakuji are regarded as exceptionally successfully examples of symbiotic relationship of architecture and sculptural "nature."

Nowhere else in Japan has there been such a density of cultural outpouring as the area around Kyoto.

Proponents of the city say that Kyoto is the richest treasure house of their country. The old imperial city has more than 1,500 Buddhist temples, monasteries, and gardens, two hundred Shinto shrines, feudal pavilions, and palaces.

Japanese emperors ceased holding court in Kyoto in 1868 when Tokyo became the new capital and seat of the "kings of the heavenly realm."

*The image of old Kyoto is one of carefully restored medieval temples and palaces. Shown (clockwise) are: the ornate roofs of the Helan Shrine, an animal sculpture at the Fushimi Inari Temple, Japanese garden art, and the Golden Temple.*

# The forbidden city of the Vietnamese emperors in Hue

*Palaces and tombs along the perfume river remind of former might*

ASIA

VIETNAM

**Hue**

*Indian Ocean*

**ROUTE**

Flights from Hanoi and Ho-Chi-Min City (former Saigon) to Hue. Rail connections with both cities

**BEST TIMES**

June–July

**ACCOMMODATIONS**

Century Riverside and Huong Giang Hotels, both in Le Loi Street with view of palace

Burial mounds and tombs come into view even when landing at Hue. The city is surrounded by graves, and the tombs of the emperors are closer to the palaces and pavilions of the former emperors. The other dead are buried by the thousand in circular mounds surrounded by stones. Alongside these there are smaller graves for children and even smaller ones for miscarriages. Rank and status were once observed even unto death in Vietnam's old imperial capital of Hue.

The city lies on the Huong Giang or perfume river, one of the most heavily fought over parts of the realm of Annam, which is largely the same as the present borders of Vietnam. Towards the end of the seventeenth century, Hue was created as a fortress town, then known as Phu Xuan, which was ruled by a succession of local strongmen until 1804 when the Emperor Gia Long made it the center of his Nguyen dynasty.

Emperor Gia Long had a "forbidden city" built on the site of the citadel as a personal residence along

the lines of the Beijing model. Surrounded by high walls and a moat, the palace complex of Hue was a fortress within a fortress. Architects and garden landscapers went to considerable pains to create harmony between the structure and nature. When the emperor left his palace he could stroll through landscaped gardens with little streams and waterfalls, artistic islets, pavilions, fine residences, and temples.

The rulers had the main entrance to Dai Noi (the emperor city)

extended with a Noon Gate, the pavilions of which are two storeys high, with roofs covered in green tiles, except the middle one, which is golden. Immediately behind the gate one came to the throne room, or Palace of Ultimate Harmony, decorated with red and gold lacquered wood carvings. Three flights of steps lead via a colonnaded walkway to the throne of the emperor of Annam. The last member of the Nguyen dynasty to hold office was Emperor Bao Dai who was deposed in 1955.

### Stone grave guardians

The six imperial graves of Hue are gems of architecture. The tomb of Emperor Gia Long and Empress Thua Thien Cao is sober in style: just two simple stone sarcophaguses that blend with the surrounding

landscape. Other rulers had more ostentatious tombs built during their lifetime. The grave of Emperor Minh Mangs is guarded by stone elephants, horses, warriors, and civil authorities. Emperor Thieu Tris is entombed in a temple surrounded by water, and Emperor Tu Duc had himself placed in a burial pavilion spanning a brook, supported by columns. This had been his favored place for meditation, where he could find peace.

Many buildings and their artistic treasures were lost during the various Vietnam wars. In February 1968 the Vietcong hoisted their flag on the imperial tower in front of the Noon Gate but the Americans and South Vietnamese regained control of the city two weeks later, until the Communist regime eventually took it back. In the vicinity of Hue alone

some 10,000 people lost their lives. Circular burial mounds that are gradually being covered with tropical lushness are a last reminder of them.

# The beauty of Angkor Wat

*One of Asia's finest cities lies deep in the Cambodian jungle*

The pagodas of the royal temples of Wat rise out of the landscape above the Khmer capital of Angkor like golden peaks. This once large and prosperous city lies in the northwest of Cambodia. At the beginning of the eleventh century the population of Angkor was one million, and the city boasted many pagodas and countless shrines to the Hindu gods. It must have been the most beautiful city in all Asia at that time. The Chinese diplomat Chou Takwan saw princesses riding elephants shielded from the sun by red canopies, caught the scent of jasmine in the air, and heard music played by cymbals, flutes, and gongs.

The Khmer king Suryavarman II surpassed all the existing buildings when he had a new temple built in Angkor between 1113 and 1150. In an area of about 240 acres surrounded by a 650-foot-wide moat, he had a new sacred quarter established. At its center are the five pagodas that tower like man-made mountains of sandstone blocks to a height of 213 feet. The pagodas symbolize the universe and the mythical mountain of Meru.

This enormous Asian sacred center was dedicated to both the Hindu god Vishnu and Suryavarman II, who permitted his people to worship him like a living god. As a symbol of his majesty he carried "the golden sword of Indra." Consequently, in reliefs around the temple compound, portrayals are found of mythical episodes from Suryavarman's life as well as the Hindu legends of holy men. It is said that he saw a nine-headed heavenly snake each night beneath the tallest pagoda of the temple, which took on the form of a beautiful girl so it could copulate with the king. According to his decrees, Suryavarman was buried at the temple.

## The jungle takes over

The sophisticated city with numerous reservoirs for water and cleverly irrigated rice fields that were cropped two or three times each year flourished up to the fourteenth century. Angkor was invaded by Thai warriors and the king of Siam's soldiers set fire to the city, so that it was abandoned in 1431 and gradually forgotten. The jungle gradually reclaimed the land, covering Angkor Wat, together with the other temples and the ingenious irrigation system.

It was not until 1860 that the French researcher Henri Mouhot rediscovered the walls and pagodas in the Cambodian jungle. He described it as more impressive than any find in ancient Greece or Rome had ever been.

Later expeditions revealed new riches among the ruins spread over several square miles of jungle. Many of the buildings that were badly eroded were restored by French archaeologists and protected against further damage. When the German television journalist Hans Walter Berg visited Angkor in 1957 he considered the pagodas to be "more balanced, more harmonious, and more impressive than the Hindu examples." He also noted the fascinating way that lush vegetation was embracing the majestic art, damaging it, yet at the same time supporting it.

Much of the restoration work at Angkor was undone during the bloody Cambodian war in the 1970s.

Many of the statues and reliefs from the golden era of the Khmer were intentionally damaged at this time by their barbaric descendants.

In 1987, the restorers were able to return to work at the temple of Angkor Wat and the other important sites in the vicinity.

*The holy site of Angkor Wat, surrounded by a 650-ft-wide moat (top left) was started in the 12th century in honor of the Hindu god Vishnu and the Khmer king Suryavarman II. He was worshipped by his subjects as a living god. In the past 100 years archaeologists have discovered numerous other temples in the vicinity of the palace temple compound, including Pré Rup (top right) and Bantea Srei (bottom right)*

# Where the Emerald Buddha changes his raiment

*Bangkok's royal palaces and the temple of Wat Phar Keao*

ASIA

THAILAND

**Bangkok**

*Indian Ocean*

**ROUTE**

Express ferry from Menam Quay in Ta Chang

**BEST TIMES**

November–February

**ACCOMMODATIONS**

Hotel Sukhotai 13/3 Sathorn Tai Road

**ALSO WORTH SEEING**

Wat Pho and Wat Saket temples, National Museum, Jim Thompson's house

Boats laden on the Menam River with bananas for cooking, golden pagodas aglow in the sunlight, white shrines to the spirits beside every road, gaggles of monks in saffron robes, blue and jade-green statues of the holy ones between scarlet columns—old Bangkok is a feast for the eyes of the beholder. Despite its population of seven million, expanding industry, and skyscraper hotels juxtaposed with the elegant temples, the Thai capital maintains its cherished traditions and retains its incomparable charm.

This metropolis on the banks of the Menam River was founded by the Chakkri dynasty which assumed power in the old kingdom of Siam through a coup by the officer corps of the army in 1782. The dynasty still rules and the present Chakkri king, who was crowned Rama IX in 1950 is King Bhoemibol. Together with his Queen Sirikit, this constitutional monarch has helped his country to become one of the major tourist centers of Asia.

For those visiting Bangkok who appreciate art, King Bhoemibol has opened up much of the royal palace. His ancestor Rama I started building it on the east bank of the Menam towards the end of the eighteenth century. The palace compound covers about 370 acres with a Buddhist monastery and temples and the Chedis pagoda that is gilded with gold leaf.

One of the older buildings, dating from 1783, contains a pagoda of five tiers. This was the first coronation chamber of the Chakkri dynasty and it contains the black throne of Rama I, decorated with mother-of-pearl, a second throne, and the king's bed. Angels are depicted on the green walls floating heavenwards from lotus flowers. The Thai call Bangkok, Krung Thep or "city of the angels."

## Animals stand guard

Of the four additional palaces, the most impressive is the "great palace of the Chakkri dynasty." It is also the most curious architecturally, being built under British architects in 1876 during the rule of King Chulalongkorn as something of a replica Renaissance castle but with the addition of Thai elements such as pagodas from which heavenly green snakes emerge. These pagodas are in turn topped with smaller, more pointed ones.

The nearby sacred quarter of Wat Phar Keao or "monastery of the Emerald Buddha" is one of the most impressive examples of Thai temple building. Twelve enormous sculptures of Yaks guard the six entrance gates. These are partly harbingers of happiness but also act as guardians. Other buildings have other animal sculptures in bronze or stone of elephants, cattle, lions, and mythical creatures. A rectangular hall with external walls of blue and gold and tiered roof, decorated with small bells, contains the most revered spiritual symbol of the kingdom. The Emerald Buddha rests on a thirty-six-foot-high plinth. The Buddha is just over two feet tall and is carved from a single piece of jade.

In 1784, King Rama I proclaimed that the Emerald Buddha represented the holy guardian of the Chakkri dynasty. Devout Thai followers built the Bot, a special temple specially for the Emerald Buddha, which is enhanced with twelve symbolic animals adopted by Buddhism from the Hindu god Vishnu. To protect the Buddha a small golden and gem-encrusted home was created for him. The fortunate traveler may chance to visit during the three seasonal ceremonies attended by the Thai king. These festivities are for the rainy season, the hot season, and the cool season. It is at these times the holy guardian of Thailand changes his raiments.

*To commemorate Buddha's death 2,500 years*

*A Buddha at Wat Phar Keao (monastery of the Emerald Buddha). The temple was built next to the royal palace of King Bhoemibol and Queen Sirikit in the late 18th century.*

ago the temple roofs and golden Ghedi pagodas and the beautiful facades and the colorful guardians of Wat Phar Keao were carefully restored.

# Java's temple of the many Buddhas

*Borobudur is a major goal for pilgrims*

SEA OF JAVA

JAVA
**Borobudur**

*Indian Ocean*

**ROUTE**

By air to Jakarta, internal flight or train to Jogyakarta. Bus to Borobudur (25 miles)

**BEST TIMES**

April–October

**OPENING TIMES**

6 a.m.–5 p.m.

**ALSO WORTH SEEING**

Prambaman Temple, crater landscape on the Dieng plateau

The court astrologers were commissioned to seek every spot in the kingdom where the male sun penetrates the female earth. Horoscopes were studied, calculations made, sequences strictly observed, and finally it became evident: the divine copulation occurs on a dome-shaped hill in a fertile region of central Java.

And so it was that midway through the eighth century the best possible site was found on which to construct a model of the mythical mountain of Meru, around which according to Hindu belief, the whole world turns.

### Eighty years to build

Ten thousand coolies were needed to build the temple on the chosen hill with its nine different levels. For eighty years they piled the enormous volume of 74,082 cubic yards of precisely cut stone on top of each other without even a fistful of mortar until the original hill had been turned into a man-made mountain.

The form of this temple underwent even greater influence from Buddhism when this religion conquered Java. Buddhas in bronze, stone, and as reliefs were placed along the nine terraces. When completed in 830, this holy place was known by the Buddhists as

Borobudur, which means "many Buddhas."

To the many Buddhist pilgrims traveling to Borobudur the yellow-brown temple mountain seemed an unparalleled sacred wonder of the world. Ascending the nine levels in a clockwise direction they were told to climb the "three stairways of being" which lead from the earthly to the heavenly world. After this, pilgrims would pass thousands of relief tablets illustrating the life and teaching of Buddha. Beyond this many niches contain figures of Buddha and his disciples leading up to the three highest platforms of the temple where there are seventy-two stupas

(bell-shaped stone structures, each of which contains a stone Buddha).

At the top of the temple, pilgrims encountered the largest stupa and the only one that is empty, symbolizing the absolute peace and enlightenment of nirvana.

Until the middle of the tenth century, Borobudur was an important place of pilgrimage for Buddhists in the Indonesian archipelago, but later the faith became centered on eastern Java, where Buddhism enjoyed a new period of growth. When the Merapi volcano erupted in 1006 Borobudur was badly damaged, statues were toppled, and the temple was covered in a thick layer of lava. Soon the jungle reclaimed the temple and this great monument was lost for centuries.

## Successful restoration

Its rediscovery in 1814 is entirely due to the British Governor-General of Malaya, Sir Thomas Stanford

Raffles who wanted to find out the meaning of the clearly carved rocks he discovered beneath the lush foliage. In the decades that followed, parts of Borobudur were uncovered. The temple had suffered greatly, most of the bronzes had disappeared, and many of the statues were headless.

From 1907–1911 the Dutchman Theodor van Erp organized the first systematic restoration. Meticulous

photographic documentation was made of the entire structure which aided its restoration in the twentieth century to its former condition. Once more as a thousand years ago, Buddhist pilgrims journey to the earthly representation of the heavenly mountain of Meru. It is said that if pilgrims stretch out their hand in the niches they may expect great happiness.

*Hundreds of Buddhas adorn the 9th century holy shrine of Borobudur (many Buddhas). The larger Buddhas are housed in bell-like stupas (top left) while others are arranged in niches in the walls along the processional route up the temple mountain. Reliefs (top right) depict scenes from the life and teachings of Buddha. For centuries Borobudur was lost beneath the jungle before its rediscovery in 1814.*

# Samarkand – the paradise of the Orient

*Under Tamerlane it was the great trading city between the Orient and Occident*

ASIA

UZBEKISTAN

**Samarkand**

**ROUTE**

By air to Tashkent, local flight to Samarkand or by rail on the Trans-Caspian railway from Tashkent to Samarkand (approx. 190 miles)

**BEST TIME**

October

**ACCOMMODATIONS**

Hotel Afrosiab

**ALSO WORTH SEEING**

Oasis city of Tashkent, Buchara and Chiwa

On his campaigns against half of Asia, the Turkoman Mongol conqueror Timur the Lame surpassed even his famous predecessor Genghis Khan in ruthless destruction. He is better known in the west as Tamerlane, a corruption of Timur Lang (Timur the Lame). The list of medieval cities plundered and destroyed by his hordes is almost endless. Untold riches, but also skilled craftsmen were captured and returned to his capital Samarkand. His building lust reflected his megalomaniac tendencies, but he was determined that Samarkand should become "the paradise of the Orient."

In Tamerlane's time, the metropolis in what is now Uzbekistan was already 1,500 years old. Long before the first millennium, the routes of the caravans carrying silk from China met at this fertile oasis on the Zeravshan river. Paved roadways led to the great market where valuable cloth, hunting falcons, fur, tapestries, and gems were traded. In 751, the craftsmen of Samarkand made paper from rags, enabling the production of academic literature, dictionaries, and encyclopedias.

When Tamerlane chose Samarkand as his residence, the city was still recovering from the aftermath of occupation by Genghis Khan. To give the city a focal point, Tamerlane had a personal mausoleum built, the Goer-i-mir or royal tomb. The main part of this structure is still intact with its cylindrical boxed roof with grooved domes simulating flower buds. Travelers approaching Samarkand from any direction first saw the cobalt and turquoise main dome standing at 111 feet, so that it rose above the horizon like a gemstone lit by the sun.

## Ostentatious entrance to Goer-i-mir

One of history's major architects, Muhammad bin Mahmud of Isfahan, built a thirty-nine-foot-high gate at the entrance to the Goer-i-mir, which is covered with a mosaic of glazed earthenware in bright colors. The motifs of the decoration represent the planets, sun, flowers, leaves, and fruit. Beyond this gate one entered the inner court bordered by the mausoleum on one side and by a madrasah or Muslim college and accommodation for students on the other. The Goer-i-mir was completed in 1405 and established the central Asian style of architecture for the next century. When Tamerlane died shortly after this, he was laid to rest in his mausoleum.

## The mother-in-law mosque

One of the finest pieces of sacred architecture in the Orient is the great Bibi Chanym Mosque, which Tamerlane had built for his wife's mother. It took ninety-five elephants four years to drag the blocks of stone from mountain quarries to be cut to shape by a team of five hundred stonemasons. Meanwhile artisans were forging the main entrance gates "from seven metals." When completed, the huge "mother-in-law" mosque possessed a large hall for prayers, and its four hundred domes were supported by hundreds of marble pillars and other supports.

Tamerlane drove people from their homes in the center of the city in order to raze them to create a large covered bazaar for merchants and tradesmen. Within a few years this new main market developed into the most significant trading center for the exchange of goods between the Orient and Occident, overflowing with riches from both hemispheres.

Under Tamerlane's cousin, Ulug Beg, an astrologer, the great bazaar was relocated and the area was transformed into a large open area known as the Registan. Later this was cordoned off on three sides with towers exuberantly decorated with mosaics.

Tamerlane's vision of "a paradise of the East" was fulfilled in part through his buildings and those of his successors, and the metropolis experienced a great period of flourishing trade. In 1941, archaeologists opened Tamerlane's tomb and found the skeleton of strongly built man with Mongolian skull, red beard, who was lame on the right side of his body.

*The madrasah (above and bottom right) is one*

*three Muslim colleges. The towers denote the area of the Registan, most beautiful center of Samarkand where the great bazaar was held.*

# Arabia's first skyscrapers

*High-rise building in Shibam along the Incense Road*

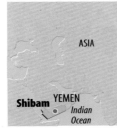

ASIA

**Shibam** YEMEN
*Indian Ocean*

**ROUTE**

By air to Aden. Local flights from Aden or San'a' to Shibam

**BEST TIMES**

October–May

**ACCOMMODATIONS**

Shibam Guest House, Sam City Chalets (near Saiyun)

**ALSO WORTH SEEING**

Sultan's palace in Saiyun, San'a'

The view looks all the world as if someone has tried to model New York City in a sand pit. On closer examination you realize the scale is smaller and it is not sand but clay bricks from which Shibam's slender skyscrapers are built. But these buildings were withstanding sandstorms long before America had its first high-rises. Caravan travelers were telling tales as early as the third century of this town of "tall houses" sited at the south of the Arabian peninsula.

## Building with clay bricks

Fugitives from Schwaba, that was put to the torch and razed around 250 AD, founded the town of Shibam in an area 1,300 feet by 1,600 feet on a hill in the Wadi Hadhramaut. Here they built five hundred dwellings close together to an unbelievable height for the age of almost one hundred feet. Perhaps they could have built even higher but they were not permitted to do so.

Of course some of the houses have been rebuilt over the centuries but the basic form of the dwellings and town remained the same. Today's builders in Shibam still work in the traditions of their predecessors of the tenth century.

They continue to use sun-dried bricks of clay. If the walls lean too far because of sandy subsoil they just build a new upright wall. The narrow format of the homes has also remained unaltered.

The mud-colored or lime wash skyscrapers were often provided with a finely carved gate as the sole form of ornamentation. The lower levels tended to be used for storage or as shops, the middle floors for the children and women, while the upper floors were reserved for the men and their guests. The roof gardens provide a fine view of the lush valley of the Wadi Hadhramaut, except during the rainy season. The valley is a thousand-foot-deep rift in the Dschol Plateau.

During the wet season the groundwater rises to the surface, enabling cultivation of date palms

and oasis cultivation of various types of cereal and vegetables. The town's wealth though was founded on its judicious position astride one of the major caravan routes of the Arabian Peninsula, the "Incense Road."

## Incense trade

Around the middle of the third millennium BC caravans carried oliban along this route (a form of gum resin) from the gum olibanum tree, from Hadhramaut and Dhofar in the southern province of Oman. When heated, the yellow and brown resin emits an aromatic fragrance. This incense was used as part of death rites in Egypt, and the Greek and Jewish temples also burned oliban.

Both Roman and Byzantine ceremonies were inconceivable without the use of incense, and its aroma still wafts today through both Roman Catholic and Orthodox churches.

Besides oliban and the greatly valued myrrh, many other treasures were also transported from the Mediterranean along the "Incense Road," such as gold from the legendary Ophir in Africa, cloth from Yemen, and herbs and gems from India. Arab slavers probably used the route for their trade too. In the third century the wealth of Shibam made it the center of the Hadhramaut kingdom.

In the ninth century, the importance of the Incense Road waned

and so too did the fortunes of the Hadhramaut kingdom. Shibam has barely changed in the past thousand years.

*The center of Shibam with its white stucco mosque (top right) takes the traveler back 1,000 years, if you ignore the mopeds, power cables, and lamp post next to the small mosque. The 500 or so homes of the inner town are on six to eight floors. Houses are rebuilt in the traditional manner with sun-dried clay bricks , when they fall into decay. In the oasis gardens outside the town palms, cereals, and vegetables are cultivated.*

ASIA

YEMEN

San'a' Indian Ocean

# San'a' is still the "pearl of Arabia"

*Dried sandstone and unique windows set the town's style*

**ROUTE**

Regular flights from Europe to San'a'

**BEST TIMES**

October–May

**ACCOMMODATIONS**

Al Gasmy Palace Hotel (inner city), Rawdaw Palace (8 miles N)

**ALSO WORTH SEEING**

Dar al-Jahar national museum (former residence of the Imam, 9 miles NW); Shibam in Wadi Hadhramaut

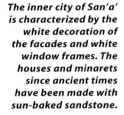

*The inner city of San'a' is characterized by the white decoration of the facades and white window frames. The houses and minarets since ancient times have been made with sun-baked sandstone.*

Many a traveler on their first journey across the Yemeni highlands felt certain they were witnessing a mirage. Shimmering sandy forms rose up out of the dust clouds in the oppressive heat. Coming near it was possible for the traveler to see white ornamentation on the brown facades of buildings, arabesque trellis work, and window frames with stucco reliefs, and small brown and white-painted minarets.

The town that lay before him was San'a', rich in sages, pearl of the Arabia, a city of commerce, silversmiths, alabaster carvers, and weavers of fine cloths.

The origins of the town go back at least 2,500 years to the Yemeni kingdom of Sheba, of Biblical fame and renowned for its great queen, whose rulers selected a fertile area to create as a stronghold. The fortress, at a height of 7,700 feet, developed into a trading place for farmers and craftsmen who were protected by a wall running for over seven miles which was over thirty feet high and up to sixteen feet wide. It is from these defensive works that the name San'a' is derived, meaning "well-protected." An armed watch guarded the seven heavy timber towers.

In spite of a great deal of rebuilding and much new construction, the city has retained its medieval appearance, in part because the same

traditions have been retained for the facades of the buildings. The first step in construction is to create a foundation from large blocks of stone. After this the walls are erected to heights of four to six storeys, using blocks of sun-baked sandstone. The diversity in form of the windows is surprising. They are circular, arched, square, or vaulted. There are line courses of white masonry between each storey of the building.

## Daylight filters through alabaster windows

The buildings of 65–100 feet still retain their traditional colors. Window frames are lime-washed white, in common with the decorative line courses and trellis of the upper windows. When lamps are lit at dusk the effect is magical. Colored glass in many windows shimmers and the traditional alabaster windows reflect a milky glow.

San'a' also reflects the various religions of the people who have lived here in the 2,500 years since it was founded, as conquerors overran the city's walls. The first temple was built at the time of the kingdom of Sheba when the Israelites, who were the kingdom's first silversmiths, built a synagogue. This was replaced in turn by a church for Coptic Christians, and ultimately used for

the brick mosque built by Arab conquerors in the seventh century. The Al-Kabir or "great mosque" has a stone recalling the Kaaba of Mecca. Today as capital of Yemen, San'a' has about one hundred mosques with forty-five snow-white minarets rising above them.

Apart from the city wall and the main Bab Al Jaman Gate of the seventeenth century, San'a' is a modern city with a population approaching a million. Medieval spinning and weaving shops have developed into modern cotton industries. There is a university with departments for Islamic law and education. There is an international airport and a radio station. The palace of the Imam reminds one of the occupation under the Ottoman Empire. It now serves as a Yemeni museum.

Tools fashioned from flint and obsidian demonstrate that humans hunted on the plateau enclosed within the walls of San'a' during the Stone Age.

# Mecca's most sacred shrine

*Every Muslim must make a pilgrimage to the Kaaba at least once in his life*

**ROUTE**

By air for pilgrims. Non-Muslims are not permitted entry to Mecca or Medina

**BEST TIME**

The hajj (pilgrimage) takes place during the 12th month of the Islamic calendar which shifts 11 days each year in relation to the Gregorian calendar

In the Islamic month of Dhul each year the same spectacle can be witnessed. Millions of Muslims from every corner of the world gather in the inner court of the great mosque in Mecca. They proceed around the cloth-draped tablet of stone that is the Kaaba. Their procession ends at the southeastern corner of the cubic structure where they kiss the Black Stone, said to be given to Abraham by the Angel Gabriel.

Long before the prophet Muhammad was born in Mecca and founded Islam in the seventh century, the long slab of basalt rock had been the focal point of religious worship. Arab tribes revered what is now presumed to have been a meteorite as a fetish sent from heaven and encased it for safe-keeping within the almost fifty-foot-high Kaaba (Arabic for cube), a windowless building with a flat roof supported by three pillars. Muhammad incorporated veneration of the Kaaba into his doctrine, which taught in common with Judaism and Christianity that there was only the one true God, Allah. From that time on he called the Kaaba "the house of God" and said the Black Stone was Allah's gift to humankind.

## Islam unites Arabia

Before Muhammad ("the praised one") died, the new religion had spread throughout Arabia, uniting hitherto divided peoples, and so provided a political counterweight to the power of Byzantium and Persia.

When the prophet died at Medina in 632, a growing throng of pilgrims came to Mecca. Pilgrims from Egypt took to bringing black cloth with them each year as festive drapery for the Kaaba shrine.

In 700 AD the Caliph Walid I built an arcade surrounding the Kaaba, with marble pillars and mosaics of gold leaf. Gradual extensions led to the present-day two tiered promenades leading to the great mosque, beside seven minarets. The compound includes such sacred treasures as the Sensem springs and well which legend says the archangel Gabriel caused to gush water, taking pity on women. Elsewhere, at the Makram Ibrahim, a tile is displayed bearing an imprint of Abraham's foot.

Current Islamic doctrine requires that all adult Muslims shall undertake a pilgrimage to Mecca at least once in their lives. The only impediments that are recognized as appropriate excuses are illness or poverty. The ceremonies are strictly ordained. When the pilgrims arrive they must walk around the Kaaba seven times and kiss the Black Stone. Other rules require them to walk seven times between the holy hills of Al-Safa and Al-Marwa, which are connected by a long covered walkway. They must also make the longer walk to the Arafat Plateau, which pilgrims do from midday until the evening even in the burning sun in order to affirm their service to Allah. Pilgrims must also gather forty-six stones in a place called Musdalifa and take them to the three "pillars of Satan" at Mina the following day. The three pillars of different sizes are said to represent the devil in three guises. In the next three days pilgrims must cast stones at the pillars. Finally pilgrims sacrifice an animal such as a lamb and once more circle the Kaaba seven times before returning home.

The annual hajj poses major problems for Saudi Arabia and private enterprise was long since unable to cope. Today's pilgrims arriving by air, train, car, or on foot are catered for by the army which creates a temporary city outside Mecca for the millions of pilgrims who attend the hajj each year.

*Around one million pilgrims visit Mecca each year for the annual hajj. On arrival and before departure they must walk around the Kaaba seven times. The Kaaba, which is hidden beneath black drapes, is located in the courtyard of the great mosque. The aerial photograph below sets the overall scene.*

# The second wonder of Ephesus

*Archaeologists uncover a lost city port on Turkey's west coast*

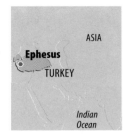

## ROUTE
Lies 56 miles south of Izmir. Dolmus (mini-bus) from Kasadasi beach 12 miles and 2 miles from Selçuk

## BEST TIMES
May–June and September

## ALSO WORTH SEEING
Ancient Priene, Milet, and archaeological museum in Selçuk

One of the original seven wonders of the world stood at Ephesus on Turkey's western coast but it was swallowed up by the earth. In the past century though archaeologists have been uncovering a new wonder that was once a thriving commercial port city. Ephesus is one of the largest and probably the most beautiful of all the ruined cities in Asia Minor dating back to the height of the ancient Greek and Roman civilizations at their peak.

The city's history goes back to the second millennium BC when vessels plying the Aegean could anchor in the harbor of Ephesus. The Lydians and later the Phoenicians established trading posts there. The nearby mouth of the Kaytros (now the Kucuk Menderes) and a caravan route leading to inner Anatolia stimulated the handling of goods through the port. Grateful for the improvement in their fortunes, the inhabitants erected a shrine at which they could worship the Earth Mother and goddess of fertility, Cybele.

### Awe-inspiring Artemisium
Fertility rites were also central to the building by the Ephesians of the largest of all Greek temples in the sixteenth century BC. This temple

*The Greco-Roman theater at Ephesus has space for 24,000 (above). The Hadrian Temple (right) was reconstructed by archaeologists from the original materials. Its fine entrance gates date from 130 AD. Next to it is a "house of pleasure."*

was dedicated to Artemis, daughter of Zeus, who is represented as a beautiful woman with many breasts. The temple, which took 120 years to build, is praised by the Greek writer Plinius as "the noblest, greatest, and most wonderful sacred place on earth." The area of the Artemisium must have been at least four times the size of the Parthenon on the Acropolis of Athens. Its roof was supported by 127 columns and the temple was regarded as one of the seven wonders of the world. The temple was so impressive and famous in 356 BC that a psychopath named Herostratus, who wished to be remembered in history, set fire to it. A new temple on the site was eventually damaged by the Goths and the remaining stonework was used by stonemasons for other buildings.

### Harbor silts-up
The majority of the superb Ephesian buildings that have been uncovered date from Greek, Roman, and Byzantine times. These are the remnants of an economic and cultural center that once housed 300,000 people but became doomed to decline as the harbor silted-up and the city was regularly plundered by marauders.

The center of the archaeological exploration has revealed a marble promenade over 1,700 feet long that is flanked by colonnades. Part of the city's most prominent building has been reconstructed by experts with the help of the findings they have made. The most advanced stage of reconstruction was achieved with the magnificent temple of Hadrian from

130 AD with its adjacent "house of pleasure." South of this marble walkway archaeologists have successfully reconstructed the famous Celcius library. About seventy percent of its two-storey facade with its 50-foot-high inner courtyard and parts of the gallery were rebuilt using the original materials. This fine example of Roman public architecture dates from the second century.

Nearby the library a Greek assembly or market-place has been unearthed. The square of 360 feet was bordered by a double row of pillar-fronted shops. Also close to the center are the impressive ruins of a Greco-Roman theater with seating for 24,000 in sixty-six rows.

Ephesus also contains early Christian structures. It was here that St. Paul the Apostle delivered his sermons and St. John the Theologian died there. There is a basilica above the probable grave of St. John where a council of the church declared Mary to be the mother of God in 431, making a strange link with the Ephesians' earlier cult of the earth mother. In the nearby Nightingale Hills, which provide a view to Selçuk, there is a small house that has been enlarged to form a chapel, where it is claimed St. Mary the Madonna died.

There is no proof of this claim but the Vatican did declare the "House of Mary" to be a place of pilgrimage in 1892. A Catholic Mass and Ascension of Mary is held there each year.

*Artemis, daughter of Zeus, was worshipped in Ephesus as fertility goddess, represented as a many-breasted earth mother.*

# The white beauty of Pamukkale

*In Turkey hot springs create nature's work of art*

ASIA

**Pamukkale**

TURKEY

*Indian Ocean*

**ROUTE**

E87 for 150 miles S of Izmir

**BEST TIMES**

May–June, September

**ACCOMMODATIONS**

Pamukkale Hotel (with thermal baths, not exclusively for hotel guests)

**ALSO WORTH SEEING**

Ancient city of Aphrodisias

The mercury in a thermometer rises to more than 104 degrees Fahrenheit (40°C) on many summer days in central Turkey, so it is surprising to suddenly encounter a large area apparently of glacier ice. The blinding white expanse reminds the Turks of cotton fields ready to harvest, and so they call this strange phenomenon of nature Pamukkale—the cotton castle.

## Chalk deposits create terraces

The sparkling white apparition is caused by hot springs. The water that drips and constantly flows down in countless gullies to the valley almost three hundred feet below is rich in calcium carbonate. As the water cools calcium carbonate is deposited, forming a white precipitate of chalky-flakes. In the course of thousands of years thick layers of calcium deposits have formed a series of terraces down the hillside to the valley below over an area of almost two miles into the valley.

The thermal pools that are supplied with mud from the springs and large pools of warm water were soon understood to have healing powers and this probably explains the establishment of the city of Hieropolis nearby in the second century BC. The residents of this city used the hot water in a Roman bath house. Perhaps those taking to the waters then also purchased souvenirs such as branches, leaves, and pebbles covered with layers of Pamukkale calcium carbonate.

*As the water cools from 95°F (35°C) deposits of calcium carbonate are formed.*

*Thermal springs have deposited calcium carbonate that has formed stepped terraces of 300 feet in depth over thousands of years. People have bathed in the hot springs since ancient times for their health. Ancient buildings of the ancient city of Hieropolis were hidden beneath the snow-like chalk.*

A less pleasant natural phenomenon near the hot springs was described by the Greek geographer Strabo in the first century. In his seventeen-volume *Geographica* he refers to a cave that produced toxic fumes that was fenced off to prevent people from inhaling the gases. Strabo also relates an account of the neutered priests who served the fertility goddess Cybele. They lowered sacrificial animals into the cave which were immediately asphyxiated. The eunuchs themselves were reputed to be immune to the fumes, thereby demonstrating their holiness.

## Necropolis for craftsmen

Later the area around Hieropolis became prone to earthquakes and plundering. Parts of the ancient buildings disappeared beneath a thick layer of pebbles and flakes. In the 1880s German archaeologists began excavations, and this was later continued by Italians. A thermal building was uncovered close to an old bathing pool that dated from the second century. This is now the Pamukkale Museum. Not far from the poisonous caves, Plutonium, described by Strabo, archaeologists found the ruins of a temple to Apollo.

Among the objects from the classical period are the remains of an octagonal structure erected in the fifth century as a monument to St. Philip the Apostle who is assumed to have met a martyr's death at Hieropolis, an amphitheater with a frieze with mythological designs, and one of the largest ancient necropolises, with references on the grave inscriptions to weavers, dyers, and other craftsmen.

In recent years Pamukkale has become a significant Turkish tourist attraction. Numerous tourist coaches stop here and the white terraces are often thronged with people. Guests who can afford a longer stay will find comfortable hotels with their own thermal baths. Physicians recommend the steaming springs for rheumatism. The greater the flow of water that is diverted to the hotel baths the less there is to create further deposits on the famous calcium

carbonate terraces. Slowly the appearance of snow or ice will surely turn brown.

# The pillars of Baalbek

*Ruins retain grandeur*

ASIA

SYRIA

Baalbek

*Indian Ocean*

**ROUTE**

By air to Beirut or Damascus, frequent coach (or hire car) to Baalbek

**BEST TIMES**

April–May, September–October

**ACCOMMODATIONS**

Hotel Palmyra (richly traditional Middle Eastern-style)

**ALSO WORTH SEEING**

Zahlé (town in a beautiful setting with waterfalls), Zedernhain in the Lebanese mountains (along the A27 towards Tripoli)

*The Roman Temple of Venus is a masterpiece of the stonemason's craft. The horseshoe-form floor plan is unusual. The building dates from the first century.*

A bronze statue in The Louvre in Paris shows the gold-helmeted god Baal. Other artifacts from early excavations in the Middle East depict Baal with bull's horns or armed with a club and spear. The god Baal, or Lord, once held sway among the Semitic divinities over the rain and fertility. Historians point to Baal rituals associated with Baalbek (city of Baal), the famous site of ancient ruins in the Lebanon.

More than thirty temples of the pre-Christian era must lie in the valley between the green hills and bare peaks of the Anti-Lebanon Mountains, buried beneath the ruins of later temples and places of worship. According to inscriptions in Assyrian, Baalbek was inhabited more then 3,000 years ago and then called Bali. The high god Baal was also worshipped as Hadad among the Phoenicians who turned Baalbek into a trading city. The Greek conquerors followed the Phoenicians, who identified Baal as their sun god Helios. At that time the city was known as Heliopolis, the sun city.

Around the time of the birth of Christ the city was occupied by the Roman legions of Caesar Augustus. The Romans regarded Baal/Helios as the same as their own god Jupiter. The Romans built an enormous temple to Jupiter upon an Acropolis which was already under construction by the Roman's predecessors. By bringing together the best of their architects and

sculptors the Romans created one of the most impressive sacred buildings of the Eastern Roman Empire. It was in harmony with Phoenician, Hellenic, and Roman styles and was hailed as a new wonder of the world.

Visitors to the temple, measuring 885 feet by 393 feet, entered via a wide set of steps which led to an entrance hall and a hexagonal inner courtyard with colonnaded arcades. This courtyard contained a multitiered altar flanked by two granite pillars, one pink and one gray. A further set of steps led to a larger temple set on a twenty-three-foot-high plinth covering an area greater than 8,300 square yards. The upper area rested on fifty-four pillars which were each seventy-two feet high. The temple was dedicated to a special local version of Jupiter,

distinct from the customary Roman Jupiter, nicknamed Optimus Maximus Heliopolitanus. Sometimes his image resembled that of his predecessor Baal.

## The horseshoe-form Temple of Venus

Wars and earthquakes have left nothing but rubble of the area in front of the enormous temple complex, which was never wholly completed. Parts of the Jupiter temple were excavated by German archaeologists between 1900 and 1905 under the patronage of Kaiser Wilhelm II. Some of their finds were spirited away to the Pergamon Museum in Berlin. Of the fifty-four tall temple columns, only six are left intact, their capitals linked by a single slab of shaped stone. A few of

the pillars of the colonnaded arcade are also still standing.

The Roman Temple of Venus at the southern corner of the acropolis is astonishingly well preserved. Apart from its unusual horseshoe-form floor plan, this temple is a smaller version of the Jupiter temple. The high entrance arch is a magnificent example of the stonemason's craft in its own right with interwoven acanthus leaves, poppies, grapevines, and ivy. Here too Middle Eastern and Roman forms merge happily. The temple itself is bounded by two rows of Corinthian columns and a wall of the interior arcade contains a decorative niche.

Also worth seeing at Baalbek, which is now a minor town of about 20,000 people, are the smaller Mercury Temple, an amphitheater,

and the remains of the old city wall. The ruins in this historic place are still fascinating and evidence of the great beauty that Baalbek once was before earthquakes and wars, which have continued into recent times, destroyed so much.

*Of the 54 huge columns of the Jupiter temple (top left) only 6 remain with their capitals joined by a single piece of crafted stone. Construction of the 886 feet by 393 foot temple started at the beginning of the Christian era. A row of pillars (bottom right) are part of the Temple of Venus.*

# Damascus the paradise

*The story of this oasis city stretches back for 6,000 years*

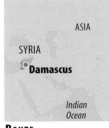

ASIA

SYRIA

**Damascus**

*Indian Ocean*

**ROUTE**

By air to Damascus

**BEST TIMES**

April–May, October

**ACCOMMODATIONS**

Cham Palace (Sh. Maisalun, about 20 min. to the inner city)

**ALSO WORTH SEEING**

National Museum, view from Mount Jabal Qassyun

Nothing is more like paradise as the Arabs imagine it than Damascus. Its old oriental quarters and beautiful location, surrounded by good soil for growing at the foot of the Anti-Lebanon mountain range have been praised by generations of poets. There is a story about the prophet Muhammad that he had experienced the city as so not of this world that he refused to enter. For humankind there is only one paradise and it is not on this earth. Hence the founder of the Islamic faith broke off his

journey to Damascus when he reached the southern suburb of al-Qadam, leaving his footprints, which long remained visible.

Damascus owes its well-being to the Barada River that created a natural oasis between the mountains and the desert. Six thousand years ago the first people settled here because of the water, and they in turn attracted others until a small village community grew into a city. No other place in the world has such a history of continuous human habitation. Arab historians regard

Damascus as the first city culture that arose. Its history is very much older than any European city.

## Stage for biblical events

Countless stories associate this biblical place and holy Islamic city. Abraham, progenitor of all the Semites, is said to have been born here. Cain murdered his brother Abel, St. Ananias healed Saul of his blindness that happened on the road to Damascus and caused the unbeliever to become St. Paul the great apostle.

Major Mediterranean cultures helped to build the palm-shrouded oasis city surrounded by mountains. The Aramaeans built a temple beside the Barada to their god Hadad. The Romans constructed a temple to Jupiter. Christians added churches. If the core of the old city were to be excavated behind its wall with seven towers, traces would be found of Assyrian, Babylonian, Persian, and Greek origins among the many races that have been part of the history of Damascus.

From 636 on, the city developed into a spiritual and cultural Islamic center. The Byzantine churches of the Christians were outnumbered by the mosques and Muslims colleges of the new religion. A major peak in the development of their culture was the establishment in 1154 of the Maristan Nuri dar, one of the most modern hospitals in the world at that time. Europe's first hospitals were places where the dying found some comfort. Damascus had medical staff, medical literature, and wards for surgery, orthopedics, fever illnesses, and mental disorders. Unlike the practice in Europe at that time, the hospital was a secular organization, not under clerical supervision.

Among the Eastern-style bustle of the old inner city, where swords of the famed Damascus steel and golden ornaments are offered for sale, there are some thousand or so beautiful arabesque buildings standing shoulder-to-shoulder.

The Omajjaden Mosque is a leading example of Muslim architecture in Damascus. Built in the eighth century, it is enclosed by a wall extended from a Jupiter temple. In its inner courtyard there is a hexagonal structure resting on six pillars that is decorated in the Byzantine style. In former days, the state treasure was stored under the dome of this mosque. A triple-nave prayer hall contains a relic sacred for both Muslims and Christians: the skull of St. John the Baptist, revered in Islam as the prophet Yahua.

*A number of major Mediterranean cultures left their marks on the Syrian capital of Damascus. At this site (top left) were once Aramaic and Roman temples, and Christian churches. The two photographs above show the decoration above the entrance and the entranceway to the Amajjaden Mosque, guardian of a relic of St. John the Baptist.*

# Trail's end for the caravans

*Aleppo is one of the Orient's oldest trading cities*

**ROUTE**
Internal flight, bus, or rail from Damascus

**BEST TIMES**
April–May, October

**ACCOMMODATIONS**
Amir Palace (close to inner city), Baron Hotel (legendary but antiquated service)

**ALSO WORTH SEEING**
National Museum

When the caravans glimpsed the red walls of the mountain fortress of Aleppo on the horizon they knew they were nearing their goal. Halfway between a major crossing point on the Euphrates and the Mediterranean, protected by a citadel, was one of the most important trading markets of the Orient.

Goods brought overland by camels in the caravans such as Chinese silk, Indian herbs, African ivory, or masterpieces from the hands of Yemeni silversmiths would fetch a good price here because there were always plenty of customers.

The earliest known information about this northern Syrian trading place dates from the second millennium BC. Like Damascus, Aleppo (or as the Arabs call it Halab), is one of the longest continuously inhabited cities of the Orient.

Long before our western calendar, rulers of the kingdom of Jamchad selected the location as a residence for its fertile land. A succession of conquerors have lived there since: Hittites, Assyrians, Greeks, Romans, and Arabs. All of them used Aleppo as a provisioning place and trading post between Mesopotamia and Europe.

### The citadel as emblem

As capital of the province of the same name, Aleppo today is still an important trading center even though the focus for east–west trade has shifted to the products of

*The only road from the citadel of Aleppo leads through a square watchtower and from there across an eight-arch bridge over the moat.*

modern textile and consumer electronics industries. The souk of the inner city, with its more than seven miles of covered shopping lanes, is one of the largest of the Middle East. And just as when the caravan trade flourished, every alleyway has its caravanserai or khan, the traditional inns for traveling merchants. The city also has special hotels for tourists.

Major attractions and perhaps the emblem of Aleppo is the citadel, located on a hill rising 160 feet above the town. The origins of this fortress at the crossroads of caravan routes is lost in the mists of time. Thousands of years before Christ, a Syrian-Hittite temple stood on this hill as a place of worship to the god of weather and Hadad, the holy man of the city.

The Greeks used this obvious defensive position and look-out spot

for an acropolis, and this was in turn used by Arab rulers to protect their royal residence.

A bridge of eight arches leads from the lower city across a deep moat to an angular tower in the middle of the fortress wall. Remains of the former royal residence behind this wall can still be seen, and the throne room has now acquired new domes and two mosques.

### Christians punished

The former cathedral of Aleppo is a magnificent Byzantine influenced structure, located in the city center, below the citadel. It is now the Hallawiya Muslim College which teaches Islamic theology. A Muslim judge had the cathedral and three other Christian churches expropriated in the twelfth century and put to different uses to punish the Christians for the activities of the

crusading Knights Templar. Since that time, Armenian and Greek Christians have only possessed small places in which to meet for prayer.

The most outstanding structure, both literally and figuratively, is the Omajjaden Mosque that was built in the eleventh century. Its 147-foot-high minaret and the four upper ledges with continuous banded inscriptions of texts from the Koran is regarded as one of the finest medieval monuments in Syria. Like the citadel, its slim, four-square tower has become a landmark of the city, the population of which is estimated at half a million.

UNESCO has proclaimed the historic heart of Aleppo, its citadel, and caravan drover's beacon as cultural heritage monuments that must be protected for all of humanity. It is a heritage steeped in thousands of years of history reflected in

its mosques, old Christian quarter, Muslim colleges, caravanserai, souks, beautiful tombs, and treasury of arabesque architecture and decoration so evocative of the Orient.

*The Greeks created an acropolis on the top of a 160-ft hill. The city below this citadel was an important trading center in the 2nd millennium BC. Today, the principal religion is Islam. Christian churches still exist, such as the small Armenian prayer meeting house pictured here.*

# Jerusalem, the Holy City

## Sacred for Christians, Jews, and Muslims

ASIA
ISRAEL
**Jerusalem**
Indian
Ocean

**ROUTE**
Buses 1, 2, 38, 99

**BEST TIMES**
April–May, October

**OPENING TIMES**
Temple of the Rock and Al-Aqsa mosque: daily 8 a.m.–3 p.m. (Ramadan 8 a.m.–11 a.m.). No tours on Fridays

**ALSO WORTH SEEING**
Burial chapel, the Wailing Wall, Mount of Olives Church, Yad VaShem Holocaust Memorial

*Interior of the burial chapel built and consecrated by the Knights Templar in 1194.*

The shrines of the three great monotheist world religions are nowhere else so cheek by jowl as in Jerusalem with its Christian Holy Sepulcher, the Jewish Wailing Wall and Temple Mount, and Islamic Temple of the Rock. For centuries the adherents of the three faiths have inhabited the walled inner city of Jerusalem. It was traditionally a place of religious tolerance, although a city of radical contrasts and violent upheavals.

The current capital of the state of Israel is built on the site of a very old settlement. Jerusalem was the seat of kings from as early as the second millennium BC, belonging to the Egyptian pharaohs. In about 1000 BC King David of Israel and Judah stormed the city that was defended by Jebistes, rebuilt it as his royal residence, and proclaimed it the holy city of Jewry. His successor, King Solomon, had a palace built in the "city of David" and a large temple which later bore his name.

### Holy place in triplicate

New conquerors came and went, until 37 BC when the Roman senate appointed Herod the Great as King of the Jews, as recounted in the

Bible. About seventy years later the new Christian era found its first adherents among this city of Jews. In the fourth century Jerusalem became the holy city of Christianity when one of the first churches was built on the spot where today we find the Church of the Holy Sepulcher.

### Slaughter of 70,000

In the seventh century, Caliph Omar I conquered Jerusalem and proclaimed the city as Islamic. The new religious center was created on the temple mount from where the prophet Muhammad is said to have ascended into heaven.

During the first Christian Crusade in 1099, the Duke of Lorraine, Gottfried Bouillon slaughtered 70,000 Jews and Muslims as

heathens. After Gottfried's death, his brother Baudouin I was crowned King of Jerusalem.

The importance of Jerusalem to the three religions remains a bone of contention among fanatics to this day.

For a time Jerusalem was divided between Israel and Jordan with barbed wire marking the demarcation between them until the Six Days War when Israel occupied the left bank of the Jordan. In 1980 Israel's parliament declared all Jerusalem to be the capital of Israel, thus aggravating conflict with the Muslim Palestinians and their sympathizers throughout the Arab world.

In spite of the explosive political situation, pilgrimages to the holy city

by groups from each of the three religions normally pass off entirely peacefully. For Christians the main objectives are the Church of the Holy Sepulcher, the place where Christ was crucified and laid to rest in the rock tomb. The church was consecrated by the Knights Templar in 1149 and was built on the site of the earlier "Church of the Resurrection" dating from 335.

The holiest place for Jews is the Wailing Wall, which is all that remains of the great temple from the time of Herod and Christ. The name has stuck with non-Jews because of the gestures of lamentation which Jews make when they pray at the sixty-foot-high wall.

The adjacent temple mount or Hram esh-Sharif, which covers almost one-sixth of the inner city, is the largest Jewish section of Jerusalem. Today the Al Aqsa Mosque, with its golden domes and seven naves, stands on the former temples of Solomon and Herod. The Arabic name means "farthest point," recalling that this was the farthest point the prophet Muhammad came away from Mecca.

*Muslims during Friday devotions at the portal of the Al Aqsa Mosque with its golden domes rising above everything. The holy Islamic quarter occupies one-sixth of the ancient inner city. The 60-ft-high Wailing Wall (bottom right) is the main focal point for devout Jews. It is all that is left of the great temple of Herod.*

# The Dead Sea or the Sea of Lot

*Salt eliminates life in the world's lowest sea*

ASIA

ISRAEL

• **Dead Sea**

*Indian Ocean*

### ROUTE

From Jerusalem 19 miles E, from Amman 22 miles SW

### BEST TIMES

March–June, September–November

### ACCOMMODATIONS

Moriah Dead Sea Resort

### ALSO WORTH SEEING

Masada, Qumran

Millions of years ago the sea poured into a deep fault in the earth's crust where today the boundary lies between Israel and Jordan, forming the Dead Sea, almost fifty miles long and up to eleven miles wide. Its surface lies 1,312 feet below normal sea level and the bottom of the sea on its northern edge is twice that depth.

### Shore is surrounded by steep cliffs

Most of us have seen the photographs of people floating effortlessly in the Dead Sea, perhaps even reading a newspaper. Because of the abnormally high salinity of the Dead Sea at around thirty percent it is impossible to sink. It is also quite difficult to swim and virtually impossible to do the crawl or butterfly stroke.

The salts in the water—mostly magnesium, sodium chloride, and calcium chloride—make life impossible for all but a few organisms such as nitrogen and sulfur bacteria and germs which break down cellulose. The shore is also a lifeless desert with a steep rocky cliff of almost two thousand feet and a shoreline encrusted with salt with

just a few wadis, or small valleys which breach the high cliff face where some vegetation gains a temporary foothold.

In Hebrew, the Dead Sea is known as *Yam Hamelach*, the Salt Sea. One of the Arabic names is *Bahr Lot*, the Sea of Lot, named after Abraham's cousin who lived in Sodom and whose wife was turned

*Evaporating water deposits a crust of salt crystals on the shore.*

into a pillar of salt when she turned back to witness the destruction of their sinful city. In antiquity the Greeks and Romans called it the "Asphalt Seas" because a substance known as "Jewish glue," a high-quality bitumen, arises from its depths and can be recovered easily from its surface. From about 150 BC until their defeat by the Romans in 68 AD a devout community of the Jewish faith was established on the northwest shore. Excavating the remains of this ruined settlement, which includes many caves, following initial discoveries by Bedouin, archaeologists in the mid twentieth century found more than six hundred manuscripts of great significance for biblical scholars. The Dead Sea Scrolls are written in Hebrew, Aramaic, and Greek on leather and parchment and also inscribed on strips of copper.

The only water entering the Dead Sea comes from the Jordan river and a few small mountain lakes and there is no outflow. Because of the relatively low flow of fresh water into the Dead Sea, the almost total

absence of rainfall, and the extreme temperatures that can reach 114.8°F (46°C) in summer, fresh water entering does not change the salinity of the sea. Ever increasing levels of water are being taken from the Jordan for irrigation so the level of water in the Dead Sea is expected to drop sharply in the near future. Because of this Israel has plans to prevent the Dead Sea from drying up by creating an inlet from the Mediterranean into the Dead Sea

that could also act as a hydro-power plant.

One of the many features of this deepest landscape on earth is the unusually high level of oxygen in the air. At the same time, because the sun's rays have to penetrate further through the atmosphere the level of ultraviolet is reduced so that it is possible to sunbathe for longer without burning.

*This aerial photograph (top) shows the Dead Sea as a backdrop to the Jewish mountain-top fortress of Masada, whose inhabitants killed themselves so they would not fall into the hands of their Roman enemy in 73 AD. The Dead Sea Scrolls were discovered at Essene on the northwest shore, a community of a Jewish brotherhood destroyed by the Romans. The level of the Dead Sea (bottom right) is 1,312 feet below that of the world's oceans.*

*Entrance to the rock tombs. The Nabataeans created temple facades in front of the tombs of their kings and sculpture in the rock face.*

# Petra – city of rock of the Nabataean kings

## Tombs and temples of a lost nation

Suspicious Bedouin kept their eyes on the traveler clad in Arab garments who called himself Ibrahim ibn Abadallah al-Schami and who said he was on a pilgrimage to the grave of Moses' brother Aaron. The stranger, who was in the valley of Petra, fifty miles south of the Dead Sea, spoke excellent Arabic but his Swiss-German was even better. Without the subterfuge Johann Ludwig Burckhardt would not have succeeded in his quest. In August 1812, he was the first European to reach a fascinating ruined city via an ancient caravan route in what we today call the kingdom of Jordan.

Through Burckhardt the West learned of the former capital of the Nabataeans. These nomadic people settled a plateau enclosed by mountains in the second century BC that was only accessible by means of a narrow pass. In the course of the following three centuries Petra (Greek for "rock") developed into a trading center at the crossroads of various caravan routes. In that period numerous monumental structures and tombs were hewn from the rocky cliffs of their settlement, lying at just under three thousand feet above sea level. Art historians consider the sculpture of Petra to be a coming-together of Oriental and Hellenic traditions.

### Well-preserved tombs

Burckhardt gained no more than a superficial impression of all this. Suspicions among genuine Muslims grew and he was soon forced to leave. Soon afterwards though British, French, America, German, and later Arab archaeologists followed in the search for Nabataean history, who were already in decline by early in the second century when the Romans occupied the rock city and made it a citadel for their province of Arabia.

Among the well-preserved structures from Nabataean times is the Qasr al-Bint Fira'un temple (fortress of the pharaoh's daughter) with its seventy-five-foot-high walls. This temple was built at about the first century and was dedicated to the high god Dhushara and his mother al-'Uzza. A forty-foot-square altar in front of this temple was probably used for fire rites and animal sacrifices. Archaeologists gave the second most imposing structure the name of "Lion's Claw Temple" because of the inscriptions on the columns they unearthed.

The fine facades and temple like tombs carved out of the rock at the edge of Petra are particularly well preserved and restored. The craftsmanship of these anonymous sculptors, whose work has exposed different colored layers of sandstone, demands the greatest respect.

The most successful of the facades in artistic terms is the "red" facade of al-Khazne, the "treasure house," in which the Bedouin sometimes vainly search for the legendary "treasure of the pharaohs." Its facade is 131 feet high and eighty-two feet wide, covering two of the levels hewn from the rock. The entrance at ground level has six columns with Corinthian capitals and at the upper level there is a circular rock pavilion housing a statue of the Egyptian goddess Isis. Other sculptures include amazons, lions, Nabataean goddesses, and figures from Greek mythology. The consensus is that this magnificent example of a building carved from rock is the burial chamber for one of the last of the Nabataean kings.

Quite unlike the days of Burckhardt, strangers today have no need to disguise themselves in order to gain access to these sacred and beautiful rock tombs in the rock-hewn theater that is Petra. The city lying behind the narrow Siq al-Baris pass is now firmly established as a tourist attraction.

**ROUTE**

Via the "King's Road" 175 miles S of Amman, or 81 miles N of Aquaba (buses from both cities)

**BEST TIMES**

May–June, September–November

**ACCOMMODATIONS**

Petra Forum Hotel

**ALSO WORTH SEEING**

Siq al-Barid pass (Little Petra) 5 miles N; former Knights of the Cross fortress, Shaubak, 25 miles N

*The Nabataeans carved grand facades and sculptures in the rock at the entrance to the rock tombs of their kings.*

# AUSTRALIA

# Australia's red heart

*Uluru or Ayers Rock is a sacred place for the Aborigines*

Caught in the light of the setting sun its is as if a giant statue of molten lava is supine. In the late evening the enormous monolith of the fifth continent glows its brightest red. Almost six miles in circumference and 1,142 feet high, Ayers Rock, as it was formerly known, dominates the skyline southeast of Alice Springs in central Australia. It is the world's large single piece of isolated rock.

Its origin dates back 600 million years when the erosion of the mountains left deposits that hardened into a an enormous mass of sandstone. About 400 million years ago this mass was pushed upwards by the earth's crust, forming the monolith now known by its original Aboriginal name of Uluru. The monolith has been weathered smooth. Another rock outcrop called Kata Tjuta was similarly formed nineteen miles to the southwest in the violet-blue mountain range known as the Olgas.

The English name Ayers Rock commemorated a former Australian Premier, and the name Olga too is of English-speaking origin. Since 1977 the original Aboriginal name Uluru has been used for the rock and the national park in which it stands. This name means "place casting shadow." The Olgas are known to the Aborigines as Kata Tjuta or "many heads." In the traditional stories passed down by word of mouth by the original inhabitants of Australia, Uluru and Kata Tjuta were formed in the original creation of the earth by the spirits, along with the other mountains, and rivers, and people, and plants. The spirits named them in their song which called everything to life.

One of the interesting Aboriginal "dream time" legends refers to an ancestor who fashioned a large sand dune into the form of a sleeping whale, which became Uluru.

## Caves and cult

The Pitjantjatjara tribes long ago painted murals in caves and crevices in Uluru depicting archers, lancers,

mighty horned heads, feathers, and leaves. The oldest drawings are linear and geometric. Some caves are considered holy places that are forbidden to woman and young men who have not yet passed through their initiation rites.

The pools of water at the foot of the monolith are also considered sacred places. This is where the rainbow snake Ungud lives, the mother of all living things, who provides the rains and ensures that women are fertile. In an annual rite of the Ungud cult during the rainy season, the murals depicting the creator snake must be retouched or repainted. Ungud's benevolent influence must not be interrupted.

Aborigines and the government have waged a long legal battle over the ownership of the Uluru national park area and the access of tourists. The government returned it to Aboriginal ownership in 1985 who

then leased it back for ninety-nine years to the Australian National Parks and Wildlife Service. It was added to the World Heritage list of unique and precious sites in 1987.

*Nature produced an enormous sandstone monolith in the desert of central Australia. The 1,142-ft-high rock is the largest monolith in the world.*

# Sydney's graceful shells

*The Opera House is still one of the most daring buildings of our age*

Indian Ocean

AUSTRALIA

**Opera in Sydney**

South Pacific

### ROUTE

Buses and trains to Circular Quay, Sydney Explorer Bus to the Opera House

### BEST TIMES

November, February–March

### OPENING TIMES

Daily performances 9 a.m.–4 p.m.

### ACCOMMODATIONS

The Sydney Regent, 199 George Street

### ALSO WORTH SEEING

Harbor Bridge, Fort Denison, The Australian Museum

All manner of descriptions have been given to the Sydney Opera House, ranging from broken eggshells, giant mussel shells, huge billowing sails, or a collection of band stands. In any event the Opera House is the most daring piece of architecture constructed in Australia.

Its beginnings were a light overture, just to warm up, moving on to a dramatic dissonance, and ultimately reaching the finale after a great crescendo.

The world's fifth continent was acutely aware in the 1950s that it lacked an Opera House or fine concert hall of the highest standing. A competition was announced to architects to design an opera house fitting for a city of three million people. In 1957, the Danish architect Jorn Utzon won the commission with his design using great expanses of glass sheltered by great but slender sails that impressed the judges.

### Fifteen times over estimate

The first and second acts yielded the customary surprises that befall grandiose projects. There were problems when additional land was needed on the Bennelong Peninsula. There were engineering problems concerning the placement of the 220-foot-high roof arches that are supported by concrete columns and tied with 219 miles of cable. The commissioners were appalled at the cost. The Danish architect quarreled with his clients and departed in a huff. Four Australian architects were hired to replace him. Meanwhile local politicians were bickering about the plan and the conviction was growing that the entire project was lunacy.

The original estimate for the construction had been seven million

Australian dollars but the building eventually cost 102 million dollars. A lottery arranged to finance the project—prizes included free tickets—had to keep being extended for extra years. Of course the building was not completed within the planned five years but took sixteen years before the work was

finally ended. All these troubles were soon forgotten. Although there were many who initially regarded the design as far too avant-garde, no one now really questions the undoubted beauty of the Sydney Opera House. Its form is unusual but surprisingly successful. A million white tiles cover the arched forms to give the building a special radiance which is enhanced by the play of light of the floodlighting after dark. There is also the sparkling topaz color of the French glazing, covering 66,984 square feet of king-sized windows.

Inside the curvaceous form of the structure there is more than just an opera house of world stature. Beneath the daring and elegant roof there is a theater, concert halls, and a movie theater making it one of the most advanced multi-media buildings of the world that graces Port

*The first place ship's meet on entering Sydney Harbor is the Opera House. This avant-garde structure is sited on the Bennelong promontory with the city rising up behind it.*

Jackson, Sydney's harbor. It is a masterpiece of architecture that no-one who sees it can forget.

The Opera House became Sydney's new landmark. The first immigrants—convicts who had been transported from England—were disembarked on January 26, 1788 by Captain Arthur Philipp at this very spot.

*Behind the floodlit Sydney Opera House looms the former major landmark of Sydney Harbor— Sydney Harbor Bridge with a span of 1,650 feet.*
*The glow of the shell-form roof of the Opera House is due to over 1,000,000 tiles imported from Sweden.*

# The coral world of the Great Barrier Reef

## Tiny polyps create the world's greatest structure

**ROUTE**
International flights to Queensland coast: Rockhampton, Mackay, Prosperine, Townsville, and Cairns but also to Hamilton Island. Launch from mainland to the Island

**BEST TIMES**
March–May, September–November

**ACCOMMODATION**
Hamilton Island (Whitsunday Towers Apartments), also Hinchinbrook Island Resort and Lady Elliot Island Resort

They may only be tiny invertebrate organisms but no other living creature has created so large a structure as the coral polyps. In the space of twenty-five million years they have constructed a huge reef of more than 1,250 miles in length that is equal in size to Great Britain, putting the polyps in a league of its own in the construction stakes.

The manner in which the reef is formed is quite simple. The tiny polyps excrete calcium carbonate that forms a hard tubular structure. The proliferation of these creatures in colonies leads to the formation of a coral reef. It takes a few million years for a reef to extend across just several hundred yards as has happened along the coast of Queensland.

In reality the Great Barrier Reef consists of about 2,500 separate reefs, although the space between them is too narrow and shallow for larger vessels.

### Paradise for fish

The reef is not only the largest structure on earth made by living creatures, it is also by far the most colorful. Depending on the species of coral polyps and the rate of decay of the reef it takes on a myriad assortment of colors. The blue and brown antler-like corals are plentiful. Stone coral is brilliant white while other corals that resemble plants are dark pink, light pink, and mauve. In addition the coral is colonized by symbiotic algae such as the purple calcium algae, mottled anthozoa, yellow fungi, and complete tapestries of green algae cling to reefs that polyps have abandoned. The sea life here has adapted its colors to camouflage themselves against this rainbow environment with wide-mouthed soldier fish for example sporting blue stripes on a yellow ground.

Zoologists regard the Great Barrier Reef as the largest living organism on earth. Over its 1,250 miles the coral "fishes" for its prey using threads and tentacles, surrounding minute organisms, closing its murderous snout over fish, sharing a meal with other polyps in the colony. Marine biologists recognize some three hundred different species of coral, four thousand different types of mussels, and more than 1,500 different species of fish such as manta rays, sharks, and large black marlin living amid the reef.

Above the surface of the sea the reef has much of interest too. There

*A tourist boat carefully approaches the coral reef of the Great Barrier Reef. Diving here immerses you in a fascinating and colorful world.*

are some six hundred paradise-like islands and islets and partly flooded coastal land that has formed from weathered remnants of coral on which coconut palms and other tropical plants grow.

## Snorkel paradise

Many of the islands, which generally have magnificent white beaches for sheltered bathing in lagoons, can be visited by tourists. They are all superb places for snorkeling or diving deeper. On some islands it is possible to walk through tropical rain forest. There are places to stay ranging from camp sites to luxury hotels.

A serious threat to the ecology of the Great Barrier Reef has come from Asian fishermen who have been systematically working the reef for some thirty years.

Since 1938 Australia has applied strict quotas on catches. About ninety-eight percent of the reef is included in the Great Barrier Reef Marine Park which was the first marine reserve on earth.

*Marine biologists consider the 1,250-mile-long reef to be the largest living organism on earth. The coral is densely populated with many tiny polyps, mussels, snails, and fish. When the reef dies, new coral colonies cover the earlier layers.*

# Pyramids of the pharaohs

*World's largest tombs at Giza, near Cairo*

Giza
EGYPT
AFRICA
Atlantic Ocean
Indian Ocean

**ROUTE**
Taxi or bus (line 9, 900, 901) to Giza, 6 miles SW of Cairo

**BEST TIMES**
October–April

**ACCOMMODATIONS**
Meno House Oberoi (at the foot of the pyramids)

**ALSO WORTH SEEING**
Sakkàra Cemetery 15 miles SW of Giza

Thousands of tourists jostle with each other year in year out, crouching through narrow and claustrophobic passageways, coughing nervously, all to view an uninteresting vault about 328 feet long, seventeen feet wide and nineteen feet high. The walls and ceiling are of polished granite, and there are no paintings or inscriptions. Just one simple unadorned sarcophagus in the western end without a lid. This is where Cheops, pharaoh of the fourth dynasty was entombed 4,500 years ago. It was from this resting place that the mighty ruler, preserved as a mummy, would ascend to heaven.

## Marvel of the ancients

The Egyptian cult of the dead brought about the construction of a larger structure than humankind had previously attempted. The Pyramid of Cheops is a man-made mountain, erected in the desert as an act of faith. Cheop's subjects piled 2,400,000 blocks of stone averaging 2½ tons each, in the certain knowledge that this would render their pharaoh-god immortal and that they could follow after him. Once the peak of the pyramid—at a height of 482 feet—glistened gold against the blue sky as it reflected the sun, celebrating the sun god's daily fusion with the ruler of the earth. Today the pyramid is almost thirty-three feet lower. The pyramids were once sheathed in fine limestone, until this was removed in the thirteenth century to use as building materials.

To the southwest of the Pyramid of Cheops is another for his son Khafre (c. 2520–2494 BC), built on the same rocky ledge but with the addition of a Sphinx as guardian for

the city of the dead with features resembling his own. The stern eyes are turned towards the east and the rising sun. A third pyramid for his son and successor Menkaure (2490–2471 BC) is further to the west. This is the smallest of the three pyramids.

From a distance these three pyramids look entirely intact, but closer up it is apparent that for hundreds of years they were regarded as useful sources of building stone. Yet the pyramids have withstood man and nature for thousands of years. The pyramids of Giza and the Sphinx are the oldest of the seven wonders of the ancient world and the only one remaining today.

For thousands of years people have sought secrets associated with these structures. In 820, Caliph Abdullah al-Ma'um was the first to

penetrate the interior of the Pyramid of Cheops. Legend has it that the chambers contained weapons that would not rust, glass that could not be bent, and priceless treasure. The caliph brought together a team of engineers, architects, and craftsmen to search the secret of the tomb. They carefully probed the entire structure but failed to find a secret entranceway so they forced a way in to the royal chamber.

They found no buried treasure. This had probably been removed by robbers within five hundred years of the pharaoh's death. The fact that they took everything, including the lid of the sarcophagus, gives rise to continued speculation down to our present age. Could the burial chamber be just a decoy? Was the pharaoh in reality buried elsewhere? Even the greediest of robbers tend to leave some traces behind them such as wreckage, scraps of wood or metal, removing only items of value or usefulness. Archaeologists found nothing in the pyramid of the ancient judge and the sarcophaguses were empty in other pyramids too.

It seemed at last as if luck had improved when the British Army officer Howard Vyse opened the Pyramid of Menkaure in 1838 and found a sealed sarcophagus. Curbing his curiosity, Vyse shipped it to England where its contents would be revealed. The ship ran aground on the coast of Spain and the sarcophagus was lost forever.

*The great pyramids at Giza are just 6 miles from Cairo. These enormous structures were built 2,500 years before Christ by the pharaohs Menkaure, Khafre, and Cheops. The Sphinx still guards the eastern end of this city of the dead. This sole surviving member of the seven wonders of the world is Egypt's major tourist attraction.*

# Ramses II and Abu Simbel

*UNESCO saved the desert temple from inundation*

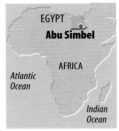

EGYPT
**Abu Simbel**

AFRICA

*Atlantic Ocean*

*Indian Ocean*

### ROUTE

Internal flights from Cairo or Aswan. By rail (15 hours) Cairo–Aswan, then 169 miles by coach to Abu Simbel

### BEST TIMES

October–April

### ACCOMMODATIONS

Nefertari Hotel (near temple and out of sight of the Nasser Dam)

### ALSO WORTH SEEING

Aswan, Luxor

Traveling by camel along the Nile through the Nubian desert, the Swiss explorer Johann Ludwig Buckhardt made a surprising discovery in May 1813. In a brief note in his diary he wrote: "My eye fell on the visible portion of four colossal statues...They stood in a deep hollow cut into the side of a hill. Unfortunately they were almost buried in the sand that the wind blows here just as if water dripping into a basin. The head and breast can be seen of one statue above the sand. The statue next to it can hardly be seen because the head is missing and the torso is covered up to the shoulders with sand.

Of the other two statues, only their headdress is visible." Buckhardt had discovered the temple of Abu Simbel.

## Playing with the sun's rays

It was more than a century, in 1907, before the 101-foot-high facade of the temple in this remote spot could be cleared of the sand and seen in the full glory of which Buckhardt had seen such a small part. There are four figures, each portraying Ramses II seated on a throne. The pharaoh-god looks east across the shimmering waters of the Nile, towards the rising sun. Between his legs are the smaller figures of his mother, his favorite wife Nefertari, and some of his numerous children.

The interior of the temple has been carved out of rock to a depth of 164 feet. There are larger-than-life reliefs depicting Ramses slaying his enemies, riding in his chariot, witnessing the chopping-off of the hands of his enemies, and offering incense to the gods. On the rear wall of the temple, regarded as the most sacred part, are four giant figures of Ramses and three divine companions. Twice each year— usually before and after the winter solstice—the rays of the sun penetrate the front entrance to illuminate the statues on the rear wall.

A little north of Ramses' temple there is a smaller one which is cut into the rock; it is dedicated to Ramses' wife Nefertari and the god Hathor.

Why did Ramses build these temples so remote from his residence in the Nile delta? Anthropologists suspect that it was a demonstration of his piety, in order to make him loved by gods and his subjects, and to guarantee his fame spread also to Nubia, disseminating Egyptian customs and ideas there.

The work to save these temples 3,200 years later was every bit as imposing as their original construction. The Aswan Dam had been built to store water from the Nile for irrigation in a lake 312 miles long to make the desert fertile. The temples of Abu Simbel are only 175 miles upstream and would have been inundated. UNESCO appealed to the world to come to the rescue. Aid came from all over the world in the form of funds and proposals of how to tackle the task. This led to the creation of an Abu Simbel joint venture which cut the temple into blocks each weighing approximately

twenty-two tons in order to raise them 210 feet and then put them together again like a puzzle. Far from the nearest civilization, the greatest international construction site of the age took shape with two thousand specialists—stone cutters from Italian marble quarries, German engineers, French mathematicians, Egyptian archaeologists, U.S. explosives experts, and crane operators from Sweden. In May of 1965 the

first block was lifted by a mobile crane. More than one thousand blocks, mostly cut by hand, were transported to the new location and fitted together again. Even the detail of the trick with the sun's rays on the back wall was meticulously retained in the reconstruction.

*Four colossal 65-ft-high statues depicting Ramses II guard the Temple of Abu Simbel. The smaller figures represent his mother, favorite wife Nefertari, and his children. At the most sacred part of the temple on the back wall are four more statues of Ramses and his divine companions. When the Aswan Dam was built the entire Temple and smaller Hathor Temple were cut into sections and moved to higher ground in 1963–1968.*

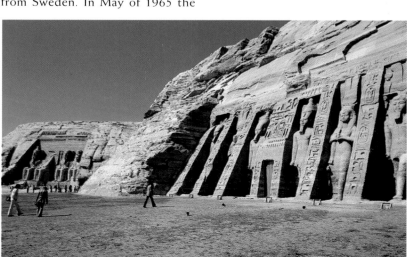

# Thebes: city of a hundred gates

*The pharaohs took hundreds of years to build the Temple of Luxor*

The red granite needle points to the heavens like a finger. The obelisk is eighty-two feet high and it honors the gods and the pharaohs, is guardian of the temple gates, and a monument in the desert. Once there were two of them but its twin has traffic circulating around it in the Place de la Concorde in Paris. The diplomat Bernardino Drovetti held that: "Antiquity is a garden owned according to the laws of nature to he who reaps and stores its fruits."

Drovetti had the 260-ton needle, erected on orders of Ramses II in the thirteenth century BC, transported from Luxor to Paris in 1836 as a present for King Louis-Philippe.

In those days the looting of art and antiquities was not especially frowned upon. Egypt was regarded as a great storehouse of treasures and both collectors and thieves plundered them at will.

There was plenty of it anyway. At Karnak and Luxor alone on either side of the Nile there were ruins of great antiquity covering the flood plain for as far as the eye could see. Nearer in the Valley of Kings, well-wrapped secrets could be chosen at will from the tombs of the great. "Returning from Egypt to Europe," critic of culture and clergyman Fedinand de Géromb wrote with sarcasm in 1831, "one cannot properly show oneself without a mummy in one hand and a crocodile in the other."

## In honor of a name

Nowhere in the world though has left behind such extensive and impressive ruins as Thebes, queen of all cities. This metropolis in Upper Egypt sat on the right bank of the Nile, During the flourishing of the new kingdom of the eighteenth and nineteenth dynasty, in around 1500 BC, this was the hub of the world, center of power, and guardian of art and commerce. Long after Thebes' fortunes had waned, Homer praised "Thebes of the hundred gates."

Rulers sought to express the glory and their fame in overwhelming structures. Consequently the 853-foot-long Temple of Luxor arose on the banks of the Nile which generations of pharaohs continued to build. They created impressive colonnades, pillared galleries like forests of papyrus, chapels of granite for their sacred barges, sculpture for gods and pharaohs, reliefs of hunting scenes and feasting, and an avenue of animal-headed Sphinxes leading to the next temple. The tip of the needle tells us to whom this enormous structure was dedicated: "The ruler of the world, Sun, Guardian of Truth, has caused this building to be erected in honor of his father Amon..."

The ancient Egyptians were not fussy when it came to choosing their gods. More than two thousand different deities populated sacred places across the ages, and they also liked to adopt gods from other people. Many gods were neglected or even ousted. Around 2000 BC Amon became fashionable as god of wind and air. He developed into Amon-Ra, the Sun God, and the cult of Amon-Ra became the state religion. Presents heaped wealth upon his supporters. His priests owned the most fertile land in sixty-five different places and employed a labor force of ninety thousand. The kingdom possessed a merchant fleet and a string of temples reaching to Nubia (northern Sudan). For important rituals, the pharaoh himself acted as high priest and pleaded at great ceremonies for the Nile's blessing and for fertility for the soil.

### King of peace, Ramses II

High up on the needle of the Temple of Luxor, Ramses the Great (Ramses II) can be seen making offerings to Amon. This pharaoh was the most important ancient Egyptian ruler, a victorious conqueror in his youth and later king of peace during his sixty-six year reign. he was an untiring builder and supporter of his own fame. His monumental representations have molded the image we have formed of Egypt in the pre-Christian era. The sculptures and paintings at which we now look in awe are a mere shadow of the former glory. At the foot of the Luxor temple there is an inscription which shows how it once was: white stone, gates made of gilded acacia, with the name of Amon set in gems.

*Two Ramses figures sit enthroned wearing double crowns (see detail bottom right) beside the solid needle that marks the ancient entrance gate. Originally this pharaoh had 6 large granite figures placed here. The twin of the needle now stands in the Place de la Concorde in Paris. The 260-ton obelisk was shipped to Paris in 1836.*

197

# Sahara: a sea without water

*This desert covers almost one-third of Africa and is still growing*

Sahara

AFRICA

*Atlantic Ocean*

*Indian Ocean*

### ROUTE
From Fez: by bus to Erfoud (265 miles/2 days) or flight from Casablanca to Fez and Er-Rachida and on to Erfound (50 miles). From there 33 miles to Merzounga oasis at the Erg Chebbi

### BEST TIMES
March–April, October–November

### ACCOMMODATIONS
Les Dunes d'Or in Merzounga

### ALSO WORTH SEEING
Rissani: tomb of the ancestors of the ruling Alaouit dynasty

In the beginning was the earth, the Bible says, and the earth was without form. In a few million years from now the earth may be desert once more, because the arid regions of the world are constantly expanding. The largest of them all is the Sahara, an enormous ocean of sand and rolling pebbles.

Covering at least 3,475,000 square miles, the Sahara stretches from the Red Sea to the Atlantic coast of Morocco and from the Mediterranean to the Sahel—almost one-third of Africa. But the desert is not uniform. Only parts of it consist of sand dunes. There are also rocky canyons as in the Tell Atlas Mountains of Algeria, with endlessly varying expanses of eroding stones, volcanic craters, and very small green islands of oases.

## Once real waves rolled here

The impression of void and formlessness, to hark back to the Bible, is strongest in the flat desert of pebbles, which the Arabs call *regs*. A carpet of wind and storm weathered gravel reaches to the horizon. Describing such a reg the size of both France and the Benelux countries, the scientific journalist Uwe George wrote: "What I saw was no landscape. It is the finish of all matter. In the course of millions upon millions of years everything we regard as landscape will be destroyed."

The Sahara has not always been like this. Earth's history plunged the Sahara from one extreme to another. Four hundred million years ago the Sahara was a sea that drained when the movement of the tectonic plates pushed the region upwards. Traces of this can be found in southern Morocco where there are fossils of cephalopods (squid) and the remnants of a sun-bleached coral reef. A "mere 170 million years ago"

much of the present desert was covered in forest. In those days North Africa still had huge herds of dinosaurs. In southern Morocco footprints more than forty inches long have been found in the fossil deposits of a former river bed.

When the sea advanced and receded thick layers of salt, sand, pebbles, and skeletons were left behind. During the last Ice Age some 10,000 to 25,000 years ago, the Sahara was a savanna landscape. The people of the Stone Age hunted gazelle, giraffe, and elephants using celts (hand-held axes) and spears. About seven thousand years ago tribes that reared cattle grazed the Sahara with enormous herds, as rock drawings on the smooth walls in the

Tell Atlas Mountains testify. Gradually the extent of grazing land in North Africa shrank. Lack of rain and rising temperatures turned the green savanna into dry steppe and then into desert. The Sahara desert is not without life though. Gazelle and mouflon move around close to water holes and the mercurial "sandfish" or lizards hunt insects in the true desert. There are scorpions, snakes, and gerbils. At dusk, desert mice and all manner of creatures venture forth from their hiding places.

The people who live in the desert keep trying to tap into the vast reserves of water beneath the Sahara. Wells are drilled every fifty to one hundred yards into the water-bearing layers, and the water is then led

through underground conduits to artificial oases. This ingenious scheme has reclaimed some thirty-six square miles each year but at the southern edge of the Sahara alone the desert devours 965 square miles of new land each year.

Allah could not have given a greater gift to the Bedouin than the camel. These "ships of the desert" can survive without water for considerable time provided they have been well watered first. A thirsty camel can drink over thirty gallons of water at a time, storing it in the tissue in its humps.

*Sand dunes likes this in the Algerian Sahara move slowly, pushed forward by the wind at a rate of thirty to sixty-five feet each year. Algerians call these sand dunes ergs. Eroding rocks, slowly sinking beneath their own debris, are also typical of the Sahara.*

# Fez: Mecca for the Maghrib

*The influence of this sacred center is felt throughout Arabia*

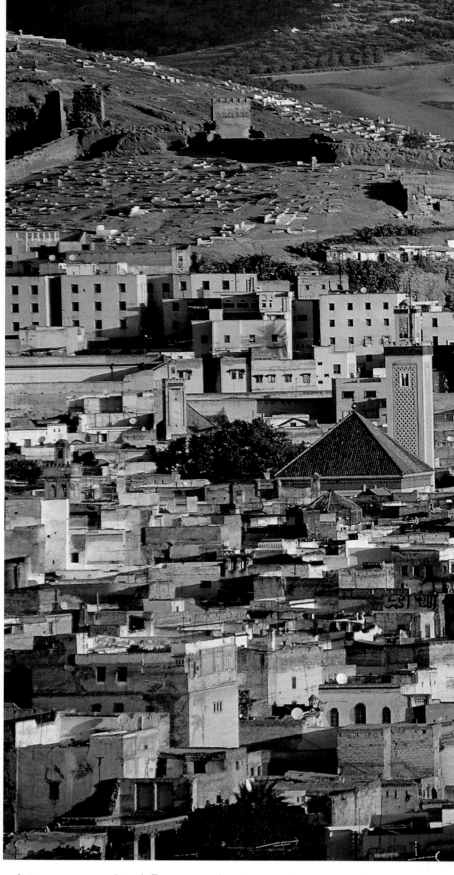

### ROUTE

International flights to Tangier and Casablanca, local flights to Fez; train from Casablanca/Rabat or Tangier to Fez

### BEST TIMES

March–May, September–November. Summer temperatures above 104°F (40°C)

### ACCOMMODATIONS

Hotel Palais Jamais in Fez al Bali (former Wezir Palace)

### ALSO WORTH SEEING

Musée du Batha (Moroccan folk art) in Fez, Moulay Yacoub thermal baths, 13 miles NW

*Each trade has its own section in the former royal palace. Tanners have worked close to the river for centuries.*

The days of glory for Fez are long gone but the city remains one of the most beautiful. Its history is not forgotten either in Fez, although the city's origins are shrouded in myths and date back to 808, just after Charlemagne had himself crowned emperor in Europe. It is said that Sharif Mulai Idris, great-grandson of Muhammad's son-in-law and successor Ali, and his daughter Fatima, founded this town with his desert riders. In the plain of the narrow valley, enclosed by mountains, on the banks of the Oued Fez, some 150 miles from Gibraltar, the men stuck their spears into the soil and established their camp. It was on this site that a walled medina was built.

This is where the most sacred place in the kingdom of Morocco stands today, the mosque of Mulai Idris II, named after the founder of the first ruling dynasty of Morocco. The mosque containing the tomb of the ruler beneath a green pyramid-form roof, with richly adorned wooden portals, is a "Mecca" for the Maghrib, a place of pilgrimage for the faithful, and may not be approached by non-Muslims or animals.

### Spanish-Moorish heritage

The brutish ousting of the Moors from Catholic Spain proved beneficial for the fledgling town. Refugees from Andalusia were experienced craftsmen, technicians, and artists. They created a Spanish-Moorish style with a new degree of perfection.

The heart of Fez-al Bali is al-Qarawiyin university and Islamic religious center combined. Fourteen beatitude towers lead to one of the most beautiful mosques of the world. There is sufficient space for 22,000 believers within the building, which is supported by 270 pillars.

To the east of Fez al Bali (the old town of Fez), the new city of Fez al Jedid spreads out on terraces. This was built in the thirteenth century and much of it is taken up with the sultan's palace, Dar al-Makhzen. The two parts of the city come together in the north, against the mountain on which the fortified kasbah is perched. Surrounded by desert or forest, the rocky Atlas Mountains, and expanses of fertile plains, Fez was once the treasured remnant of the Spanish-Moorish civilization, but the city was always more than just that. In the course of time it became the sacred and artistic center of Morocco and its light spread throughout the Arab world.

In the seventeenth century, Fez lost some of its importance. In an encyclopedia from 1896 we find: "The streets are not paved. the city is run down, dirty, and dark. At present Fez has but some 100,000 inhabitants but of the 785 mosques in use when the city flourished, only 130 remain. All that is left is a shadow of former glory." Today, with six times that number of inhabitants, Fez is hard-pressed to house them all.

A thousand-year-old Arab quarter or medina, doggedly opposes the modern world. When you wander

through the inner city, which is the true heart and soul of Fez, it is like traveling back to the Middle Ages, a pilgrimage for the senses.

## Open-air museum

Submerging yourself in this lively "open-air museum" among the teeming souks, with people swarming and shouting, you find the alleys too narrow for motor vehicles, just wide enough for a donkey or hand cart. Each trade has its own section of the town, with each category of goods kept strictly apart. In one place you will find carpets, in another gold jewelry. Shoemakers work down one narrow thoroughfare, while the tanners are established next to the river.

*The box-form houses of this ancient royal city are built on terraces on the hillside. For a thousand years this was the political, religious, and cultural center of North Africa, home to its kings, craftsmen, scientists, and artists. Visitors will still find some of the finest examples of Moorish architecture in Fez.*

# The craters of Kilimanjaro

*Africa's highest mountain is capped with snow throughout the year*

AFRICA

**Kilimanjaro**

*Atlantic Ocean*

TANZANIA

*Indian Ocean*

**ROUTE**

Direct to Kilimanjaro International Airport near Arusha (Tanzania) or via Nairobi (Kenya)

Tourist support center for Kilimanjaro tours is at Moshi (Tanzania)

**BEST TIMES**

December–March, July–October

**ACCOMMODATIONS**

Kibo Hotel, Marangu

**ALSO WORTH SEEING**

Arusha National Park, Ngorongoro National Park

Two German missionaries were told they were suffering from delusion brought on by the tropical climate when they insisted they had seen a great mountain covered with snow in darkest Africa. Their reports were met with incredulity. Snow? In Africa? Surely no snow could survive in such heat?

Scientists divided into two camps. Geographers in London agreed that these two clergymen from the Anglican Missionary Society were mistaken. In Berlin, however, the famous physicist Alexander von Humboldt was less skeptical about such a notion of a high mountain in East Africa with snow-capped peak. Soon other travelers from Africa confirmed the earlier reports of the missionaries. In 1848, Johannes Rebmann, one of the missionaries, had been the first European to see Kilimanjaro. His colleague Ludwig Krapf saw it too within twelve months.

The highest of Kilimanjaro's twin peaks is 19,340 feet above sea level, towering above the flat savanna of East Africa. Not only is Kilimanjaro Africa's highest mountain but surely the greatest single mountain on earth. The Africans call it Kilimanjaro or "the shining white mountain." Above 16,000 feet the temperature is arctic-like and the summit of the higher Kibo peak is capped with snow and ice. When the mountain was first climbed in 1889 by the Leipzig geographer, Hans Meyer and

the Salzburg alpinist Ludwig Purtscheller, they named the summit "Emperor Wilhelm Summit" but this name did not hold. The colonial powers of Germany and Great Britain drew an arbitrary line on the map to demarcate German East Africa and the British colony of Kenya but did bend the line to include Mt. Kilimanjaro within the then German colony of Tanganyika. The British got the consolation prize of Africa's second highest mountain, Mt. Kenya (17,058 feet) until they too controlled the former German East Africa.

When the former colonies gained their independence from Britain the original borders were retained so that Mount Kilimanjaro is now in Tanzania.

Authors such as Karen Blixen (*Out of Africa*), Ernest Hemingway (*Green Hills of Africa*), and Robert Ruark (*Safari*) visited Kilimanjaro and wrote about their adventures on the dark continent. Anyone witnessing the snow-capped peak of Kilimanjaro from afar for the first time is likely to share their poetic experience but the beauty and majesty is often hidden beneath cloud.

A panoramic view of Kilimanjaro can be seen from the air. The three craters of the volcano stand out as black against the icy crust. The black vent of the Kibo crater is like a giant's eye surrounded by snow, it resembles a pupil while a ring of lava is reminiscent of eyelashes. Hot sulfurous fumes escape through this eye of Kibo from the depths of the

vent. The Kibo crater is not yet wholly dormant, unlike the craters of Mawensi (16,892 feet) and Shira (12,998 feet).

### Gillman's Point is the goal

Tourists led by native guides can ascend Kilimanjaro by various routes. There are various kinds of tropical fruit, rice, maize, coffee, vegetables, and herbs cultivated to an altitude of around 7,500 feet. There is rain forest in the misty zone between 6,500 and 9,800 feet. The large trees are draped with lianas and braids, while orchids bloom on the trunks. The following three thousand or so feet are covered with great expanses of heather and the swamps of Kilimanjaro. Between 13,000 and 16,500 feet the atmosphere is arid

and the temperature may vary greatly.

Most tourists head for Gillman's Point on the edge of the Kibo crater, 18,651 feet above sea-level. Those who have been there and seen it say that the sunset is the most enchanting in Africa. The final summit of Kilimanjaro is another 689 feet higher, known now as Uhuru (freedom) Peak.

*Many species of wild animal live in the national park at the foot of snow-capped Kilimanjaro, including giraffes. Much of the savanna surrounding the volcano is used as pasture by the Masai for their herds of cattle. In the Amboseli National Park (bottom left) on the Kenyan side, there are large herds of wild buffalo and elephants. The umbrella like acacias with their broad, shady crowns, are very characteristic of this savanna landscape.*

# Ngorongoro Crater, paradise for wildlife

*Wildlife in the tens of thousands inhabits the floor of this giant crater*

It is as if nature itself has created a special reserve for the animals of Africa. The forces of nature have created the enormous Ngorongoro Crater in northern Tanzania providing grazing of ninety-six square miles for countless herds of animals, breeding ground for astounding flocks of birds, and hunting ground for almost every kind of East African predator within this vast plain surrounded by steep hills.

This unique landscape was formed by several adjacent volcanoes. Millions of years ago, eruptions and lava flows created the cauldron-shaped crater about twelve and a half miles in diameter. Most of the vast plain of the crater floor is surrounded by the cliffs at the side of the crater rising to 2,300 feet above the bottom of the cauldron, and a height of 7,480–7,906 feet above sea-level.

The fertile crater floor of the Ngorongoro is covered with acacia trees, tall grasses, an area of swamp, and a salt lake and flats called Magadi. The living conditions in these surroundings are ideal for

*Flamingos feeding in the saline waters of Lake Magadi*

almost every animal indigenous to East Africa.

The numbers of mammals such as elephant, rhino, hippo, gnu, water buffalo, zebra, antelope, and giraffe living in the crater is estimated at 20,000–30,000. This number varies because many of them also live outside the Ngorongoro for part of the time. The big cat predators roaming are chiefly lions, cheetahs, leopards, and a few of the smaller cats also.

## Traces of the first inhabitants

The saline waters of the Magadi are frequently the feeding grounds of thousands of flamingos. Flocks of Nile geese and various types of duck also land on the water. Cranes too find plenty of cover to hatch their eggs as do plovers, hoopoes, coursers, and great bustards. On the more solid ground one finds ostrich, always ready to take flight, wandering around in the world's most densely populated volcanic crater.

The paradise-like conditions of the Ngorongoro attracted upright man as far back as 3,600,000 years ago. These hominids were four to five feet tall. In 1978, the American anthropologist Mary Leakey discovered footprints of these early Africans about twenty-five miles from the crater wall. They have a species name like animals: *Australopithecus afarensis*. Because of their prominent lower jaws they have been dubbed the "nutcracker people."

Much more recently, the verdant crater floor was pasture for 10,000–15,000 Masai with their herds of around a million cattle. When the Ngorongoro Crater and nearby Serengeti National Parks were created, the Masai were restricted in their use of this habitat. Today they are permitted to graze their animals on the crater floor but not to live there.

Both the Ngorongoro Crater and the Serengeti would be seriously threatened without the strong protective measures that have been put in place. There is a small stone cairn at the entrance to the Ngorongoro Crater National Park as a memorial to the zoologist Bernhard Grzimek and his son Michael who died in an aircraft crash in 1958 while filming the legendary film *The Serengeti Shall Not Die*.

*Volcanic action formed the vast and fertile Ngorongoro Crater in the north of Tanzania, covering 96 square miles. The crater walls also act as a boundary. Just about every indigenous species of East African wild life can be encountered here, such as hyena, and water buffaloes (bottom right).*

# The thundering Victoria Falls

*The Victoria Falls on the Zambezi stride the border of Zambia and Zimbabwe*

*Mosi oa Tunya: the Smoke that Thunders. The Zambezi separates Zambia and Zimbabwe.*

AFRICA

Atlantic Ocean · **Victoria Falls**

ZIMBABWE · Indian Ocean

**ROUTE**

International flights to Harare (Zimbabwe). Local flights to Victoria Falls or via Lusaka (Zambia) to Livingstone/Maramba

**BEST TIMES**

May–September

**ACCOMMODATION**

Victoria Falls Hotel

**ALSO WORTH SEEING**

Lake Kariba, Hwange National Park, Matoba Hills National Park near Bulawayo (Zimbawe)

The British explorer David Livingstone was lyrical in his description. "This is the most marvelous sight I have ever beheld in Africa," he jotted in his notebook in November 1855 as he stood on an island in the river gazing in awe at the thundering mass of water of the Zambezi as it cascaded into a narrow gorge. Deep below he saw two rainbows against a backdrop of a dense white cloud with a "column of vapor two or three hundred feet in height" rising aloft, "the upper portion of which took on the color of dark smoke."

Crossing Africa from the Atlantic to the Pacific, the Englishman was the first European to reach the legendary falls on the Zambezi river, the largest in Africa. The sound of falling water was deafening to the point that the natives, fearful of the mighty spirits at work, dared not draw near. They called this wonder of nature Mosi oa Tunya, "the Smoke that Thunders." Livingstone had already noticed five columns of apparent smoke from a distance, as if the savanna was burning.

## Falls into nine canyons

David Livingstone named the falls Victoria Falls in honor of his queen and later the town that grew up a few miles away was named after him. Today's map of Zambia uses the African name of Maramba for the town once known as Livingstone.

The Zambezi is 1,287 miles long and the longest river in southern Africa. At the border between Zambia and Zimbabwe (once North and South Rhodesia), at the place described by Livingstone, the Zambezi's mass of water, more than a mile wide, drops 360 feet over a basalt ledge into a narrow gorge that is linked to a further nine canyons which were once receiving basins for the cascading water. The Victoria Falls consist of five separate falls: the Eastern Cataract, the Rainbow Falls, the Horseshoe Falls, and the Devil's Cataract on the western side of the geological fault.

Since Livingstone's time the falls have remain largely unaltered except for luxury hotels such as the Mosi-oa-Tunya Intercontinental and a new highway almost to the brink of the falls. A railway bridge has also crossed the narrower section of the falls since 1904 linking Zambia and Zimbabwe. A picturesque jungle track in Zambia leads to Knife Edge, a slippery rock path between the first and second canyon of the Victoria Falls.

Although the "columns of smoke" described by Livingstone are rarely seen today, and enormous mist cloud still hovers above the falls which is at its largest during the end of the rainy season when around 84,500,000 gallons of water pour over the falls each minute. The volume of water reduces to a mere "trickle" of some 4,800,000 gallons per minute at the end of the dry season.

Exceptionally lush vegetation still surrounds much of the Victoria Falls as described by Livingstone. Clouds of mist cause fine rain to fall over an area with a radius of more than eighteen miles from the falls, creating a great wealth of plant life. The entire area on both sides of the Zambezi are now protected National Parks. On the Zambian side the Mosi-oa-Tunya and the Victoria Falls National Park on the Zimbabwe side.

The tourist center for Zambia is Livingstone (Maramba), less than five miles from the falls.

*With deafening roaring, millions of gallons of water cascade into a narrow gorge 360 feet deep and 165 feet wide. The rising clouds of foam cause a fine mist to descend in a radius of 20 miles.*

## Photo credits